ALPHA
AND
OMEGA

STUDIES IN
THE BOOK OF REVELATION

BY

SAMUEL W. JENNINGS

AMBASSADOR
Belfast • Greenville

Alpha and Omega
First published 1996

© 1996 Samuel W. Jennings

Printed in Northern Ireland

ISBN   1 - 898787 77 8

AMBASSADOR PRODUCTIONS LTD,
Providence House
16 Hillview Avenue,
Belfast, BT5 6JR
Northern Ireland

Emerald House,
1 Chick Springs Road,
Greenville,
South Carolina 29609
USA

List of Contents

Introduction

What?! Yet another book on the Revelation? Surely the time has come when such books are legion, and indeed more than sufficient to meet the need of the Christians until the Lord's return. In view of His imminent coming it is all the more essential that books should continue to be written, and read, concerning the things that shall shortly come to pass.

I trust that this book will highlight some truths which we are prone to forget, truths which are essential to the understanding of this book of Prophecy; The Revelation.

1. The first of these points I wish to make is that the book was written for first century readers, as well as for the tribulation saints in the last days. This simple statement is sometimes overlooked in expositions of the Revelation. If the book is only for those in the last days; that is, future days subsequent to the Church period, then why did the Spirit inspire John to write it nineteen hundred years beforehand? Yes, we know the book of God is complete, but surely Scripture is always timely in meeting the present need. The early Christians were being persecuted in a most horrible way in the early history of the church, millions were put to death in the most blood thirsty of ways. Others took joyfully the spoiling of their goods, and

suffered physical torture as well. Peter speaks of these sufferings in his epistles. Paul speaks of conditions similar in Philippians, Thessalonians and in the Pastoral epistles. By the time John wrote the Revelation, the suffering and persecution of believers had greatly increased, it was a common pastime to cause the followers of Christ to suffer. The Book of the Revelation was first and foremost for these very believers.

2. After the Lord comes to the air for His blood bought church, God will again begin to work with Israel and the nations in judgment, but also in grace. Tribulation days shall produce innumerable believers who will be loyal to Christ and to the Word. These people shall suffer greatly, and the same book of Revelation will again come into its own, having a pertinent relevance to their situation. They will then turn to it for consolation, and for solutions to the problems arising from their trying circumstances.

3. Times of persecution produce problems and questions that would never arise in periods of peace. For example, "Must we continue to meet in church capacity"? "Does God expect church principles to be upheld in such times of trouble"? "Are we to worship the Emperor or refrain, even at such a cost, the cost of our very lives"? Or "we are praying, why is God silent to our crying unto Him by day and night"? Again, " the most faithful of believers are being cut down, the very leaders on whom we depend, why does God allow this to happen"? Whether in the early stages of the church, or in the later tribulation days, the problems are the same, believers are asking the same questions. The Revelation is the answer to these questions, all is made clear. It was so to those who suffered in the early gospel testimony, they endured largely because of this Book. This same book will be the comfort and counsel of those who will pass through the Great Tribulation, they will resort to this book and derive strength therefrom. In fact, in times of persecution throughout the history of the church, believers have automatically turned to the book of Revelation for help and comfort.

4. To see this "Problem Idea" coming out, it is necessary to understand that the book is not therefore written in chronological order, but rather

in subject order. Clearly defined sections can be detected in the book where it is evident that one subject ends, and another begins. In fact, there are seven such sections, and each subject is built around seven things such as Churches (Ch. 1-3) Seals (Ch. 4-7) and so on. In brief, each of the seven sections in the book, based upon a series of sevens is really the answer to a problem besetting suffering saints.

5. Another important point. John is very fond of Tabernacle teaching. This has often been pointed out in his Gospel, the reason being, that while Matthew and Mark look to the fulfilment of the Prophecies concerning the Christ, John and Luke on the other hand base their writings on the types of the Old Testament. Luke's is the Priestly Gospel while John favours the Wilderness. He makes much of the feasts for example, referring to the Passover more times than the other Gospels. Another example of this is he alone refers to the Feast of Tabernacles (John 7). On this ground, John constantly brings in the Tabernacle in the wilderness to back up his presentation of the Person and ministry of the Lord.

He also uses the same themes to begin and end his writings such as "Behold the Lamb of God" (John 1:29) and "The throne of God and of the Lamb" (Rev. 22:1). The first is the Lord upon the cross, and in the Revelation reference, the Lord is upon the throne.

Again, the wedding in John ch. 2, the marriage in Cana, and the presence of the Lord can be linked with Rev. 21 the Bride the Lamb's wife. The first is in his second chapter of John, the last in the second chapter from the end in Revelation. He uses this same idea also with the Tabernacle and begins his Gospel with "The Word was made flesh and tabernacled among us" (John 1:14) and ends with "The tabernacle of God is with men, he will dwell with them" (Rev. 21:3).

So, just as the theme of the tabernacle runs through the gospel of John, in the same manner it is woven into the Book of Revelation. In fact, John uses a reference to the tabernacle in order to introduce each new section, thus indicating a new beginning.

To sum up: the pattern of the Book of Revelation is as follows:-
a) There is an introduction and epilogue to the Book
b) The rest is divided into seven distinct sections

c) Each section circles around seven symbols or entities
d) Each new section begins with a tabernacle reference
e) A problem relevant to a persecuted people is the
    main theme in each section.

This book will seek to further develop these salient points.

CHAPTER ONE

Outline of the Book

The outline of any book of Scripture is most important. This helps one to see an over-all view of the picture, so enabling the reader to slot the various details into place. Every book of the Bible is a masterpiece of structure, and most orderly. This is especially true of the Book of Revelation as already indicated in the Introduction. The outline is as follows.

A. TESTIMONY ON THE EARTH. CH. 1-3
Seven Churches
Tabernacle. Lampstands
Key Word = MIDST

B. GREAT EVENTS CH. 4-7
Seven Seals
Tabernacle. Glory. Ark.
Key Word == THRONE

C. PRAYER, INCENSE CH. 8-11
Seven Trumpets
Tabernacle. Golden altar.
Key Word == REWARD

D. KINGS AND KINGDOMS CH. 11:18-14
Seven Heads
Tabernacle. Ark ch. 11:18
Key Word == CROWNS

C. MARTYRS CH. 15-18
Seven Vials.
Tabernacle. Laver. Sea.
Key Word == WRATH

B. GREAT DESTRUCTION CH. 19-20
Seven Judgments.
Tabernacle. Linen.
Key Word == WHITE THRONE

A. TESTIMONY ON THE NEW EARTH 21-2
Seven New Things.
Tabernacle of God.
Key Word == DWELL

This division seems to be genuine, and not just conjecture.

It is readily proved by the parallels one with another as suggested by the classification under Capital Letters in the chart above.

Section one chs. 1-3 is parallel with section seven chs. 21-22. This is not a mere coincidence but seems to be the design placed there by the Spirit. The whole writing is in the form of inverted parallels.

Consider these two sections labelled A.

COMPARISON OF A. CHS. 1-3 AND A. CHS.21-22.

1. I John a prisoner 1:8	I John saw 21:2
2. New Jerusalem 3:12	New Jerusalem 21:2
3. Alpha and Omega 1:8	Alpha and Omega 21:6
4. Him that overcometh 2:7	He that overcometh 21:7
5. In the Spirit 1:10	Carried in the Spirit 21:10
6. Go no more out 3:12	Unclean not enter in 21:27
7. Lamb's book of life 3:5	Lamb's book of life 20:27
8. Tree of life 2:7	Tree of life 22:2

9. New name upon him 3:12 — Name on foreheads 22:4
10. Shortly come to pass 1:1 — Shortly be done 22:6
11. Angel 1:1 — Angel 2:6
12. Words of this prophecy 1:3 — Prophecy of this book 22:7
13. Behold He cometh 1:7 — Behold I come quickly 22:7
14. John fell at feet 1:17 — John fell down 22:8
15. The churches 2:3 — The churches 2:16
16. Spirit saith, Hear 2:7 — Spirit says come 22:17

COMPARISON B. CHS. 4-7 AND B. CHS. 19-20.

1. Throne 25 times chs. 4-7 — Throne 4 times chs. 19-20
2. One sat on the throne 4:2 — Him that sat on it 20:11
3. Throne, rainbow, emerald 4:3 — Great white Throne 20:11
4. Lamb 10 times — Lamb 9 times
5. Starts with 4 praises chs.4-5 — Starts with 4 Alleluias ch.19
6. Beast on white horse 6:1 — Lord on white horse 19:11
7. Elders in white garments 4:4 — Bride in white linen 19:8
8. First mention/elders, beasts — Last mention/elders, beasts 19
9. They fell before throne 4:10 — They fell before throne 19:4
10. A Book, opened seals 6:1 — The books were opened 20:12
11. Priests unto God 5:10 — Priests unto God 20:6
12. Fifth seal, Martyrs 6:10 — Martyrs on thrones 20:4
13. Pale horse death, hell 6:8 — Death, hell cast into lake 20:14
14. Second seal, war 6:4 — War, Armageddon 19:21

COMPARISON C. CHS. 8-11 AND C. CHS. 15-18.

1. Seven angels with trumpets — Seven angels with vials
2. Heavenly scene, altar 8:5 — Heavenly scene, sea of glass 15
3. The Holy place, Tabernacle — The court of Tabernacle
4. Prayers of saints 8:3 — Song of saints 15:3
5. Fire on altar 8:5 — Glass mingled with fire 15:2
6. Trumpets, earth, sea etc. — Vials, earth, sea, etc.
7. No repentance 9:21 — No repentance 16:9
8. Delay no longer 10:6 — It is done 16:17
9. Witnesses, truth, slain 11 — Scarlet woman, false, slain 17
10. Jerusalem as Sodom 11 — Babylon as harlot 17

11. Guilty, blood of Lord 8:11   Guilty, blood of martyrs 17:6
12. Beast out of abyss 11:7   Beast out of abyss 17:8
13. Hailstones start of trumpets   Hailstones end of vials
14. Ch. 11 ends, those who destroy earth, and ch. 18 ends with the destruction of Babylon.

Chapters 12-14 stand distinct, having no section with which to compare, this is the centre of the book. The true King and the true Kingdom.

Surely this is by the wisdom and design of the Spirit of God, to indicate that the sections are distinct, separate, each having its own individual message, to encourage and comfort believers in troubled times.

Earlier it was suggested that each clear section of the book had for its theme a certain problem or difficulty that persecuted believers would encounter. Today believers in other places are suffering persecution for their faith. If this was the case in our country difficulties would surely arise. Churches would be closed, evangelism prohibited, elders and leaders would be imprisoned and killed, and many other things. Questions would then be asked by disconcerted saints, the very questions that are evident in the seven sections of the Revelation.

The several problems can easily be identified by the Tabernacle reference in each, and by the key word or idea. These would provide a summary of the problems, and of course God's answer to each one.

1. Is assembly service and testimony to continue ? Ch. 1-3 answers this, the churches had difficulties, but nowhere are they told to shut the door, and cease to function. Yes, church life must continue no matter what.
2.. Is heaven real, is God really in control? Has everything degenerated into a state of chaos which God can no longer control? Ch. 4-7 answers this. The Throne, God is in full control, all events on earth are predetermined in heaven.
3. In troubled times the dear saints pray, but why are the prayers not answered, why is God silent ? This problem is answered by ch. 8-11 which starts with the prayers of saints at the golden altar, and the silence in heaven. God answers prayer, but he is working to a programme, when the time comes, then God will avenge his own elect who cry day and night unto Him. (Luke 18:7)

4. Why are the godless nations so strong, and the persecuting nations so powerful ? Again this is specifically addressed by ch. 12-14. It is a section all about kings, mighty kings in opposition to God, but their reign is short lived. The Lord soon appears as King of Kings (14:14).

5. Why are the cream of saints martyred, why are the most useful servants of God taken away ? The section of the Martyrs chs. 15-18 is the answer here. God is patient, but all is not forgotten, the day of reckoning will surely come to the persecutors, for example, the scarlet woman is doomed etc.. The martyrs in the meantime bow to the will of God.

6. Can God really judge the world, have things gone so far that judgment cannot be meted out? Two great chapters full of the judgments of God come in here, namely ch. 19-20. Yes, God can and will judge the world, every enemy shall be subdued.

7. Is it all worthwhile? There seems to be no end to suffering and difficulties in the faith. Better to eat and drink for tomorrow we die as 1 Cor 15:32. The bright glories of ch. 21-22 fully answer this problem, all is worthwhile, "Write, for these words are true and faithful". (21:5). The Glorious day will surely come.

This is the main thrust of the book, and it gave wonderful light and strength to a people passing through fiery trials in the early church days. In the future Great Tribulation, the same consolation shall be derived from this Book of Revelation. The same is true in any times of persecution occurring in the interim.

CHAPTER TWO

The Double Introduction

The beginning of this magnificent first chapter is dealt with most efficiently by many of the expositions of the Revelation now available. Because of this the remarks here shall be brief and very much to the point.

The first thing to notice is that there are two introductions, the first is in verses 1-3 and the second appears in verses 4-8, each has similar features.

a) The Person of Jesus Christ, the object and source of the material, so verse 1 and verse 5

b) The channel is John, His servant John verse 1
   John to the churches verse 4

c) The receivers of the message again in both, His Servants verse 1
   The seven churches verse 4

It is very simple to see the reason for the double introduction, the first is to the whole book of Revelation, "Blessed are they that hear the words of this prophecy" (Verse 3). Note, "all things that he saw", this would include all the visions of the book.

The second introduction is to the Seven churches and therefore relates to the scenes of this chapter and the seven letters of chapters 2-3.

With this before the reader it is easy to see the simple but masterly structure of this first great chapter.

A. An introduction to the whole book of Revelation v 1-3
B. An introduction to the seven churches. v 4-8
B. The experience of John, the Seven golden lampstands v 9-12
A. Vision of the Son of Man. v. 13-20.

It is evident that the vision of the lampstands is related to the second introduction, that is to the seven churches of which the lampstands are symbols. Whereas the vision of the Son of Man is related to the first introduction, and therefore to the whole book of Revelation.

To take the tenfold symbolic description of the Son of Man as applying only to the seven churches is most misleading, the teaching contained therein, the symbolic picture is applicable throughout the whole book. For instance: -

1. The Son of Man appears again in ch. 14:14 with something in His hand and something on His head, a sharp sickle in His hand and crowned with a Victor's crown.
2. The thought of His apparel, the garment is again referred to in Ch. 19, the Lord is clothed with a vesture dipped in blood.
3. The golden girdle is again referred to in Ch. 15:6 this time associated with angels, seven angels are described as having their breasts girded with golden girdles. The thought is common to both passages, judgment cannot be set aside by love, the breasts, speaking of affections, are girded.
4. His head and hair white as snow, His head appears again in ch. 14:14 as being adorned with a victor's crown, and also in ch. 19:12 as crowned with many diadems.
5. Eyes as a flame of fire, is again mentioned in ch. 19:12, "His eyes as a flame of fire".
6. His feet like unto fine brass, the feet being a symbol of judgment. This idea is found in ch. 16:20 "the winepress was trodden without the city", and the terrible judgment of Armageddon is depicted there.
7. His voice as the sound of many waters. There are two main references to this symbol of power in the Revelation, "And I heard a voice from heaven as the voice of many waters" (Rev.14:2). "And I heard

as it were the voice of a great multitude and as the voice of many waters". (Rev. 19:). The people of the Lord take their character from the Lord.

8. He had in His right hand seven stars, this already has been referred to, so no comment is needed, except to state that stars are used extensively in the Book to convey truth.

9. Out of his mouth went a sharp sword with two edges. This is part of the description of the Lord as seen in ch. 19:15. The power of the word in judgment is the thought in both places, here to the church, there to the nations.

10. His countenance was as the sun shining in his strength. This idea is repeated with an angel in ch. 10:1 which some propose is the Lord. The face of our Lord is again alluded to in ch. 20 etc.. All this would suggest that the tenfold description here is extended beyond the letters to the churches and is therefore, as the first introduction, related to the whole book.

CONSIDER THE FIRST INTRODUCTION V 1-3

It is interesting to see how John introduces each of his group of writings. The Gospel is an exposition (John 1:18) The only begotten Son who is in the bosom of the Father hath declared,(expounded) or given an exegesis of Him. The first Epistle is called a declaration, "That which we have seen and heard DECLARE we unto you" (1 John 1:3) the same word as "told" used so often in New Testament. So, the Gospel of John is AN EXPOSITION, 1st John is a DECLARATION, but this final book is A REVELATION. Now a declaration or an exposition is to all that care to listen, many or all may reject, this is grace coming out. However the Revelation has a prepared people to receive this message, namely the servant, this is the purpose of God. Declaration is for all, but Revelation is for those who prepared beforehand can grasp it. Paul is an example, he was set apart for the revelation of the Son. (Gal. 1:15-16).

The Revelation of Jesus Christ, this title immediately emphasizes the Lord as seen when upon the earth, He made and proved wonderful claims, but they were rejected by the nation. A cross was given instead of the rightful crown. This is the Revelation of that person, His vindication to Israel and to the world, the blessed Lord is all that He claimed to be.

The things that John saw of v 2, are all the events preceding and subsequent to the great unveiling, namely the Lord's return to earth in glory.

The channel, God, Christ, Angel, John, servants. The servants are not inferior to the servant John, just as Christ is not inferior to God. In one N.T. sense all believers are bondservants, as the word should be. However in another sense the word is used of those specially called to a specific service as John was here, and the servants are the final end of the channel. Bondservant is found 70 times in the Gospels, 30 times in Paul's church epistles, and 14 times in the Revelation. So nothing can be made of this as being a distinct people apart from those of other dispensations.

Shortly means speedily, once the hand of God moves, all will be quickly consummated.

Now John bears witness, that is to the bondservants. This is the principle of 2 Tim. 2:2 things heard, then passed on to other faithful men. Three ideas are used to describe the one thing.

1) The Word of God, indicating the source is God, this is the formula for prophecy in the O.T. so therefore bodes of heavy tidings.

2) The testimony of Jesus Christ, He is the grand Subject.

3) Finally, "All things that he saw", not the words only but signs, visions, the withal to make the matter clearly understood, "eye gate is better than ear gate" as the saying is.

The Book has many titles even in its own pages. The Revelation of Jesus Christ, this Prophecy, (1:3) this Book of Prophecy (22:19), The Word of God, Testimony of Jesus Christ. These are but a few, others appear later in the book. Each of course suggests a different character of the book itself.

The suggestion is attractive that the Word of God is a reference to the Gospel of John, where the Lord is described as the Word. The Testimony of Jesus Christ being a reference to the Epistles, and the things that he saw being the Revelation. However, good as this sounds, the threefold title seemingly is in reference to the present book.

Verse 3 is the first of seven beatitudes in the book, and the only one that contains a promise. "He that readeth" is singular, and "they that hear" is plural, this would suggest the public reading of the book. While it is largely a book of symbols, yet it is the keeping, and not the understanding that brings the blessing.

Genesis, the first book of the Bible, Satan challenges; the last book of the Bible, he causes one to neglect, suggesting, "It is too difficult".

THE SECOND INTRODUCTION V 4-8

This second introduction is obviously to the seven churches, so stated in verse 4 and the said churches are named in verse 11.

Prophesy is important, but first things first, the testimony for the present is always paramount to God. This introduction contains a greeting, the character of Christ, a thanksgiving for grace, a prophecy v 7 and a claim from the mouth of the Lord.

The Trinity is presented, God, as in the language of Jehovah, always, eternally present, so He is in control in spite of seemingly adverse circumstances.

"Which is", again repeated in 4:8 "which was", also in 11:19 "which art", the emphasis is different each time, but here IS comes first, because of the circumstances of the suffering saints in tribulation. God is a present help.

The Holy Spirit is seen symbolically as Seven Spirits before the throne. There is little reason in making this to be the seven presence angels of ch. 15, and much less the angels to the seven churches, Ch. 3:1 would dispense with that idea, there the Seven Spirits injecting life into a dying church. The fact that this is placed between a reference to God and the Lord Jesus would indicate this to be the Holy Spirit. The Holy Spirit is seen here in various characters and graces.

a) Seven, being the completeness of the Spirit's work, He always completes things, the revelation of all truth etc..
b) Before the throne, as always representing God, coming out from the throne.
c) The Spirit joins in the divine greeting of grace and peace.
   This formula is mentioned again in ch. 3:1, 4:5, and 5:6.

The Holy Spirit is seen in the Gospels as to come (John 14-16), in the Acts as having come and sealing the believers, and in the epistles as indwelling the church. Here in the Revelation the Spirit is seen as governmental, before the throne.

Verse five is a beautiful threefold view of the Lord Jesus.

1) The faithful witness, all counsels fully declared.
2) The first-born of the dead, as this He inherits all things.
3) The ruler of the kings of the earth. All things are subjected to Him.

The first is the past, His witness in the flesh, the second is the present, the place He now occupies, and the third is yet future.

Again, the witness is the Prophet, the First-born from the dead suggests the Priest, and the ruler is the King of course, the threefold way in which the Lord often appears in Scripture.

One may add, the witness was for God, the first-born is for saints, and the ruler is for Israel and the nations. The witness is on the old earth, the first-born is the appearing in glory for the church (Col. 1:18) the king is linked with the coming Millennium.

The first-born has the connotation of the double portion, and this is seen in His inheritance in the saints and in Israel with the nations as here, heaven and earth.

In spite of present tribulation, John writes to rejoice in the great love of Christ, and his redeeming work. Loved us and washed us from our sins by his blood.

Verse 6, the work does not stop there, believers are made kings and priests unto God, perhaps a Kingdom of priests would be a better way to put it. The holy priesthood that Peter speaks of is the priesthood here, and the royal priesthood would suggest the kingdom as here, the witness to the world without. This is present access to God, the believers were looked upon by the ungodly as the off scouring of the earth, but to heaven they belonged in that holy place. The epistles use priest-like language often, Eph. 5:1 and Rom. 12:1 speak of our offerings, and the Philippian epistle especially speaks of the gifts they sent to the beloved Paul as sweet savour offerings. Peter speaks of the spiritual sacrifices in the spiritual house and that holy and royal priesthood already referred to. (1 Peter 2:1-8). Many a one has dominion but lacks glory, the Lord Jesus has both, and has brought believers into blessing as depicted in this first doxology.

The prophecy is in verse 7, His coming and the effect. The coming with clouds would be literal, that is from the sky, just as a cloud hid Him at His ascension in Acts 1, so the clouds shall be the means of His manifestation when He returns. "Clouds are His chariots" is written in Psalm 28 describing the majesty of the Lord.

The every eye seeing and the mourning could be on a double level. It is true all eyes shall see Him, not all at once, rather over a period of time, and all unbelievers shall mourn because of Him. However the reference seems to be to Israel in the day of their repentance.

a) Every eye, that is the living of Israel when He appears.

b) They that pierced Him, that is, carrying the sins of their fathers.

c) "Kindreds" would be better rendered "tribes", meaning the twelve tribes of Israel represented in the last days.

d) Mourn over, is repentance. All this is a fulfilment of the prophecy of Zech. 12:10-12, the looking upon the One they pierced, and every family mourning apart.

Verse 8, who makes this threefold claim, God or Christ? These are true of both the Father and the Son, but the indication is that the Lord Jesus is the speaker being linked with the previous verse, the great event of His coming.

a) The Alpha and Omega, the first and last letters of the Greek Alphabet, would then suggest the Lord is the beginning and end of all revelation, the Word as in John ch. 1. This occurs again in verse 17 and in ch. 22:13. The beginning and the ending of verse 8 is omitted in most versions.

b) Which is and which was and which is to come. Equality with Jehovah of verse 4. Divine, yet distinct personality. This is The Lord God, and is used in Genesis 2 of His relation to His creatures.

c) The Almighty, a title that connects with the provision of God for His own, the power on the side of God, similar to the Lord of Hosts in the O.T. So used in 2 Cor. 6:18.

This passage forms an inverted parallel and presents encouraging consolation to the churches in difficulties.

A. Which is, was and is to come verse 4

B. First advent of Christ, his love and death. verse 5

C. Believers a kingdom of priests

B. Second advent of Christ, glory and reign verse 7

A. Which is and was and is to come verse 8.

Such then is the second introduction contained in this first chapter and so used to the seven churches and develops into chapters 2 and 3.

CHAPTER THREE

The Seven Lampstands

John was in the Spirit, he heard a voice. In experience one is the outcome of the other, the words of our Lord can only be communicated if the Spirit is there. Such is the teaching of 1 Cor. 3, the natural man cannot receive the things of the Spirit, as he has no indwelling Spirit within to make him understand and appreciate Divine things. The mind of God is always conveyed by the Spirit to those who possess the Spirit. However, in this passage the experience goes even beyond possessing the Spirit, it is rather the Spirit possessing the man, John was in a spiritual condition, a vessel ready for the communication that God would have him learn. Again the thought no doubt carries the idea that John was favoured by a special visitation of the Spirit, with a view to receiving the Revelation. Most likely both these things are true of him.

He turned, the voice of the Lord is bound to have effect in some way, he turned, as Moses turned to see a burning bush in the desert long before this.

THREE GREAT SYMBOLIC PICTURES

He saw seven golden lampstands which speak of the seven churches in question, his book was to be addressed to them. These assemblies were more important than he realized, the Lord would have him face the churches and contemplate them. Many dear believers today have done the reverse and turned from the local aspect of church testimony to other workaday things. The churches are very necessary to God, they are the outlet of all His truth. John also saw the Lord in a wonderful symbolic way, a significant tenfold description for the meditation of all His saints.

The third picture is the stars in the right hand of the Lord, the importance of these three pictures he was about to learn.

There is great matter here, the three things go together, the person, the lampstands and the stars. All three are inseparably linked together. This can well be illustrated by the ancient tabernacle in the wilderness. God began with golden vessels, the ark with its mercy seat, then the golden table and lampstand, all speaking of the revelation of God in his glorious attributes, but further of His Beloved Son that would come into the world. (Ex. 25). These precious vessels however must be sheltered, they cannot be left in the open to the fury of the elements, they must have a house, so God then gives instruction for the making of the tabernacle and the tent of covering. Strictly speaking, the tabernacle was the house composed of the ten glorious curtains which in turn was covered by the tent of goats hair, all this is found in Ex. 26.

All is now complete, that is the vessels and house to contain the holy furniture, but it must function, its services and worship must be maintained. To fulfil this, finally God gives instruction concerning the vessels of approach, the golden altar, the laver and the priest with his garments of glory and beauty, anointing oils and so forth. To sum up, furniture is there made according to the God given pattern, the house is there to contain all these and the necessary priesthood is there to make all function for the glory of God.

In the same way the threefold symbolic pictures that John saw are related. The glorious Person is there, the lamps shine unto Him, and the stars are in His right hand, the lamps and stars are unto His person. The son of God has come in answer to the golden furniture of the tabernacle, such a revelation of grace, love, wisdom and power, the Son declared the Father. "God who at sundry times and in divers manners spake in times past unto the fathers by the prophets hath in these last days spoken unto us in His Son". (Heb. 1:1-2). God was in Christ reconciling the world unto himself. Also the Spirit has come down at Pentecost, Divine Persons have been revealed. Such an astonishing revelation must be housed and protected and that is where the churches come in, of which the lampstands are the symbol. There would have been no such thing as churches if Christ had never been incarnate and the Spirit had not come. The churches are supposed to contain the revelation of Divine Persons, and so answer to the teaching of the tabernacle and tent coverings in Ex. 26.

However this is not enough, all must function unto God, leaders are needed, those who are called to responsibility, and willing to take that place. This no doubt is the significance of the stars, just as our Lord is likened unto a star in royalty, one who leads, so these are under stars, those who lead. These are called angels or messengers, and are addressed in the letters to the churches. God has revealed himself in the beloved Son, and the Spirit, this must be contained in the churches, the practice and outlet of truth, and all must function under the leadership of teachers, shepherds and those with the quality to take responsibility. All must then function to the glory of God.

The lampstands must first be considered.

THE METAPHOR OF THE LAMPSTAND

There are eight metaphors of a local church in the New Testament. Seven appear in the words and writings of Paul and are as follows:-

1. The Flock -   Acts 20:28 As touching shepherd care
2. The Tillage -   1 Cor. 3   As touching Fruit, increase
3. The Building -   1 Cor. 3   Thought of Edification
4. The Temple -   1 Cor. 3   Thought of worship, holiness
5. The Body -   1 Cor. 12   The idea of Unity and diversity
6. The Bride -   2 Cor. 11   The affection for the Lord
7. The House -   1 Tim. 3   Thought of Order, discipline

These are followed by the Lampstand as in this chapter. Here the chief concept is Testimony. Note the first and last, the Flock and the Lampstand, the first is what the Lord is for the believer, and the last is what the believer ought to be for the Lord.

1) John is learning, even in old age, the importance of the local church testimony, he was made to turn as if to suggest his face and heart were in a wrong direction.

2) The churches come first in this book that speaks of the purposes of God, in keeping with Ephesians chapter 1 which presents the church as the chief thought in the mind of God; all was proposed before time began.

3) Prophecy, as touching Israel and the Nations cannot proceed to fulfilment until the church programme is completed and the church raptured to heaven.

4) The Lord's chief place today is in the midst of the lampstands or churches as Lord of all, all must be unto Him.

5) The main epistles in the N.T. were written to churches such as Romans, Ephesians, Corinthians etc.. God would impress upon His people the importance of church testimony.

This last church metaphor in the Bible suggests many salient features, and could well be considered under three main headings.

1. Relative to the Godhead.
2. Position and function.
3. Maintenance and supply.

The Godhead has been revealed, hence the church relationship, but they have a service to perform, and all must be supplied if continuance is to be upheld.

1. RELATIVE TO GOD HIMSELF

The first thing that presents itself is the material the lamps are made of, GOLD; twice over the fact is stated that they were golden lampstands (verses 12,20). Gold, as ever speaks of Divine glory; that which is of God and that which represents God, such as the extensive use of gold in the tabernacle. The gold used in the ark, mercy seat, table and lampstand of the tabernacle all witness to the Divinity of our Lord Jesus when He would be manifested in this old world. Now these lamps are made of gold, simply teaching that each N.T. church is Divinely established. God Himself is the source of all such churches, they are planted by God Himself, howbeit He uses men in this labour but the increase is of God. It appears that the word "election" in 1 Thess. 1:4 is not that of the individual, rather the church, "Knowing brethren beloved of God your election" (R.V.). The point is that it is Paul that has this knowledge, and not the believers that formed the church. Paul is speaking of the work that went into the planting of that assembly, and it was evident by the presence of the Holy Spirit that God had foreordained that a church should be planted in that locality. This is no doubt true of every N.T. constituted church, and this wonderful fact is indicated by the gold of the lampstands. When Paul addresses the church of God at Corinth, not only is he denoting the location of the gathering, but also that God is its source, and it ought to be characteristic of the ways of God. As he puts it in 1 Cor. 3, Paul planted, Apollos waters, but God gave the increase. This means that the gathered believers do not own the church, they are responsible to serve in that which belongs to God Himself. True, we do read of churches to the saints, but that is not ownership, rather composition, composed of believers only. The same can be said of churches of the Gentiles in Romans 16:4. It is therefore good to keep in mind that the church belongs to God and is Divinely planted, no matter how weak and small the testimony.

RELATED TO CHRIST THE LORD

1) He is in the midst, all should shine unto Him, each holy exercise of worship, service etc. must always have Christ as its object. Ephesus had missed this vital requirement, to their great loss.

2) He alone can discern the spiritual condition of each church, and discipline accordingly if need be, He is in the midst and knows all things, each letter carries the searching statement, "I know."

3) This Lordship is beautifully taught in Romans 14, all the believer does or says affects the Lord, no man liveth unto himself. The Lord is either pleased or grieved by the behaviour of His people. This is individual, while the lampstand unto the Lord is collective. Each company gathered in the church capacity must do all unto the Lord. This is Lordship, and speaks of authority, headship is somewhat different and speaks of sustenance, Christ is presented as head of the body and all subsistence comes from Him as the head. Christ is never called the Head of the churches in Scripture, rather Lord of the churches, and Head of the church which is His body. So the lampstands must function as unto the Lord, this the chief calling.

RELATIVE TO THE HOLY SPIRIT

The Spirit is seen of course in the oil which is one of the many symbols that present the Spirit in Scripture, and the reason why the rendering "Lampstands" is more accurate than "candlestick". A candlestick depends on its own resources for light whereas the lampstand depends on an outside source, the oil of the Holy Spirit. As the lamp is useless without the oil, so the church cannot operate without the Spirit. An assembly, no matter how gifted, really depends upon the influence of the Holy Spirit to operate unto the Lord in testimony and service. First Corinthians has often been described as the "Charter of the Church", and many of its chapters are saturated with teaching concerning the Spirit as to His working in the believers. When it comes to teaching and learning, the Holy Spirit is essential as is clearly seen in ch. 2, there the Sprit is mentioned seven times, and is therefore a requisite for all communication of Divine truth. Again, when it comes to the activity of gifts and dedicated ability as in ch. 12 the Spirit is mentioned 11 times. How could any Christian seek to exercise any God-given gift or learn the Word apart from the Spirit of God ? This is the lesson in the oil, a lamp cannot give light without it, no more can an assembly function apart from the Holy Spirit.

So the gold speaks of God himself as the source of the assembly in the first place. The church is there for the Lord, His glory in principal, and all thrives by the oil of the Holy Spirit.

2. POSITION AND FUNCTION

The most obvious point in this connection is the fact it is a LAMPSTAND. Lamps are useful things and serve the purpose of giving light. The metaphor used here by the Lord therefore implies that the world is in darkness. Very often this sobering fact is stated in Scripture, one reads of the kingdom of darkness, of people that sit in darkness, and the fact that men love darkness rather than light. The testimony of God to the World of darkness is often presented with the thought of light, hence John the Baptist was a shining light or lamp. The Lord Jesus is the light of the world, and He taught the disciples that they were the light of the world, taking His place in testimony after His resurrection. Paul also designates the believers of Thessalonica as sons of the light and sons of the day. (1 Thess. 5:5). By sons of the light he speaks relative to their union with Christ, as sons of the day he has in mind the eternal day of God to which all Christians are destined. Sons in Scripture speaks of character and inheritance etc.. The believers therefore should reflect the character of the One to whom they belong, and the place for which they are bound. Each Lampstand represents a church in testimony for God in the dark neighbourhood where its lot is cast.

However, the testimony of God is very embracing, the local church is the outlet for all the revelation of God, Paul is thus minded when he speaks of the church as the pillar and ground of the truth. All N.T. truth is under three headings, first there is GOSPEL TRUTH, much of this is found in the Gospels and in some epistles but especially Romans and Galatians. The gospel preacher should be well versed in the gospel parables of our Lord in Luke, and especially in the great salvation passages in John, and very much so in the epistle to Romans and Galatians.

Another section of the revelation is CHURCH TRUTH, and it is precisely this which is presented in the lampstands, as well as in Corinthians and in the prison epistles of Paul. Many dear saints are zealous for the gospel but are very ignorant and negligent of church truth. As previously stated in these notes John himself had his back to the churches, implying that his heart was not where it should have been, the back would be turned on that which is considered unimportant.

The third division of revelation is PROPHECY, the coming events that God will fulfil according to His own purpose, and all through Christ. So many believers have no interest in prophesy at all and look with disdain upon all such teaching, yet a great proportion of the Bible is given to prophecy.

These three cardinal truths have been summed up by others as The CROSS, the CHURCH and the COMING.

Another function of the lamps is to shine upon the Risen Lord, He is in the midst, and as suggested earlier He must be the prime object of all activity and witness. The disciples were commissioned in Luke 24 to be witnesses of these things, that is, the things concerning salvation, but this is further developed in Acts ch. 1, where the Lord speaks of them as being Witnesses UNTO ME, saying "Ye shall be my witnesses". As the lampstand in the tabernacle shone upon itself, so the believer, as the branches with their shining witness, is unto Him.

SEVEN IS COMPLETENESS

There are two numbers used in Scripture to convey a continuing process, the number 7 as the days of the week, then to a new beginning, the same idea with the number 12 as the months in the year. Seven is therefore completeness, nothing can be added as the subject is complete in itself. Such is the revelation of the matter concerning churches, all is complete and nothing is to be added or further revealed. Hence the fact that there are seven lampstands conveys this concept. It is sad today when puny man seeks to add to the perfection that the Lord has left for the believers of the church age. Others of course are busy taking away from it. All the truth is in the Word, but whether man has discovered it all or not is another matter. Much gold is buried in the mines of the earth, but all has not yet been brought to the surface.

It would be an excellent exercise to set aside all traditions and to enquire in the Word as to the matter of church fellowship, and to bow to the perfect will of God in this respect.

This is made clear in Colossians ch. 2, all the treasures of wisdom and knowledge are revealed in Christ and the believer is complete in Him.

THE AUTONOMOUS BASE

The reading is clear that the lampstands were separate from each other, and not as a candelabra, or as in the tabernacle, the Lampstand and its branches. The Lord is walking in the midst of them, thus each is on its own separate base. This is significant, informing of the autonomous churches as seen in the book of Acts etc..

As the standards in the camp of Israel in the wilderness, each was in its own place and all responsibility rested with each tribe to its own standard. The fact that there was an angel for each church bears out this thought, each is responsible for its own government.

Also the fact that a different letter was sent to each emphasizes this concept, each is responsible for its own recovery or whatever else may be required by the Lord.

Yet all were unto the Lord, He was the centre and all must be unto Him. Consider the Nazarite in Israel, there were no doubt many but each one was unto the Lord. Christ was in the midst of a sort of semicircle and all related unto Him.

3. THEIR MAINTENANCE

Chiefly their maintenance would depend on the oil, this has already been considered as the presence and power of the Holy Spirit necessary in every church testimony.   The learning as seen in 1 Cor. 3 was the responsibility of the Holy Spirit as are also the gifts in ch. 12.

However there are necessary conditions for the Spirit to work, the wick must be clean, the Spirit is sensitive, and can be grieved, hence the channel can be choked and no power forth coming. He is not called the HOLY SPIRIT without significance.

Also there needs to be a constant supply of oil otherwise the outcome will be as of the ten virgins of Matt. 25 whose lamps were going out because of the lack of oil. All these are searching lessons, there are conditions to which the Spirit is attracted and in which He is free to work.

THE ANGEL

Here is another side of the maintenance, the angel who is held very responsible for some of the conditions that prevailed, "Thou sufferest that woman Jezebel" and so on. Also being called upon to act in the recovery etc.. Now what is this, who is the angel ?

It cannot be a literal angel, because these are churches, and Colossians distinctly teaches that such are not dependent on angels but are in direct contact with the Head, even Christ. The angel seemingly stands for a group of people in each church, even as the lampstand itself represents many people, even so the angel represents a plurality of believers, who else but the overseers of each church. These are representative as the elders that came to meet Paul at Miletus, and as such are responsible.

Again it would imply that these are teaching elders, those who know the Word and the way to recovery, such was the prophet of old, he was the channel of the Word from the mouth of God leading to repentance and recovery.

These are seen as stars, and stars are used of teachers in Dan. 12:3 and false teachers are likened unto wandering stars in Jude 13. So the teaching body seem to be indicated in the angel, and are for the preservation and progress of the church.

The angels are in the right hand of the Lord and as such are controlled by Him, and not by the angel of another church, the autonomous thought again.

In conclusion, the lampstand teaches many things;

1. Relationships, that of the church to God, the Lord Jesus and the Holy Spirit.
2. The position and function of a local church, to shine in testimony in the world to the last.
3. The maintenance of each church, by the oil and the angel, one speaking of the Spirit, and the other of the teaching feature, all with a view to sanctification for the use of the Lord.

CHAPTER FOUR

The Vision of the Son of Man

A few remarks are necessary on John at this stage. Although he was separated by distance from the dear believers, yet he had an affinity with them. He was one with them as a family, even a brother, and as a partaker in tribulation. Actually, he was more so, likely being banished for his faith, and like them he waited for the coming kingdom of our Lord Jesus. The term "in Jesus" is characteristic, he suffered rejection as the Lord did during His ministry. (Verse 9). Although he was separated from them, for they were on the mainland and he on Patmos; his thoughts were obviously with them, and especially their gathering on the Lord's Day to remember the Lord in the breaking of bread.

The Lord's day, mentioned in verse 10, is suggested by some to be John being projected into the Coming Day of The Lord. This cannot be, strictly speaking: the Day of the Lord begins with the coming in glory of the Son of Man, and therefore is not until ch. 19:11 of this book. All the rest of the material up to that point covered in the Revelation is but precursory leading up to that climax. This is made clear in the preaching of Peter on the day of Pentecost, when he stated that the sun would be darkened and the moon turned to blood BEFORE THAT GREAT AND NOTABLE DAY OF THE LORD COME. (Acts 2:20). Now the signs in the sun and moon are subsequent to the Great Tribulation and all the other things that proceed from it. Therefore the greater part of the material in the Book of Revelation treats of the events leading up to the Day of the Lord. It is more in keeping with the passage to consider the Lord's Day as we know it now, that is the first day of the week which was for the Christian. Upon the first day of the week the Lord was raised from the dead, the Holy Spirit came at Pentecost, the believers met to break bread and the collection was taken. (1 Cor. 16:2).

John, one with the saints but not present with them because of circumstances, was therefore alone. This being so, he is nevertheless in the state required for the exercise of remembering the Lord, he was in the Spirit, the exercise was there no doubt to the pleasure of the Lord. Now more may be contained in this phrase as suggested earlier, but this no doubt was very much the case. The Lord rewards John for this exercise and condition, by a special drawing near of Himself as depicted in this passage. Such a principle, and such a hope for those who, because of infirmity and other circumstances beyond their control, cannot meet with the dear believers but are confined to rooms, beds, and hospitals because of infirmities. Others may be interned in prison camps etc.. To these the Lord often draws near, and many testify that their spiritual experience more than compensates for the restriction in which they found themselves. Such is the case with John in Patmos on the Lord's Day.

FOUR DESCRIPTIVE PICTURES OF THE LORD
IN REVELATION

Four times the Lord appears in this book and is described in symbolic language. Chapter one, as the Son of Man; chapter 5 as the Lamb before the throne; chapter 14 as the Son of Man upon the white cloud and finally in chapter 19 coming upon the white horse. These four pictures are linked in numerous ways, and the more one looks, the more one sees the comparisons and deep mysteries that are embodied in these four great passages.

a) In the first two visions the Lord is seen standing, this is always with a view to service in the Bible.

b) In visions three and four the Lord is seen sitting, upon a white cloud in ch. 14 and upon a white horse in ch. 19. Sitting carries the thought of JUDGMENT, and so in these latter visions.

c) The first two contain the lovely thought of "Being in the midst", of the lampstands and of the throne respectively.

d) In all four pictures there is something in the hand of the Lord, the stars in the first, the book in the second, the sickle in the third and the rod in the fourth vision.

e) As the hand, so also the head is seen in all four visions, His head and His hairs were white like wool as white as snow, the seven horns and seven eyes of chapter 5:6, the victor's crown upon His head in ch. 14 and on His head many diadems in ch. 19. Many other comparisons can be detected by a careful examination of the four passages, but this will suffice to see that the Spirit has left these apparent connections. Each idea of course presents a different character of Christ as meeting the different circumstances and conditions that prevail.

THE TENFOLD SYMBOLIC PICTURE

1. "The Son of Man" would speak of the humanity and compassion of Christ, also His humility, rejection, vindication, coming glory, and the ability to reign and to subject all to Himself to the glory of God. All this and much more is contained in the title of The Son of Man. Such characteristics of Christ are seen throughout the Revelation in His relation to the earth and the nations.

2. The garment down to the foot. Garments in Scripture speak of office and character, and two men were so clothed in Israel's past history with garments to the foot. The High Priest in the tabernacle days, and Eliakim, the governor in Isaiah ch. 22:21, here the Lord is seen officially as the Priest of His people and also as governor. Eliakim is a type of Christ as the passage in Isaiah goes on to expound, using the language used of the Lord to the church at Philadelphia, "He that hath the keys of David, and he shall open and none shall shut, and he shall shut and none shall open".

3. The girdle is also linked with the priest and administrator as seen in Ex. 28 and Isa. 22. This speaks of service, and in both these offices the Lord serves His beloved people. Also he will be the righteous governor in the Millennial kingdom.

4. His head and hair would declare His wisdom, the quality to judge and rule, similar to the Ancient of days seen in Dan. 7:13. Here indeed is the power and wisdom of Christ as stated in 1 Cor. 1:24.

5. His eyes as a flame of fire. This is a symbolic conveyance of the omniscience of Christ, He sees all, He knows all, and nothing is

hidden from His all searching eyes. "All things are naked and opened unto the eyes of him with whom we have to do". (Heb. 4:13). Fire is ever the sign of judgment, righteous judgment in keeping with the nature of God.

6. His feet like unto fine brass as if they burned in a furnace. This speaks of His power to take up judgment, the firmness with which sin must be met. Note, the eyes see the need for the judgment and the feet carry it out accordingly. Many good men can see the need for discipline but have not the power to carry it out, the Lord does not fail in this. Brass ever speaks of righteousness as dealing with man in responsibility. In the holy of holies and in the holy place of the tabernacle, God is seen in intrinsic holiness symbolized by the gold, but in the court where man is responsible, brass was the material of the altar and laver.

7. His voice as the sound of many waters. This speaks of power in Psalm 93:4. "The Lord on high is mightier than the noise of many waters, yea than the mighty waves of the sea".

8. He had in His right hand seven stars. This speaks of His authority, holding all things secure for God. This symbol is most important as used in the Lord's approach to Ephesus in Ch. 2:1 and to Sardis in 3:1.

9. Out of His mouth went a sharp two edged sword. The power of His word in judgment is depicted in this, also to discern what is to be disciplined and what is to be encouraged. "For the Word of God is living and powerful and sharper than any two edged sword" (Heb. 4:12) This of course is the spoken word, the Lord shall consume by the word of His mouth. He speaks the word and it is done, as often in His miracles recorded in the Gospels. It is interesting to see that the Word as a sword immediately follows the stars, they represent teachers in Scripture, and the bond between the two is evident, the teacher must teach His Word and nothing else, the Lord's messenger with the Lord's message.

10. His countenance was as the sun shineth in its strength. Again His power and majesty is in view, His right and ability to reign as the sun of righteousness by and by.

There is a moral order in the description, first He is seen as Man, the way the revelation of grace came. Then He appears as Divine, as the Jehovah, the Ancient of days, followed by His ability to judge as seen in the eyes and feet. Then finally as the One who would bring to fruition all the purposes of God in power, to judge and consume all enemies, and to set up a kingdom in righteousness. These latter would be official glories.

From a devotional standpoint this portion is precious. Consider the contrast in the glorified Man here to the Man of humility as depicted in the Gospels.

Garment to the foot - The short seamless tunic. John 19:23
Breast girded - He girded himself with a towel John 13
Head white - Nowhere to lay his head. Matt 8:20
Eyes as flame - Eyes that wept. John 11
Feet as brass - Feet pierced John 19
Voice as waters - Voice not heard in streets Matt 12:19
Stars in hand - Hands often in service in Mark
Sword of mouth - Gracious words proceed out of His mouth
Countenance as sun - Visage was so marred

Another order can de discerned in the remarkable description here from a practical viewpoint.

1) The Son of Man and the garment and girdle speak of experience. This is needed for all rule and authority. Even the priest had to be taken from among men, so as to have experience in the things that concern man. This thought naturally comes first.

2) The head and hair speak of wisdom, experience is not balanced without wisdom. How to apply lessons learnt is a great art indeed. This comes next.

3) This is followed by the power and willingness to set things right, seen in the eyes and feet, both carrying the symbol of fire.

4) Now follows the word, the voice as many waters, and the sword out of the mouth. He speaks with authority and power;
everything falls into place as God ordained.

5) Finally heavenly things, the stars and the sun. Both are spoken of as rewards in Scripture. "They that turn many to righteousness shall shine as stars for ever". (Dan. 12:3). "Then shall the righteous shine forth as the sun in the kingdom of their Father (Matt 13:43). This then is promotion and reward, as to His servants in Matt. 13, so to Himself here.

Now this can well be illustrated by a manager in a workshop as follows.

1) He must be a man of experience er he can take control, as befitting the Lord in this passage.

2) He must have the necessary knowledge of that product or whatever business the workshop is engaged in. A novice will not do.

3) He must be able to speak with authority, that authority coming out of his experience and knowledge, and people are bound to listen, there must be subjection to his word if production is to be maintained or increased.

4) He now speaks, and with power as a sword, as many waters, and all will instantly obey him, thus all things operate smoothly and the goal in production is reached.

5) Finally, all is rewarded, and the righteous manager will see that good men have the place they deserved. This seems to be the order here, and is most practical. Would that churches would run their affairs and activities as the example of the Lord here. He will control and bring to fruition the eternal counsels of God both now and in the last days.

INTRODUCTION TO WHOLE BOOK

As earlier stated in these notes, this vision is an introduction to the whole book of Revelation and not to the seven churches only, although the symbols from this are used extensively. The sword out from the Lord's mouth and eyes as a flame of fire are found again in ch. 19. Many other allusions from this vision of the Son of Man are further developed in the Revelation. Nevertheless, the seven churches can take many lessons from this wonderful vision, and in a special order that may not be detected in a casual reading.

This must now be considered.

THE VISION AND THE SEVEN CHURCHES

The tenfold symbolic description falls into two groups, those that are used in the way the Lord introduces Himself to the churches, and those which are not so used, but silent. The symbols used in the addresses are as follows.

Walking in midst of the lampstands, to Ephesus.

The seven stars in his hand, twice, to Ephesus, and Sardis.

Sword of mouth to Pergamos.

Eyes as flame of fire, and feet as brass to Thyatira.

Five in all, as stars are used twice, so exactly half of the symbols are used by the Lord in His addresses.

The way they are used is most instructive, and much truth is no doubt contained therein. The churches fall into three categories.

1) Those with nothing in them to condemn as Sardis and Philadelphia.
2) One that is condemned rather than commended, Laodicea.
3) Those that are both commended and condemned for some things.

Now it is to this last group that the symbols are taken from the vision and used in the opening address to each church, namely four, Ephesus, Pergamos, Thyatira and Sardis, these four are both commended and condemned. To these only are the five points so used and therefore carry an important meaning.

It would seem that these points are so used then to ENCOURAGE THE GOOD and to JUDGE THE EVIL, as these peculiar churches are firstly commended for their steadfastness etc. then condemned for their neglectfulness. Now consider:-

1) Ephesus, the Lord as walking in the midst of the lampstands. This carries the thought of nearness, intimacy, complete knowledge as being able to discern true condition. The church at Ephesus had many things to commend, their toiling, discernment of evil men and abhorrence of such, steadfastness in the truth, and the hatred of the Nicolaitanes. By the Lord so near, as walking in the midst of the lampstands, they can take courage of His approval and by His help, strive all the more in these graces. However, the nearness of the Lord also detects the fact of their having left their first love, and this turned out to be a very serious defect indeed. By His walking so intimately with them His accessibility is ready to be used to their recovery. Also the mention of the stars are a warning not to seek to control other churches, all control is in His hand. This will be more fully dealt with in the consideration of the letter to Ephesus. However, the mention of the stars in His hand encourages leadership.

2) Pergamos, and the two edged sword from His mouth. This indicates good in the correction of false doctrine. The church was being handicapped by the doctrine of Balaam and that of the Nicolaitanes, the sword, speaking of the Word can correct all this. The sword is used in judgment on the teachers of such erroneous doctrine, the teachers of such will suffer discipline of some sort (2:19). The same

sword of the Word of God is the way to correction. The truth manifests and removes the error, "to the law and to the testimony, if they speak not according to this word it is because there is no light in them" (Isa. 8:20). Such is the way the symbol is used in Pergamos.

3) The Eyes as fire and the feet of brass to Thyatira. Division existed in this church along with many other defects, but worst of all, "The depths of Satan"(2:24). The eyes as fire can discern this, which the wisest of men would fail to see. The fire will also devour the evil, and the Lord shall crush the offenders with the feet of brass. The Lord can discern their problems, and read their motives. He also is the answer, as in ch. 5 He appears with the seven eyes speaking of perfect intelligence. Colossians ch. 2 carries this thought, there the Lord is the answer to every false teaching and doctrine which would plague the saints of God. "In whom are hid all the treasure of wisdom and knowledge".

4) In Sardis, the Lord is seen holding the seven stars and the Seven Spirits of God, both taken from the vision of ch. 1. How encouraging to the dying church, the fact of the Spirit of God, the channel of life. Also the responsibility of leadership as seen in the stars. It is encouraging to know that the stars are held by Him, all is not lost, if they are willing, new life can be injected into that church.

This seems to be the pattern in which the points taken from the vision are used in the addresses to the churches. The order is steadfast; only in the churches that are both commended and condemned is language borrowed from the great vision of chapter one.

THE OUTCOME OF THE VISION UPON JOHN

1) John fell at the feet of the Son of Man, in the days of His flesh he leaned upon His bosom. The human body of Christ in the Gospels is now, by resurrection and the ascension placed in the glorified state. God has given Him glory, Paul also was confronted with this on the road to Damascus, he fell down upon the ground before the glorious Lord. Stephen saw the Lord in heaven, he did not fall to the ground, because already he was entering into that company of the spirits of just men made perfect. How wonderful, on the brink of death he was prepared for the heavenlies.

2) John fell as a dead man, similar to the soldiers that guarded the tomb of our Lord, at the appearing of the angel they became as dead men

(Matt 28:4), they were not on resurrection ground. John is on resurrection ground but not yet on the ground of glory, that was yet to come.

3) The Lord laid His right hand upon him, the hand that held the stars, speaking of security, power and authority, "kept by the power of God" as Peter would say. John himself was a star, a bearer of the truth as shining in the darkness, so the right hand was laid upon him, the Lord preserves those carriers of the Word until their task is finished.

4) The cheering words, "Be not afraid" ... The voice of many waters, without the touch and the voice John would remain as dead, even so it is with the gospel message, the dead shall hear the voice of the Son of God and they that hear shall live (John 5:25). To John this is the touch of identification and the Word of compassion, all is well.

5) The first and last, among other things is indicative of "Always being present", before all things and after all is folded up, just another way of saying "I am always with you."
He is the beginning of all, He sustains all and He finishes all.

6) A few more wonderful statements are made, these to do with His achievements, "I am He that liveth and was dead." That state of death he willingly entered into, manifesting the love that could not be quenched. The very state that so many dear saints were entering into in the Book of Revelation. The state of death that John was in by figure. The Lord entered into death and destroyed it. The mysteries of His death are unfathomable, but the reason for that agonising death is well experienced in those who believe. To such the sting of death is removed.

7) Behold I am alive for evermore. He now occupies the place of glory, He liveth after the power of an endless life. Never again shall the lord be subjected to that which is the penalty for sin. Sin and death are finished for the believer through Him.

8) Amen, (R.V. has "therefore"), the result of this entering into death and resurrection, means the Lord has power over the underworld, He has the keys of death and of hell. He has the power to release, this is demonstrated to John, the Lord has the key, not man or Satan. A key of David is mentioned in chapter 3:7, there it refers to power over the political and material world, here reference is to the spiritual world.

9) John is now commanded to write, to go on with his service, the view of the glory has prepared the servant. Such was the case with Isaiah,

after seeing the glory, he was commissioned to preach (Isa. 6) similarly with Paul; the Lord of glory appeared, he fell to the ground, after adjustment is made to his spiritual condition by conversion, he is commissioned as a chosen vessel.

The three things of verse 19 are often used to divide the book of Revelation, but this division obscures the subject matter which really is the message of the Book, as seen earlier.

THE STARS AND ANGELS OF THE CHURCHES

Much has already been noted on this subject but a few remarks here would not be out of place.

a) Stars are a symbol of teachers (Dan. 12, Jude 13) and of leaders, for the Lord Himself is seen as the Star out of Jacob, meaning the king (Num. 24:17), and the root and offspring of David the bright and morning star (Rev. 22:16). Teaching elders are here presupposed.

b) The word "angel" really means "messenger". When angels appear in Scripture they are messengers representing the living God. In another sense, the believers thought that Peter was dead and that Rhoda had seen his spirit or angel, that which represented Peter (Acts 12:15). These angels are used in this sense here, representing those messengers who handle the Word of truth and representing God. Such were the teaching elders in the seven churches.

c) The angel is addressed each time, "unto the angel of the church", they are part of the testimony, a literal heavenly angel could not be so. The angel in each case is either commended or condemned with the church "I have something against thee (The angel) thou hast left thy first love". If literal angels they would then be fallen angels and immediately banished to Tartarus (2 Pet. 2:4).

d) They are spoken of as part of the church, " But to you I say, to the rest that are in Thyatira." (2:24 R.V.) Also in 2:13, "My faithful martyr who was slain among you", the angel is part of the church at Smyrna as was Antipas.

e) In the last three letters the angel is not distinguished from the church as in the first four, but is addressed throughout. This fact may intimate that the management in the churches were losing position and authority at that early stage.

From all this it is the better suggestion that the angel is the leading and teaching element in the churches.

CHAPTER FIVE

An Introduction to the Churches of Asia

A very small island, Patmos, about 10 miles long, with approximately 37 miles of coastline, situated about forty miles from the mainland and sixty miles from Ephesus is the setting for the grand tableau of scenes that make up the Book of Revelation. It may be of little esteem in the eyes of the world, but it is the setting of the great movement of God in revealing His will for John, the future and the destiny of all nations.

John is separated from the churches of the saints, he is lonely, longing for Christian fellowship, but the sea isolates him from the beloved saints. One day, there will be "No more sea" (21:1) and the time of separation will be over.

The reason for this isolation is given as John being there, "For the word of God and the testimony of Jesus Christ". (I:9). This could be interpreted in two ways.

1) Banished there because of his Christian beliefs, John is being persecuted for both righteousness sake and for the Sake of Christ (Matt. 5:10-11). The enemies of the gospel had therefore deported him to that lonely island.

2) The other thought is that the Lord so ordained him to be there alone for special dealings, perhaps he was there on a visit or went on his

own accord as Paul upon conversion went into Arabia for a season. Either way, he was there, and the Lord gave the wonderful messages to pass on to the churches.

In a sense he was in good company, as often men of God were taken aside for special teaching in the Spirit. For instance :-

Joseph in the prison became the revealer of secrets.

Moses at the burning bush in the wilderness learnt the Name of Jehovah, and the purpose of delivering the people of Israel.

David who was often afflicted became the sweet Psalmist of Israel.

Daniel, exiled from his Nation and home, was the first to learn of God's programme in "The Times of the Gentiles" and passed this on in his inspired writing.

Ezekiel also in exile, in a prisoner of war camp saw heaven opened, and became the channel through which we received exceeding great prophecies concerning Israel, and the nations.

The apostle Paul while in prison wrote the Prison Epistles revealing the staggering truth concerning the Church as the body of Christ.

John follows in the footsteps of these great men to whom God in the silent place, reveals His mind and purpose with ever-lasting effects.

CHURCHES IN A PROPHETIC BOOK?

Why read of churches in the only prophetic book in the New Testament ? Several answers could be given to this question.

1) Judgment must begin at the house of God (1 Pet. 4:17), and of course the churches filled that place, both then and now, being God's testimony on earth.

2) The subject of the church is important, there can be no fulfilment of any prophecy of Scripture without it, all God's purposes can only come to consummation if the Church is in existence. Therefore the churches come first in this prophetic book.

3) The ways of the Lord are not only doctrinally intelligent, but also practical, this can be seen in the first chapter of our Bible, all works are in consideration of Man and the place of his subsistence. Consider

the apostles, in difficulties over doctrine, when all was ironed out, a stipulation was made "To consider the poor" which Paul and his company were already determined to do (Gal. 2:10). In every N.T. book a section or more is given over to practical application, this principle follows in the first 3 chapters of the Revelation.

4) The church is the consummation of all God's plans, through it the Lord will bring about all He has proposed, and the church shall have the chief place.

5) Consider the part this book would play to the first readers going through a terrible period of persecution, as stated in the introduction and because of this, encountering many problems. The first three chapters of this book deal with the first great problem, MUST CHURCH LIFE CONTINUE ? The letters to the seven churches certainly answer this in the affirmative.

The early Christians were most active in gospel witness, and successful to the extent that it is said that the churches in Asia numbered 500 or more. If that be so, why are only 7 chosen here for the special communication from the Lord, and why this particular seven ? The simple reason is that a singular condition existed in each church. Paul wrote to seven churches, two epistles to two of them making in all nine church epistles. In the studying of them it can be learned how they began in those early days. John also writes to 7 churches, not as to how they started, rather as to how they fared. All in Asia had turned away from Paul (2 Tim. 1:15), but later, as recorded in these churches, some are turning away from the Lord.

Each of the churches hold forth their testimony under different circumstances, some are suffering, some are not and so forth. Also the spiritual condition in each is vastly dissimilar. This difference can be summed up in a word or two as follows.

Ephesus was doctrinally sound but missing the needed affection and motivation as unto the Lord. A MISGUIDED CHURCH.

Smyrna is suffering trial, persecution is their lot, howbeit there seems to be no error in doctrine. A PERSECUTED CHURCH.

Pergamos is a hotbed of teaching, but alas, quite a lot of it is false. Therefore, AN ERRING CHURCH.

Thyatira is quite progressive and active, predominate in works commended by the Lord, but, sad to say, factions exist. Therefore, A DIVIDED CHURCH.

Sardis had many activities in the past, some had ceased, others were about to cease, yet a few believers remain faithful and exhibit Life. A DYING CHURCH.

Philadelphia was not large in numbers or gift, yet faithful in that which they had. A WEAK CHURCH.

Laodicea gloried in riches as far as the world is concerned, but were experiencing poverty in the riches of God.

A MATERIALISTIC CHURCH.

THE CATCH PHRASE

The varied condition of each church can be summed up in a "catch phrase" that occurs in each letter, words that are patently set in contrast.

In Ephesus. LOVE (2:4) AND HATE (2:6) if their love to the Lord had been as strong as their hatred of error, all would have been well.

In Smyrna, the catch phrase is POVERTY AND RICHES. (2:9). Poor as to this world but rich as touching the world to come.

Pergamos. The two words HOLD AND CAST (2:14). They were holding personally to things that were having an adverse effect on others, casting them down to be idolaters.

Thyatira. The catch phrase occurs in verse 19, LAST AND FIRST.

There is progress in this church in spite of the divisions, their last works had eclipsed their first.

Sardis. LIVING AND DYING (3:1). The profession of the Name was present, but the process of death was at work.

In Philadelphia the catch theme is OPEN AND SHUT (3:7). Opportunity is given them by the Lord, an open door, and no man can shut it.

Laodicea. This one is well known, HOT AND COLD (3:15). The lukewarm condition, they were spoilt for the world, yet of little use in the service of the Lord.

This catch phrase in each letter is most important, it sums up very neatly the condition as in the sight of the Lord.

DIFFERENT PERILS IN EACH

As well as all this, each church is in danger in some way, and again these dangers are so dissimilar from each other.

Ephesus is in danger of being removed, the ceasing of the testimony altogether, the removal of the lampstand.

Smyrna is in danger of discouragement, the Lord cheers them with the great "Fear not", discouragement is very defeating.

Pergamos. The danger in that church was the heresy that was being held by so many, again the effects were very far reaching.

Thyatira. Depletion in numbers by death and the discipline of the Lord - a perilous condition in which to be.

Sardis. The testimony is weakening, and in danger of dying out altogether, the process of death is at work.

Laodicea. Time was running out for them, they were about to be spewed out by the Lord, his denunciation is very serious.

Thus, all the churches were in peril in some way, some from without, others from within.

The unmistakable reason for the differences prevailing in each church is the lesson for churches today. All these conditions are evident in many churches in the present day, therefore help is available to such in the reading of these letters.

Overshadowing all is the main problem, "Is church life to continue if some or all of these adverse conditions exist"? Yes, none are called upon to close the door, only the Lord can determine that. Such a voice to churches everywhere in these last days of church testimony.

THE OLD TESTAMENT BACKGROUND

Each of the seven letters are based upon an Old Testament passage or book. This is quite evident in some, Pergamos for instance, the wilderness journey is beyond doubt the foundation of that letter, the reference to the Manna, Balaam, Balak etc.. It is so with all the messages, and the Old Testament background is there to convey to the reader the fact that the same sins and hindrances can cripple believers today as in Old Testament times. It is therefore profitable to examine the distinct O. T. reference in each letter, and this will we do if God permits.

THREE WAYS TO VIEW

These church letters can be viewed in three ways.

1) Essentially, as they existed in their time, the historic circumstances that surrounded them, and the internal problems with which they had

to cope.   Adding to this the different dealings of God with each church.

2) Prophetically. The word "Mystery" (1:20) suggests that some deeper scheme lies beneath the surface.   This is the favourite way of interpreting these letters to the churches, most, if not all the commentaries on Revelation follow this idea.   The details of this can be seen in the Tableau at the close of this chapter.

However, a few words of explanation are needed on this subject. The section is one of three double panoramic pictures in the Bible.

A. Gen. 49, the Blessing of the sons by Jacob, is a panoramic view of Israel's history right up to the Millennium as seen from a national stance.

B. In Deut. chapter 33 Moses blesses the tribes of Israel, again a wonderful picture of Israel's future history, only this time from a spiritual viewpoint.

A. From Dan. ch. 2 using an image made of metals, God gives a picture of the times of the Gentiles, this from a national viewpoint.

B. Again in Dan. 7 the same nations are viewed from a spiritual angle this time by the picture of wild monstrosities of beasts.

A. In Matt. 13 from the parables of our Lord, again a panoramic view of the church appears, that is outwardly, with regard to profession etc..

B. The series is complete with Rev. ch. 2 and 3 where the church is seen from a spiritual point of view.

Summing up, two sections to do with the Nation of Israel. Gen. 49 and Deut. 33, one is outward, the other inward.

Two sections to do with The Gentiles, Dan. 2 and 7 and again one is outward, the other inward.

Two sections given to the church of God, Matt. 13 and Rev. 2-3 following the same pattern, one outward, the other inward.

The Word of God therefore traces the future of the Jew, Gentile and the church of God in an historical and spiritual way.

THE STRUCTURE OF THE LETTERS IS AMAZING

They form inverted parallels, that is, the first and the last have the same features. The second and sixth follow suit. The third and fifth again are so alike, and the middle one, Thyatira stands alone. Why this structure? a few answers could be given to this question.

1) To present the prophetic view as already stated.
2) To aide the memory, in order to to keep in mind several features.
3) To highlight the centre, the most important part, in this case the church of Thyatira is the most important.
4) To give two sides to the same truth.

This structure can be seen in the summary at the end of this chapter.

Another feature of the letter structure is that the seven are divided into a three and a four. This feature is uniform in the "Sevens" of the Bible, and throughout the Book of Revelation this factor can be seen many times.

In the first three, the Promise comes after the appeal to hear, this is reversed in the final four, the appeal comes before the promise.

Again the first three promises are related to life, the promise to Ephesus is "To eat of the tree of life", and that of Smyrna "the overcomers' shall not be hurt of the second death. That of Pergamos is "To eat of the hidden manna", which sustained life. The Lord spoke a great sermon on the Manna and the life He gave (John 6). The last four are all in the relation of Christ to his Father, God. Thyatira, the promise is to rule with Christ as he received of HIS FATHER. To Sardis, the promise is that the overcomer among other things shall be confessed by Christ before MY FATHER. The next to Philadelphia is to be made a pillar in the temple of MY GOD. Finally to Laodicea, the promise is to sit with Christ on his throne even as He is sat on HIS FATHER'S THRONE. The first three emphasize LIFE, and the final four deal with INTIMACY. It is clear therefore that the letters are intentionally divided into a three and a four.

A GREAT AREA OF TRUTH

1) There is much here for the analytically minded, there are 17 distinct titles of the Lord Jesus in the two chapters containing the seven letters, besides many other titles in chapter one.
2) The Lord presents Himself to each church in a different but suitable way, He is the answer to all the difficulties that exist in churches. If only the dear people of God would grasp this, there would be less leaning upon feeble man, and less failure would be forth-coming.

3) The Discernment as in Ephesus is another important feature, He alone can discern the full spiritual condition of any church.

4) The Lord encourages as in Smyrna, He is the source of all comfort and fortitude.

5) The Lord warns as in Pergamos, oh that the dear saints would listen to the warnings from Scripture that the Lord brings home to the heart.

6) He chastens as in Thyatira, He is Lord of the churches, and in His hand is power to righteously discipline, and all with a view to recovery.

7) He will hold out incentives as to Sardis, the promise, "they shall walk with me in white, for they are worthy".

8) The Lord blesses as to Philadelphia, all blessing comes from Him, He alone can give the open door of opportunity.

9) He appeals, and challenges as in Laodicea. "I counsel thee", "behold I stand at the door and knock". How wonderful that the Lord should so appeal to a lukewarm church.

DANGERS TO THE CHURCHES

PRACTICAL DANGERS exist in the subtle formalism of Ephesus, and in the discouragement of Smyrna. Also the laxness, idolatry and fornication of Pergamos. The deadness of Sardis, and the materialism of Laodicea, lessons can be learned there also.

DOCTRINAL DANGERS. The Judaism and false apostles that threatened Ephesus, there is also the legalistic doctrines suggested by the "the synagogue of Satan" in Smyrna. The terrible deeds and doctrine of the Nicolaitanes that were disquieting Pergamos. Then the awful doctrine of Balaam, compromise with the world, that was also afflicting Pergamos. On top of all this, the horrible doctrine of Jezebel, spiritual perversion, that was afflicting Thyatira. These dangers existed then - both in a practical and a doctrinal sense, and they still exist in various forms today in several churches of the saints.

THE ACTIVITY OF SATAN

The hiss of the serpent can be heard behind the several practices and doctrines as seen already. Satan progressively appears in the church letters.

To the Jews, the synagogue of Satan as in Smyrna and Philadelphia. To the Gentiles, the throne of Satan appears in Pergamos. Further still, the depths of Satan as seen in Thyatira. Also he is seen in Smyrna as both the Devil and Satan, twin titles with different meanings, as well as his character of "Liar" in Ephesus. The "murderer" characteristic appears in Thyatira. If there is trouble, the devil is not far away as these letters prove.

DISCIPLINE IN THE CHURCHES

Ephesus is threatened with removal of the Lampstand of testimony.

The sword is used in some way in Pergamos, perhaps a cutting off of some trouble makers, or some other severe form of discipline.

The principle of sowing and reaping; retribution is observed in Thyatira, while the sudden unexpected discipline is described as like to the coming of a thief to Sardis. Finally, to be spewed out of the mouth of the Lord is the promised discipline to Laodicea. The Lord is in the midst of the churches, His prerogative is to discipline a church, the elders can discipline individuals only.

FINALLY, THE LORD'S RETURN

The return of the Lord is held out as an encouragement and an incentive to some of the churches. "Hold fast until I come" was a word to Thyatira. "Behold I come quickly" or soon is the stimulation to Philadelphia. The coming thief idea as to Sardis is not necessarily the Lord's return, rather a coming in with discipline at any unexpected time. The spewing out of the mouth of the Lord in Laodicea again may not by definition be a reference to the return, howbeit Christendom as such will inevitably be rejected by the returning Lord.

SURVEY OF THE SEVEN CHURCHES. REV. 2-3

PARALLELS	FEATURES	PROPHETIC
A. EPHESUS	1. Meaning Desirable	Apostolic
1. Paul Planted	2. Formal Church	A. D. 50-150
2. Paul wrote to	3. O.T. Gen. 3	
3. Stars	4. Ref. lamps, stars	
4. Left first love.	5 Love and hate	
5. Removal.	6. Promise. Tree, life	

PARALLELS	FEATURES	PROPHETIC
B. SMYRNA	1. Meaning Myrrh	Roman Persecution
1. No rebuke.	2. Persecuted church	A.D. 150-300
3. Synagogue of Satan	3. O.T. Exodus	
3. Crown of life	4. Ref. dead and alive	
4. Trial, believer	5 Poverty and riches	
5. Not hurt, death.	6. Promise, no second death	
C. PERGAMOS	1. Meaning Marriage	Church and State
1. Come, make war	2. Erring church	A.D. 300-500
2. White stone.	3. O.T. Wilderness	
3. Name written	4. Ref. Sword	
	5. Cast and hold	
	6. Promise Manna, life.	
D. THYATIRA	1. Meaning Wear Away	Papal, Dark Ages
1. Longest letter.	2. Divided church	A.D. 500-1500
2. Middle Letter	3. O.T. King Ahab	
	4. Ref. eyes, feet.	
	5. Last and first	
	6. Promise. My Father	
	Rule. political	
C. SARDIS	1. Meaning Escape	Reformation
1. Came as thief	2. Dying church	A.D. 1500-1800
2. White Garments	3. O.T. Joash	
3. Name not blotted	4. Ref. stars, spirits	
	5. Living, dying	
	6. Promise, My Father	
	Confess, Religious	
B. PHILADELPHIA	1. Brotherly love	Missionary
1. No rebuke	2. Fruitful church	Revival
2. Synagogue of Satan	3. O.T. Hezekiah	A.D. 1800-1900
3. Loss Crown	4. Ref. Faithful, Key	
4. Trial earth	5. Open, shut	
5. No more out	6. Promise, My God	
	Pillar, Religious	
A. LAODICEA	1. People rule	Materialism
1. Paul Planted	2 Blind church	A.D. 1900 -?
2. Paul wrote to	3. O.T. Captivity	
3. Creation	4. Ref. Faithful witness	
4. I Love	5. Hot and cold	
5. Spewed out	6. Promise Father	
	Throne, Political	

CHAPTER SIX

Gospel Work at Ephesus

The city of Ephesus was the capital of Asia minor, and in those primitive far off days it had grown substantially. It appears that at the time of writing the population numbered 300,000, which was indeed quite sizable. The main reason for the remarkable growth was the fact that the city possessed a busy seaport, and the main road leading to the waterfront was 70 feet wide and beautified with rows of columns on either side.

The city was famous on two counts, it boasted a marvellous theatre, being one of the wonders of that day, this drew many people to visit the city, besides those who chose to dwell there. This theatre was said to be able to seat 50,000 people, one sixth of the population of the city in fact, and is in keeping with some of the mighty auditoriums of today.

The other feature that made the city famous was the temple to Diana, the goddess that was supposed to fall out of heaven. It was because of the worship of Diana, and the profits certain people made out of this adoration, that Paul encountered such trouble in Ephesus as recorded in Acts 19. Seemingly it took 220 years to build this temple, probably the longest period ever to be devoted to one building. Its dimensions were 343 feet by 164 feet and it was surrounded by a forest of columns 50 feet high, it must have been quite a sight in those days.

As a result of these important factors the city became the centre of Art, Drama, Culture, magic books and many other things that of course led to offensive behaviour and sin of an ominous kind. On top of this, the city became the seat of the cult of Emperor worship, this of course led to vexation for the believers in those apostolic days. Another factor which must be considered, many of the Jews who inhabited Ephesus at that time, practised a sort of healing and casting out of demons, which caused some concern to the apostle Paul when he was preaching there (Acts 19:13-14).

How wonderful, that sinful city was visited by the gospel, and God planted a very healthy church for a testimony there.

The spiritual history is found in Acts 18-19. Paul visited the city on the way to Jerusalem and Antioch, accompanied by Pricilla and Aquila a very devout couple (Acts 18:19). He did some teaching in the synagogue of the Jews which was well accepted. They desired him to stay longer but he had other plans, however, he left Pricilla and Aquila there for a witness, or perhaps to establish a sort of work and went on his way to Jerusalem.

Later he returned and stayed two whole years, and the work began in earnest. A company of disciples of John the Baptist were found there, after learning the truth, these no doubt, formed the foundation of the new assembly that was planted. The Jews however turned out to be a disappointment, they behaved in an antagonistic way, and were not as favourable to the Word as previously, how fickle is man. Paul set up a preaching centre in the school of Tyrannus, and a mighty work was accomplished there it seems. Special miracles were granted from the Lord, heaven favoured the work, and it became a real visitation of grace from the Lord. The city therefore became a centre of evangelism to all Asia, being a city of culture and commerce with a constant stream of visitors from numerous places.

The work was most genuine which explains why Satan was so active in seeking to hinder the progress. The deception was seen in the sons of Sceva who professed to heal, in reality Satan was appearing as an angel of light. Further, he appeared as a roaring lion in the religious uproar in the theatre, concerning which Paul later wrote "I have fought with beasts at Ephesus" (1 Cor. 15:32). The town clerk was wise, and stilled the mob, and Paul escaped with his life. However, the gospel triumphed, the remarkable change was seen in the believers burning the old magic books and curious arts, and leaving once for all the worship of Diana. This was the reason for the uproar, not any affection or allegiance for Diana, rather the pockets of the silversmiths were emptied of profit. Such was the revival in Ephesus.

Development was soon manifested there, elders were raised up by the Holy Spirit (Acts 20:28) and a great emphasis was placed upon teaching. Visits by Apollos, Timothy, John, Aquila, Paul and many more, were the order of the day, really the cream of teaching brethren were most influential in the church. The epistle to the Ephesians is recognized as reaching the highest church teaching in the N.T.

Time makes differences, and eventually unsound teaching entered in. Timothy became the man of the hour, and managed by a visit and teaching to subdue the useless unsound doctrines that were seeking to arise. (1 Tim. 1) The Christians were sound in the faith and without the slightest hint of unsound teaching in the assembly when later the Lord dictated the letter of Rev. 2.

While in prison Paul wrote the familiar epistle to Ephesians. In that wonderful letter among other things, LOVE is found 14 times and 12 references to the Holy Spirit of God. Think of some of the Love passages.

Rooted and grounded in love
Forbearing one another in love
To know the love of Christ
Body edifying itself in love
Grace with all that love our Lord Jesus

All these references are from Ephesians. The last one is most touching.

Some time later the Lord sends the letter to the same church in Rev. 2. The trouble is not from without, they were able to endure with joy any persecution and trial that would arise. Nor is the trouble doctrinal, Timothy took good care of that, rather something subtle, deep; and hard to observe, namely, the LEAVING OF THE FIRST LOVE, which makes this first letter of the utmost importance. Even when doctrinally sound, the motive for all church activity is that the Lord must have His portion, after all the assembly is for His display even as the body is the display of the Head. Hence the church is threatened with removal, the only one so endangered, this first letter is worthy of great consideration, for any church today can fall into the same subtle condition.

CHAPTER SEVEN

The Letter to Ephesus - Rev. 2:1:7

It would be helpful to approach each of these letters with the same formula, each adhering to an order as follows.

1. Any special features, peculiar to the said letter.
2. The Old Testament background.
3. The catch phrase.
4. The way the Lord introduces Himself.
5. The information concerning each church.
6. The remedy.
7. The appeal and promise at close.

Before following this course with this first letter an important question must first be settled.

WHY EPHESUS FIRST?

Why Ephesus first? Was it because its testimony was in the capital, or was it the most sound church doctrinally ? The Lord is interested in all churches, and does not give one priority over another because of its location or merit. A longer letter was written to Corinth, which was followed by another, yet Corinth was not a capital city. There are three reasons for this Ephesus letter to appear first.

1/ The letters came from Patmos, Ephesus was a seaport therefore it would be natural to visit Ephesus first to deliver the letter. However although this is one reason it is not really what the Lord had in mind.

2/ Because of the panoramic nature of the letters surveying the whole time of grace, Ephesus would come first being the Apostolic period.

3/ Ephesus had received the most instruction of all the churches, therefore they are addressed first for they have the greatest responsibility.

"He that knew his Master's will and did it not shall be beaten with many stripes", so says the parable (Luke 12:47). Ephesus carried the greatest responsibility and therefore that church alone was threatened with removal. Light brings accountability.

1. THE SPECIAL FEATURES

These special features are most important, they show the particular instructions that the Lord would have believers know in each separate letter.

This is the only letter of the seven where the word "Apostle" is found. "Thou hast tried them which say they are apostles and are not". As more or less stated already, the reason for this is because of the panoramic outlook, being the first period, it was then that apostles would appear.

The metaphor of the LAMPSTAND is found only in this letter, and occurs twice, verses 1 and 5. Now the Ephesian believers would be familiar with metaphors having several of them in the letter that Paul wrote, the Bride, the Body, the Household and many others. Here is the Lampstand, the metaphor of the local church which they would well understand. Also, the Lampstand depends on the oil of the Spirit, again they were well acquainted with the teaching of the Spirit with the twelve references in Paul's letter.

The word EVIL is only found in this first letter of the seven. One would expect that word to occur many times because of the terrible conditions that prevailed in some of the churches, but no, the word is found only here.

Again, WALKING is found only in this letter, the epistle of Paul to Ephesus contains the word WALK 5 times in chapters 4 and 5. So again they would be familiar with the meaning.

The word LABOUR only occurs in this first letter, service is referred to in the other messages, but none use the word labour with the exception of Ephesus.

The same could be said of the tree of life, paradise and many other words, but this will suffice in the meantime.

2. THE CATCH PHRASE

The contrasting words are Love in verse 4 and Hate in verse 6.

The hate was proper, and in keeping with the mind of the Lord, "Which thing I hate" but God looks for the positive as well as the negative. Love ought to be there also, and if their love had been as strong as their hatred, then all would have been well, and no threat of removal would have existed. It is good always to have balance in the things of the Lord, and the imbalance of many well meaning believers has caused a lot of heart break. It is good to have no strong points simply because there are no weak points.

3. THE OLD TESTAMENT BACKGROUND

This O.T. background appears in all the letters, in some more obvious than others but there all the same.

Now the background to Ephesus is the early chapters of Genesis and especially ch. 2 and 3. Herein is the reason for the peculiar words that arise as noted already. Tracing this is easy.

1) The stars in His hand would remind of Gen. 1:16 "He made the stars also".

2) Walking occurs for the first time in Gen. 3:8 The Lord God walking in the garden in the cool of the day. The law of first mention draws attention to this. Walking therefore speaks of agreement and fellowship, "Can two walk together except they be agreed"? (Amos 3:3). Walking also speaks of direction, and again, is used morally to describe Godly behaviour as in the 5 references in Paul's Ephesian Epistle.

When David would make a house for the Lord, God answered "I have walked in a tent and a tabernacle" (2 Sam. 7:6). It tells that God is with his testimony on the earth. God walked in the garden with the first man Adam, but because of sin this could not continue, God drove out the man.

Later in Gen. 5 God finds a man in Enoch with whom He could walk. The pleasure of God was such in this first man to walk with Him after the fall, that He took him to glory without the passage of death. God walked in the tabernacle with Israel as they journeyed thought the desert, and here in the midst of the lampstands He is found walking with the testimony then, and now upon the earth.

3) EVIL; now it can be seen why this word occurs here alone of all the letters, it is a reference to the tree of the knowledge of good and evil in Gen. 2-3. This caught Eve and Adam, but failed to attract the Ephesian believers. So again the Genesis background comes out.

4) Thou hast tried them which say they are apostles and are not and has found them LIARS. Where were the first lies told ? Genesis ch. 3 "Ye shall not die" and many more besides. The parallel is clearly seen.

5) The word FALLEN occurs only in this letter, and again the reason is obvious, it is parallel with Genesis 3 where the fall of man is recorded.

6) The lampstand threatened with removal again savours of Genesis, God drove out the man, he was removed from his sphere of labour. Note the word LABOUR, Adam wrought in the garden, to till the ground, dress and keep it, all this involved labour howbeit of a happy kind before the fall, and the curse. All this was lost because of his disobedience.

7) The tree of life in verse 7 is a real proof of this parallel, the Lord by design would bring the two passages together, both Gen. 2-3 and the first 7 verses here.

One may ask, "what is the reason for this parallel"? The old serpent worked the same way in Eden with Adam, as later with the church at Ephesus, both left their FIRST LOVE. In Rev. 12 the devil is called the Dragon, that is his political sphere, but also the old serpent, that is in his religious sphere, and the OLD, signifies he has been at this for a long time, even in Eden, and now with the Ephesian church.

However, it was judgment in Gen. 3 there would be no reversal, no way to the tree of life, it was barred by the sword in the hand of the cherubim, speaking of judgment. Grace, and not judgment is seen in Ephesus, there is no sword, that was for Thyatira, and the way to the tree of life is still open. There was no room for repentance in Genesis but the Lord leaves room here, repent, is the exhortation of verse 5. We are under grace.

4. HOW THE LORD INTRODUCES HIMSELF

The Lord presents Himself in a twofold way in verse one, a double claim: holding the stars in His right hand and walking in midst of the seven golden lampstands.

a) This would remind the believers of the Ephesian letter from Paul. Its division is simple, three chapters to do with the believers place in the eternal thoughts of God, SECURITY would be the word to describe the first three chapters. As already noted, chapters 4-5 contain the word WALK 5 times. The Hand would speak of security, and the walking of course, is the Lord as the great example, "we ought to walk as He walked" (1 John 2:6).

b) It is noticeable also that the information is in advance of chapter 1. There the stars are ON His right hand, the hand being open, but here IN His right hand, the word suggests a closed fist, indicating security. Again, the Lord is seen as in the midst of the lampstands, but advancing here, He is now walking, still in the midst, but walking. Movement is the thought; progress, the principle of advancement that is a feature in all the Book of God. This church was actually in a backsliding state, the first works were left, the first love was left, instead of going forward they were going back. However, God is looking for advancement.

c) The stars in His right hand are significant when mentioned in this letter. This is put very strongly to Sardis that it is "He that hath ... the seven stars" but here they are held in HIS HAND. Why is this pointed out to Ephesus? According to the record in Acts 19 Ephesus became the centre of all Christian activity in Asia Minor. All in Asia heard the Word in Ephesus. There was the danger therefore of the church in Ephesus putting themselves in a place of eminence, and accordingly seeking to influence and rule over the other churches, but more serious still it takes control out of the hand of the Lord. He is LORD of the churches, none can judge, rule or control other churches save Him. This is a great lesson to learn.

d) The fact of His walking is also significant in this letter. He is described in chapter 1 as having a garment down to the foot, and a girdle, two men only in Scripture are clothed in this fashion, the priest of Ex. 28 and the governor of Isa. 22. The Lord combines both here, "a judging priest". This is in keeping with the attitude of the priest, in standing it indicates service (Heb. 10:11) but the priest as walking in the house as in Lev. 14 is judging if there in leprosy in the wall or stones of the building. Hence, a walking Priest signifies judgment. So the Lord is seen in the capacity of judging the assemblies here, again He is the only one that has the spiritual ability to do so. Such a capacity would be needed for such a task, so great in fact, it belongs only to the Lord. Most if not all wise men would have judged Ephesus as being most progressive, sound and spiritual, but there were other things there that only the Lord could discern and rightly judge. Leaders in churches have the authority in the New Testament to judge others in the assembly that have sinned, but it is out of the hands of men to judge an assembly. Things in some churches may not be to our pleasing, and unscriptural practices may exist, one can be exercised to help or stay away according to the conscience, but the right to judge that assembly belongs to the Lord alone.

5. THE INFORMATION CONCERNING THE CHURCH

They were not without problems in some form, and so has every other New Testament church, they all have difficulties in some way. It ever seems to be that peace is enjoyed for a while then some difficulty arises. Could the Lord not prevent this occurring? No doubt he could, but chooses not to do so, the reason is apparent, it is for the maturity of the saints. When the children in school learn a new subject, and are well aware of all the principles of the said subject, the teacher puts problems to them, so as to put into play that which they have learnt. The Lord does the same, experience in handling trouble, adversity, sin etc. leads to maturity. It is one thing to know the doctrines but another thing to make them work to the profit of all. Hence, problems appear in the churches of the New Testament.

a) Trouble arises in Matt 18, the first reference to an assembly testimony. There is discord and disobedience, then discipline is necessary. However government and fellowship is also present, and experience comes out of the whole situation.

b) The church at Rome had to deal with divisions, discord and a certain amount of immaturity, but it all added to their training.

c) Corinth of course had problems abundant; division, unjudged sin, abuse of the Lord's Supper, doctrinal error concerning cardinal truths and so on. Paul explains in 1 Cor. 6 that these difficulties must not be avoided, rather approached and dealt with. The church is going to have great authority in the world to come, even over angels, so they gain some of that experience now. James also agrees, his first chapter is all about trial and the great experience that comes as a result if the exercise is taken up. Back to Ephesus.

THEY HAD FOUR THINGS WITH WHICH TO CONTEND

1) Evil men of corruption were seeking to gain an entrance so as to influence in some way. "Thou canst not bear them which are evil", or evil men as the R.V. puts it. At least the believers here were clean and not defiled by the deadly evil. Of course this is the parallel to the tree of knowledge of good and evil in Gen. 3.

   Evil can come in a variety of ways, emphasis is put on this in Matt. Evil thoughts come out of the heart of man according to Matt. 15:19. He also speaks of an evil generation in 12:39 and evil things in 12:35. He also makes mention of an evil eye and many like things using the word "evil" many times. To the credit of Ephesus, they abhorred evil men.

   The church at Colosse failed in this, Gnosticism managed to make inroads, and with it all the evil practices that issued from that devilish teaching.

2) They also had to contend with falsehood in the form of professing apostles who were not genuine. They were not sent from the Lord, consequently they had no true message. The believers tried these "would be" apostles, and found them as from the father of lies, the Devil himself.

   How did they try them? Only from the Word, the teaching they had received from the various men of God who watered with the Word continually. Ministry leaves its mark, and is a very necessary exercise in every church of God.

   Galatia failed here, they were carried away with false teaching concerning the vital truth of the gospel, they went back to law and works instead of grace and the principle of faith. Error like this would not be tolerated in Ephesus.

3) Violence in some form was also present, they sustained a certain amount of suffering for the Name of the Lord. Two words describe

this suffering, the first "borne" or perseverance, a persistence in testimony and church services no matter what, nothing would move them. The second word, "patience", better "endured" they passed all tests, their faith in His Name was steadfast, they had recompense unto the reward.

4) Another enemy seeking to storm their gates was the deeds of the Nicolaitanes, seemingly the idea of a controlling body that ruled the rest, "conqueror of the people" is said to be the true meaning of the word Nicolaitanes. This of course goes against the truth of the church as a body and every member playing its part as clearly taught in 1 Cor. 12. These deeds they abhorred, as the Nicolaitane belief directly contradicted the teaching of Paul in Ephesians that Christ is the head controlling the body, and that gifts are given only by the Spirit.

The deeds of the Nicolaitanes later became a body of doctrine in Pergamos. The outcome is most detrimental, consider the following:-

a) It divides the church into higher and lower levels.

b) Also impedes any gift and development that the Spirit is promoting in the gathering. A great hindrance to growth.

c) Class distinction arises between higher ranking and the lesser saints, but God is no respecter of persons, and this would be contrary to His ways.

Well may not only Ephesus, but all churches of the saints abhor the deeds of the Nicolaitanes.

Note the world is seen in the Nicolaitanes, the flesh in the corruption, and the Devil behind the falsehood.

FIVE THINGS COMMENDED

The Lord commends before he condemns, many reverse this standard, they are habitually blind to a lot of virtues in people because of a blemish they see, and most often it is an insignificant short-coming at that. The Lord looks for the good first, He commends all such virtues as in all these letters with the exception of Laodicea where no commendation is earned.

Paul follows this procedure also, and commends first as in Corinth. However there is one epistle where he declines to commend, that is the letter to the churches of Galatia. They were in error doctrinally, whereas the church at Laodicea erred practically.

1. WORKS, LABOUR AND PATIENCE

The first thing commended is how they went about their service for the Lord. A trinity of words appear in verse 2, these are not three things rather three ways of approaching a task. WORKS are the deeds, or services such as teaching, gospel work, visiting the sick, and work amongst young people and so on. The works cover the several activities involved.

The second word, LABOUR or perseverance is the attitude adopted towards the works in the first place. The service was not approached in a half hearted way, rather whole heartedly, in a worthy manner understanding the seriousness of doing anything for the Lord. This stance is richly commended by the Lord.

The third word ENDURANCE, or patience is the exercise that waits upon the Lord to manifest Himself in blessing, to secure the service as unto Himself. God expects the servant to wait upon Him, understanding that the ways of God may not be to grant success all at once, rather to wait God's time, and God's way.

If all services in the churches were taken up with this sincerity and faith, the approval of the Lord is bound to be seen, coming forth in blessing by and by.

2. ABHORRENCE OF EVIL MEN

This has been considered already, so just a few remarks are necessary. This commendation following on the reference to service, reveals that all was pure, there was no defilement that would hinder the workings of the Holy Spirit. This also the Lord speaks of with evident approval. A different situation prevailed at Corinth, evil in many guises was able to enter into the ranks of the believers there. Here at Ephesus the new nature of the believer was at work.

3. DISCERNMENT IN DOCTRINE

Ministry was very prevalent in this church, and they gave heed to it. Alas, so much good profitable ministry falls to the ground because of deaf ears, and there is no application in a practical way in the lives of those that hear. The Lord expects His people to harken to and obey His Word as it is clearly taught. Because this feature was present in Ephesus, the unsound teaching of false apostles did not gain an entrance. All was proved, discerned by the Word.

How necessary this exercise is today, consider the failure of Joshua in not discerning the Gibonites (Joshua 9) and the far reaching effect of that loss of discernment. The same failure comes out of the story of the young man and the lying prophet, it cost him his life, he did not discern the falsehood, he rather was swayed by the fact of the man's age and seeming maturity, surely he must be right. The story can be read in 1 Kings 13.

Barnabas is the best example of discernment in the N.T. he is the one that was trusted by the church at Jerusalem to investigate the movement at Antioch, and he judges it rightly. He was able also to discern that Saul of Tarsus was genuine when all others trusted him not. Sad to say Barnabas failed in this his strongest point in the controversy in Gal. 2.

4. PATIENCE IN PERSECUTION

This also has more or less been dealt with, suffice to note that the Lord is aware of all the suffering that saints pass through, and his approval of their steadfastness is there, although it is not really seen until the Judgment Seat of Christ.

5. HATRED OF THE NICOLAITANES

So close they were to the heart of the Lord in this statement, "which I also hate". There are several things the Lord hates as Prov. 6:16 declares: "These six things the Lord hates, yea seven are an abomination to Him. A proud look, a lying tongue, hands that shed innocent blood, a heart that devises wicked imaginations, feet that are swift in running to mischief or evil, a false witness that speaketh lies, and he that soweth discord among brethren". Here is another thing the Lord hates, the ruling over the people of God as if they were a lower rank. The guidelines are found in 1 Peter 5. Elders are to shepherd and guide, not as Lords over God's heritage, rather as an example to the flock.

The epistle of Paul to the Ephesians puts great emphasis upon unity, and also the spiritual recognition of God-given gifts. That epistle was no doubt a saving feature to this church, and delivered them from that which later became a doctrine in Pergamos.

These five things the Lord commends before getting down to the grave failure that existed in that particular church. Something was missing, and shall be looked into in the next chapter.

CHAPTER EIGHT

The Defect in Ephesus

In the last chapter commenting on this first letter, remarks were made concerning the peculiar nature of this message, the O.T. background, the catch phrase, the way the Lord introduced Himself, and some information concerning the church. The information as touching the Lord's condemnation, with the remedy and the appeal with the promise, is yet to be examined.

This church has often been described as luscious and fruitful in the branches, but rotten at the roots. What man sees is almost church perfection, but the Lord sees differently, a vital part is missing, even LOVE, and so serious is this that the church is threatened with removal. This of course is the basic reason for the constant reference to Adam in the early part of Genesis, he also left his first love.

THE DEFECT IN EPHESUS

Work and labour is one thing, but more important is that the service is in fellowship with God, and worthy of his approval.

Paul acclaimed the Thessalonians as having a work of faith, a labour of love and a patience of hope. The faith love and hope yoked the outward services to the invisible God. These factors are largely absent here. Patience was there, perhaps in some degree hope also, but the love was sadly missing. Love was present, but in the wrong direction. They loved church life, and all the activity that goes with it, but the real reason for the testimony in the first place was forgotten, even love to Christ.

This can be well illustrated by a man recovering from a serious sickness, and a wife that constantly serves him, making sure everything is just right, continually removing every crumb or speck of dust, busy all day with the broom and dustcloth. He longs for her to stop for a while, and sit with him and to enjoy mutual companionship. This the Lord longed for from Ephesus.

The word used for love is the strong word "Agape", amazingly, Thyatira had this in spite of a lot of grave defects that called for correction. (Ch. 2:19). There must be balance, truth must be accompanied with love, not truth at the expense of love nor truth without love.

All is very final, "you have left", this is a strong term, it is the same term as used of a man putting away his wife in 1 Cor. 7:11-13.

The great failing in this church could be described as FORMALISM, similar to that which is rebuked by the Lord in Malachi ch. 1. King Amaziah too was characterized by formalism, the story can be read in 2 Chron. 25. He did what was right in the sight of the Lord as far as external things were concerned, but when rebuked by the prophet for idolatry he rebelled and commanded the prophet be silent.

LOVE IS IMPORTANT

The word is used 14 times in Paul's letter to the Ephesians, they therefore ought to know its value. Love is the very nature of God, not merely an attribute. God is love in the same manner and degree as God is light and God is life.

Love is the fulfilling of the law, all other commandments are fulfilled in this one, as is well demonstrated in Rom. 13:8-10.

The great 1 Cor. ch. 13 accords love the highest appraisal, without it all service, gift, and sacrifices are nothing, and come to nothing.

This truth is put in an interesting way in Col. 3:14, after mentioning many virtues, Paul sums up, "Above all put on love" that is as a garment, it must cover all things. Peter would agree, saying love covers a multitude of sins, (1 Pet. 4:8) and of course he is referring to Proverbs 10:12. This is the wisdom of Solomon. Now the Ephesians missed this important factor, they put store on lesser things to their stupendous loss.

THREATENED WITH REMOVAL

This is the only one of the seven churches so threatened, which manifests the seriousness of the offence. The discipline spoken of in 1 Cor. 11 was again because of lack of love, the abuse at the Lord's supper, and the chastisement is severe, even sickness and death. This is why the play upon words is significant, if they had loved in the degree that they hated, no such threat would be forth coming.

The Pharisees were characterized by many noble works of the law, but there was nothing in their hearts towards God. They displayed works to be seen of men, but without any inner affection towards God. Love is the better thing, yet love is never passive, but will manifest itself in selfless service to the one who is loved.

RECOVERY POSSIBLE

The comparison with Genesis 2-3 is evident, but herein lies a contrast. There was no room for repentance in Eden, but these Ephesians are under grace, therefore space is given to repent and make things right. The Lord does three things.

1) He asked them to remember their first works from which they had fallen. Those early times when with freshness of love to the Son of God, the Saviour, they burnt the books associated with their unregenerate days. That day of gladness when they left behind former things to wholly follow the Lord. How the Lord must have delighted in those early first works.

2) He then calls for repentance, self judgment in the presence of God. True repentance is confessing the sin, and condemning it in self, and being willing to make a change for the future.

3) He looks for repetition, to repeat the first works, not so much the works but the attitude in which they were accomplished.

These thoughts have been summed up by others in three appealing words as Remember, Repent, and Repeat.

There is another word however, "Removal", the inevitable outcome if no repentance is manifest. This removal is the diminishing completely of the testimony, no lampstand remaining, and seems to betoken the total close down of the assembly. It would seem that if an assembly remains, the Lord is still recognizing it in some degree, but if departure continues, then removal comes sooner or later.

THE APPEAL

The appeal is to all seven churches, each had its own letter, but is exhorted to listen to the others letters also. All the Word of God is for all the people of God. The Spirit is the means of communication, the Words to the churches are from Him, He is also the source of the power that is needed for recovery.

Each church had a certain amount of truth as brought forth in the letters, but no church had all the truth. The truth is too great for any man, or company of men to fully know it all.

It is noteworthy that the formula is repeated in ch. 13, but without reference to the churches. "He that hath an ear let him hear", the rest of the phrase "unto the churches" is omitted. The reason is clear, the churches will be no longer on the earth during the tribulation times of which ch. 13 speaks.

THE PROMISE

In the first three letters the appeal comes before the promise, this is reversed in the last four, the promise comes before the appeal to hear. This divides the letters into a three and a four, the reason for this will no doubt come out later in these pages.

This division appears also in the main content of the promises.

The first three have LIFE as a theme. The tree of life in Ephesus, not hurt of the second death (implying life, in Smyrna); and life sustaining Manna is referred to in the letter to Pergamos.

The last four all include among other things the intimacy with Christ, the things which belong to Him. To Thyatira the kingdom spoken of as belonging to Christ as from My FATHER, and the Lord speaks of confessing names before MY FATHER to Sardis. Again in the letter to Philadelphia, the phrase occurs, the temple of My GOD, and to the last church, Laodicea, the Lord speaks of the overcomer sitting with Him on His throne even as I am sat with MY FATHER in His throne. Each of the last four use the term MY FATHER OR MY GOD and speaks of the intimacy with Christ in the coming time of glory.

The overcomer in each case is the genuine believer, one who will not let go of faith no matter what. This is determined by the promise to

Smyrna, of not being hurt by the second death, which is true of every believer no matter what spiritual capacity was there or wanting.

The tree of life in the paradise of God will be true in the future. In Eden this tree had the centre place, in the midst of the garden. The woman speaking to the serpent in her mind robbed the tree of life of this position, she spoke of the tree of the knowledge of good and evil as in the MIDST of the garden. The tree of life speaks of the Life the Lord gives, it also speaks of His authority as LORD over those who possess life in Him. This will come into full realization in the glory. Perhaps there is also the thought of a present application now to feed upon the Lord, to enjoy the life given and act in the power of it.

Such is this first promise, and is the call to partake of the Living Christ they had unwittingly set aside in loving other things. A searching message to all.

Chapter Nine

The Letter to Smyrna

The dear believers in apostolic days generally suffered much persecution from their fellow men. Three New Testament churches are specially mentioned as suffering excessively for their testimony. The Church at Thessalonica was born out of much affliction. The opposition was such that the apostle Paul had to flee after a matter of just a few weeks in that city. However a great work was accomplished in spite of the affliction, and they continued no matter what the enemy did to silence the witness.

Another such church was that at Philippi, again it arose out of much affliction. In the early stages the apostles were beaten, imprisoned insomuch that he referred to it in 1 Thess. 2:2. "Being shamefully entreated at Philippi". Ten years later the letter to Phillipians was written and the persecution had not abated, and Paul used the epistle to encourage them among other things.

The third church that so suffered was that at Smyrna, to whom the Lord sent this little letter.

The mistaken idea is prevalent that suffering is needed to bring perfect conditions and revival among the Lord's people. This was not the case with the three assemblies mentioned. In Thessalonica there was unsound doctrine as to the Lord's return, also much practice of uncleanness and slothfulness, all strongly rebuked by the apostle Paul in the two letters to the said church. Again perfection did not prevail at Philippi, there was discord, discouragement, and attractions to doctrines that were very unsavoury which Paul deals with in Phil. ch. 3. The church at Smyrna did not fare any better, for discouragement of a serious magnitude was present, hence this letter.

THE MEANING OF SMYRNA

Smyrna means Myrrh, a sticky substance that was obtained by the piercing of a thorny gum tree. It was of a very fragrant odour but rather bitter in taste. Therefore it symbolizes suffering and death in the Bible, and is so used at the beginning and end of the Gospels. In Matt. 2 myrrh is included among the gifts of the wise men, the Spirit's indication of the suffering Man that had come into the world. In the burial of the Lord the beloved followers brought spices with which to anoint the body, and those spices included myrrh. A fitting witness to Christ, the Man of sorrows who went eventually to the death of the cross in obedience to the Father's will.

However the myrrh speaks of a further truth, it was used as an ingredient in the holy anointing oil for the high priest in Ex. 30. Now this again was fulfilled in the Lord Jesus as the one raised from the dead and made a great high priest after the order of Melchisedec. Consequently the figure goes into death, and beyond death, to the other side. The one who died is alive for evermore, and anointed with the oil of gladness above His fellow, that is His fellow priests. The position of the believers as placed in Christ means that they also are promised life on the other side of death. This salient point is the reason for this letter, and is the basis for the encouragement offered.

SPECIAL FEATURES IN LETTER

1) This is the shortest letter of the seven, only four verses. Why so few words to a suffering church, surely much has to be explained as to why, and how long? That is just the point, when people are suffering and dying, brevity and clarity is needed, there is not time for lengthy doctrines or expositions. Encouragement of a definite nature is required. The Lord knows this, and in wisdom dictates a short letter.

2) None of the other letters refer to Calvary except this one, the death of

the Lord appears in verse 8, the one who became dead. The reason for this is obvious, the suffering saints are facing the extreme test of dying for their faith.

3) Another peculiarity is the reference to death three times, that is the burden of the letter. The three references of course present different aspects, the death of our Lord, the death of the believer in verse 10 and the terrible second death of the unbeliever in verse 11. Such a gospel message, the two classes, the death of the saint, that eternally of the sinner, and between, the death of the Lord Jesus which separates one from the other.

4) No works are mentioned as in the other six letters. The word "works" is omitted in the R.V. and the Darby Translation, and this appears to be so in most manuscripts. The Lord does not expect services and works when the church is in peril of its life. The underground church is not expected to produce a witness etc., to the degree of such that are free and have Christian liberty. The Lord is just, and expects more from those who have opportunity and liberty to produce. This on the other hand is not a license for slackness, there must be the grasping of any opportunity that comes along.

5) There is no rebuke for the first time in these churches, the same can be said of Philadelphia. In all likelihood there was much that could be rebuked, none are perfect, but the Lord withholds this because of the suffering conditions prevailing.

When the trying time is over, then the Lord will no doubt get down to the correction of things that need to be reproved.

6) Here is the first mention of the enemy, and in both titles, the Devil and Satan. Satan is mentioned in Pergamos, Thyatira and Philadelphia, but only in Smyrna is the devil referred to. Again there is a reason for this inclusion. The devil means "the accuser" and this no doubt the enemy was busy doing while the dear believers of Smyrna were discouraged, thinking themselves useless with no works to commend them. It is always so as in chapter 12. The accuser is against the personal life of the believer, censuring their personal failure, whereas the title Satan, "the adversary" is more in opposition to the service of the believer. Both aspects then are seen here in the enemy's offensive against a weak suffering church.

7) The synagogue of Satan is mentioned for the first time in these epistles, and later is mentioned in Philadelphia. The persecution and

trouble was from a religious quarter and is described by the Lord as the synagogue of Satan.

NOTE A PARALLEL WITH PHILADELPHIA

As pointed out earlier, these first three letters compare with the last three in the form of inverted parallels, and the middle letter, that to Thyatira stands alone. Accordingly, this letter stands in relation to Philadelphia, note the similarities.

a) The Synagogue of Satan is mentioned in both, showing that the opposition was from a religious and Judaistic quarter.

b) In both letters crowns are mentioned, the crown of life to those threatened with death in Smyrna, and the warning to Philadelphia "Let no man take thy crown". One church is up against it, the crown is sure for suffering loss, the other church is faced with opportunity, "Behold I have set before you an open door" (3:8), but if the responsibility is not taken up, the crown will be lost.

c) Discouragement is a feature of both churches. This comes because of conditions from within and without in Smyrna, the same can be said of Philadelphia, little power within, and the strong opposition from without. The lesson is to get the eye off both these aspects and focused on the Lord, the feeding of the 5000 illustrates this lesson. From John's account of the miracle Philip is taken up with the great need without, "Two hundred pennyworth of bread is not sufficient for them that everyone could take a little". On the other hand Andrew is taken up with the small resources within saying "There is a lad here which hath five barley loaves and two small fishes but what are these among so many" (John 6). The eye must be on the Lord and not the weakness within or the strength that opposes.

d) The presentation of the Lord in both letters is not taken from the tenfold symbolic vision from chapter one, rather from the words that the Lord spake. To Smyrna the Lord said, "The first and the last which was dead and is alive", and are taken from chapter 1:18, whereas to Philadelphia the words of the Lord are "He that hath the KEY of David", again carried from chapter 1:18, "Amen and have the KEYS of death and hell". The Key which speaks of power and authority is paramount in both cases.

THE CONTRASTING WORDS

The catch phrase, the contrasting words are very evident in these four verses. "I know thy poverty but thou art rich", (verse 9). Things are not what they appear to be, heaven sees diversely from the man of the world, values are different. To the world the believers of Smyrna had failed in life, they were in poverty, but the world could not see the treasure that was laid up in heaven. Two Greeks words are often used to describe hardship in our N.T. One translated "poor" means just having the necessities of life, only just having enough to get by on without suffering hunger or nakedness. The other translated "poverty" is extreme want, not enough for food and clothes and shelter. Both words are used of the grace of our Lord in 2 Cor. 8:9 "Ye know the grace of our Lord Jesus Christ that though he was rich yet for our sakes he became poor (the first word, having only the necessities) speaking of his home in Nazareth, that we through his poverty (the second word, reference to his ministry days) might be made rich". This more extreme word is used here "I know thy poverty" Things are not what they appear, this can be traced right through this letter in fact.

a)   Christ is dead as far as the world is concerned, but He is ALIVE. John has seen Him.

b)   Those who say they are Jews, they had all the outward trimmings, but they are NOT, and are of the synagogue of Satan.

c)   The Emperor is casting saints into prison, so it seems to onlookers but it is the Devil and Satan, he is working behind the powers that be.

d)   The believers are overcome, they suffer the loss of goods and life, rather they are the OVERCOMERS, they overcome by obedience to death as did our Lord, they are the successful ones in the sight of heaven and the throne of God.

e)   Then this last, they are poor, in extreme poverty, but they are rich towards God. A verse in James would be appropriate here, "Hath not God chosen the poor of this world rich in faith, heirs of the kingdom which God hath promised to them that love Him". (James 2:5).

THEY WERE RICH TOWARDS GOD

"Thou art rich", this is heaven's assessment of their spiritual wealth, one may ask, "in what way were they rich"?

The answer is, THEY WERE LIKE CHRIST. The letter is filled with language and experiences that was dear to the heart of our Lord, for He had the same ordeals when in the flesh. Consider as follows:-

a)   Poverty, the Lord knew this, We through his poverty were made rich (2 Cor. 8:9).

b)   Assailed by the devil, three of the gospels treat of the temptation of Christ by the devil, and his victory by means of the Word. The Lord can sympathize with the gathering at Smyrna.

c)   Satan, the adversary, at the end of the temptation the Lord commanded, "Get thee hence Satan" (Matt 4:10).

d)   The Lord, as this church, suffered from the Jews, they were his constant enemies, especially they of the synagogues.

e)   The church at Smyrna faced prison, so like their Lord, He was taken from prison and from judgment. This again would appeal to the Lord.

f)   Some of the believers were called upon to lay down their lives in death, so true of the Lord, he entered into death by the Father's will, thus becoming the means of redemption.

g)   The meaning of Smyrna is Myrrh, and as already referred to, Myrrh is associated with the Lord in his birth, death and resurrection and anointing.

Herein lay their riches, they were like their Lord, and a kindred spirit prevailed. It is likely that they did not see this, and would have been the last to state their similarities in this way. Poverty and riches, the values of earth and heaven.

THE OLD TESTAMENT BACKGROUND

The O.T. background is very obvious, and many parallels can be found with the book of Exodus, especially the early chapters.

1) These saints were passing through a tribulation similar to the people of God in Exodus, both were in the iron furnace of affliction.

2) In both cases all is known beforehand, God foretold the affliction of Israel in Egypt in Gen. 15 and so the Lord here speaks of the future affliction to this church.

3) Satan and the devil are behind the trouble here, and so with Israel, it was Pharaoh, indeed a picture of the enemy Satan. He took up arms against God, Moses and the people in the same way as the devil does today.

4) The believers are threatened with death. So it was with Israel, the male children were to be drowned in the river, death was before them as in this church.

5) The title THE FIRST AND THE LAST is a reminder of the revelation at the burning bush to Moses. I Am that I Am, ever existing and both these titles First and Last, and I Am that I Am, are the presentation of Jehovah.

6) The time of persecution is limited in both cases. To the children of Israel 400 years are determined to them, "Shall serve them and they shall afflict them 400 years" (Gen. 15:13). To this church the period is limited to 10 days, and there is no reason why this may not be taken literally.

7) The second death is referred to in this letter, and is in correspondence with the angel of death that passed through the land of Egypt, and the first-born in each house was slain where the protecting blood was not on the doorpost.

8) The synagogue of Satan with the religious adherents are over against the magicians in Egypt, they were the religious element in opposition to the truth in both cases here.

9) The Lord is spoken of being dead and alive again and here is a nice comparison with the pascal lamb that was slain, that wonderful type of the death and sacrifice of Christ. The fact of the resurrection follows in the crossing of the Red Sea in Exodus 14, so fitting that these foundation truths are stated here to the suffering church at Smyrna. The link with Exodus is surely placed there by the inspiration of the Spirit.

What is the reason for this close resemblance to Exodus? The same message is in both passages and is encouraging to those that are in the school of suffering. The purpose of God is the reason for all, God is working according to His eternal counsels to bring his purposes to a consummation; God had a purpose for Israel in Egypt and the Lord had a purpose for this little suffering church. In both cases all ends with the glory of God.

Israel began in Exodus making a house for Pharaoh, being delivered they ended building a house for God, and He dwelt among them. Smyrna were being afflicted by the world and Satan, the likeness of Christ was manifested and they like Him would enter the glory of resurrection life. In the meantime they had functioned in a house for God, the assembly, of which the house is a metaphor in 1 Tim. 3:15. How precious to all suffering believers are these passages, a little letter but carrying great consolation, the will of the Lord be done, ending with joy unspeakable and full of glory.

CHAPTER TEN

Encouragement to Smyrna

A few details have been considered concerning this letter to Smyrna, that of the O.T. background, the contrasting phrase etc. it will profit now to reflect upon the letter itself.

The Lord presents Himself to this church in a twofold way or title, The First and the Last, and Was Dead and is Alive Again.

The first would declare His essential Deity being an O.T. title of Jehovah, the other treats of His humanity, He who entered into death and now in resurrecting power, which is New Testament revelation, So both Testaments are encompassed in this double approach. The man who died upon the cross was God.

THE FIRST AND THE LAST

This title is a reminder of the burning bush and the revelation of the Great "I Am" to Moses, speaking of covenant relationship, and God coming down to deliver His own from the hand of Pharaoh and to bring them out of Egypt into a Land flowing with milk and honey. It is remarkable that no mention of the wilderness was made to Moses, the wilderness was part of the school of God, His ways, but the land was the ultimate purpose for the people. A similar situation prevails here, the saints of Smyrna despised by this world, are being afflicted by a greater than Pharaoh, but God is for them, covenant relationship is there, and the Lord was about to deliver them. This deliverance would come in different ways to these believers, to some it meant imprisonment and death, a deliverance altogether out of this world, to others it would only be ten days, and the time of trial would be over. However to all, it would be deliverance from discouragement, God is for them, who can prevail, they shall conquer at last.

The First and the Last is used three times in Isaiah, and in most interesting contexts.

1) Isa. 41:4 Calling the generations from the beginning, I the Lord, the First, and with the the Last, I am He. The context in the previous verses is about raising up kings in the political scene, "The righteous man raised up from the east, God gave the nations before him, and made him rule over kings". (Speaking of King Cyrus that was to come). A ruler was afflicting these believers, but such are raised up of God, His will be done, and there is a purpose in it all. How fitting is this truth to the little suffering church.

2) Isa. 44:6. I am the first and I am the last, and beside me there is no other. The words that follow speak of the Lord appointing the ancient people and planning their future, meaning the future is in the plan of God, all is in His hands. Again such a consolation this would be to the dear oppressed saints to know all the future is held in the hand of God.

3) Isa. 48:12. Harken unto me O Jacob and Israel my called, I am He, I am the first, I also am the last. The context is encouraging, the Lord begins things and finishes things, the plans of God will be completed. Again, there is a purpose in everything, nothing is by chance, Israel were being refined, they were chosen in the furnace of affliction (Verse 10) and all eventually would conclude to the glory of God. When the church at Smyrna receives this epistle, and considers these things, the Lord would give them understanding, then all would be clear, they would accept the will of God. They would commit themselves as unto a faithful creator, knowing God has ALLOWED the persecution, God has PLANNED IT, and God will FINISH it, and the purpose will be glorious and eternal.

The first and Last would be also another way of saying "I am always there, I am with you". An illustration would clarify this. A person being first in a building, and the last to leave, would be aware of all that happened during that time. Some others may come in later and go out earlier, and they would not be aware that things took place before their arrival or after their departure. The lights could have gone out and on again, or some other peculiar happening. The person first and last in the building would be fully aware of all that transpired. So with our Lord, He was there when they were born, and when they were converted, He was with them in their Christian life and testimony. He was with them when they were arrested and is there in the prison with them, and will be close beside them when the time comes to die, to leave this earth for the glory. I am the First and the Last. Every believer can depend on this promise, for that is what it really is.

HE WAS DEAD AND IS ALIVE

This as the First and the Last is taken from the words of the Lord in chapter 1:17-18. The experience of the Lord in humanity, He suffered and entered into death. Death is not the end, it is only the beginning, the darkness is past, the Lord is now alive in the light and brightness of glory. Death was the end of the sufferings of the Christ, all the shame and pain ended with death, the resurrection was the beginning of the glories that should follow. Many glories are to come to our worthy Lord, and many traced in this wonderful prophetic book, but the resurrection was the first of these glories. Paul had these two blocks of prophetic Scriptures in mind when he referred to the death of Christ according to the Scriptures, and the raising again from the dead according to the Scriptures (1 Cor. 15:3-4).

Because of this experience the Lord as a Priest can succour the tried Christians. Such a support to consider that the Lord has gone before, others follow after, He is alive, so the prospect of resurrection is before the believer. Death is not the end, rather the beginning. The Lord as a Priest is interceding for all saints, especially for those in trouble that their faith may not fail. Such was the experience of an Abraham about to be trapped by the king of Sodom, but he was able to resist because he met Melchisedec. Again in the case of Peter, the Lord prayed for him that his faith fail not, his courage failed but his faith never, he always believed, he denied that he knew the man, but never could he have denied that Jesus was the Christ.

The emphasis is on ALIVE AGAIN, these believers were facing death, but the support is the Lord's own experience, death issues in life eternal, resurrection is certain. In this twofold way the Lord applies Himself to this affected church, they are held by a Divine hand, they follow their Saviour in death and resurrection.

THE COMMENDATION

They were not alone, the Lord knew their troubles and struggle, and He was with them. "I know thy Works", A.V., Works is omitted in most versions and this seems to be so in the old manuscripts, the reason for its omission in this particular letter is obvious. Because of the difficult conditions the Lord does not expect works of a plentiful nature to be present, better if they were, but the Lord makes allowances.

He knows three things about this church, first, I know thy tribulation, He was fully aware of that which occupied them causing deep discouragement, such a comfort this fact is to all suffering believers. Sometimes sorrows can be secret, known only to the person in question, but the Lord knows, and this is all that matters. He also cares, His knowledge issues in action, hence the letter.

He knew their poverty, they were destitute, the stronger word is used here denoting extreme want, likely this situation came by their goods being confiscated as the Hebrews in a similar way suffered in Heb. 10. He also knew their riches which they were unaware of, the quality of these riches have already been pointed out. Heaven was real to these believers.

a) Godliness is great gain, "profitable unto all things". (1 Tim. 4:8)

b) Giving is righteousness that remains. 2 Cor. 9:9

c) Suffering the loss of houses, brethren, sisters, fathers, mothers, wives, children, and lands for the sake of Christ and the gospel, shall receive one hundredfold. (Mark 10:29-30). The words of the Lord.

d) Again the utterance of the Lord in Matt 6, "Be not anxious what to eat, wear" etc. He uses the Word "anxious" 6 times in the passage, to help believers to trust in God's goodness. Sometimes the necessities of life are denied by God as in this church, but again there is a greater purpose in the matter, and God will see it through. These believers were laying up treasure in heaven.

The third thing the Lord knew and draws attention to, was the Jews of the synagogue of Satan. Why synagogue?

Because of the captivity Israel lost all their outward religious order, they were in Babylon without a temple, priest, and offering, but they had the Scriptures. In order to keep the Law to the fore they met together in places to read the Word of God, these places were called synagogues, "meeting places". They evolved into places of exhortation, teaching, and membership, from which one could be excommunicated as in the experience of the blind man of John 9. The Lord used the synagogues as a place to teach, as did the apostle Paul and others later. It was always a starting place in a strange city for the gospel preachers to seek a foothold for their intended work.

The synagogues nevertheless were characterized by opposition to the truth as in the Gospels and Acts, Satan had taken over, instead of the intention at the first to maintain the Word, this Word was entirely rejected, and the commandments of men were valued instead.

The Jews were God's privileged people, being in rebellion against the Lord and the gospel they were not worthy of the name Jew, hence these remarks. These Jews were not in the fellowship of the church it would seem, rather they opposed them from without, the Jew and Christian followed the same God, but the Jew rejected the latest revelation of that God while the Christian accepted by faith. The Lord charges these Jews with blasphemy, they were speaking impiously of the Revelation of Christ and the coming of the Spirit.

A similar encounter can be experienced by any church today, not the question of Jews etc. but the compromise of the Word of God.

The Word must be to the fore in every gathering of the saints. When the interest wanes, and little importance is placed upon teaching, then other things swiftly come in to replace that Word. This is a present danger to any church, and Satan was working in this direction with Smyrna. The reason for this is obvious, when in trial, the great confidence of the believer is in the promises of God in His Word, so to take the Word away from such is to leave them unfurnished, and at the mercy of their own discouragement and Satan.

In their troubles both titles of the enemy appear, the Devil and Satan, he is also seen approaching in two ways, by the tribulation as the roaring lion, and in the would be Jews of the synagogue, the enemy is seen as an angel of light.

Now the Lord puts his finger upon their actual distress, their suffering. "FEAR NONE of those things which thou shalt suffer," this is in keeping with His words in John 14:1 "Let not your heart be troubled". There were hard times in front of them, already poverty abounded but bodily harm was also forthcoming, here the Lord forearms them. Prison was before some, the Devil was active using the imperial powers to accomplish his plans. Others are facing death, the call is to be faithful unto death, "fear not them who kill the body, rather fear Him which is able to destroy both soul and body in hell", with such words the Lord exhorted His disciples in a situation like this. (Matt.10:28).

ALL IS UNDER CONTROL

All is not lost in this church. outwardly it would seem so, but the Lord makes a few remarks that give certainty to the continuance of the testimony.

a)   Some of you cast into prison, but not all. Satan is limited as always.

b)   Ten days, is to be taken literally as all the other days in the Revelation, the 1260 days of chapter 12 etc. and the one day in the experience of Israel in Esther chapter 9:1.
      There is an end in sight, as in Egypt the Lord controls the duration of the trial.

c)   Faithful unto death, is spoken to the angel representative, the elders in danger of death, the leaders are always taken first. But again to greater glory, the promise of the crown of life to compensate for such loss. Satan can bring into death, the Lord can and will take out of death by resurrection.

d)   The Divine purpose, that ye may be tried, that is, all is ordered of the Lord for the maturity of the believers. The Lord was using the attack of Satan, the trial of imprisonment and the threat of death to mature these saints, there was a purpose in it all.

e)   The incentives are seen in the crown of life, call to fear none etc. and the experience of the Lord Himself who entered into prison and death to fulfil the will of God and bring blessing to others.

REWARD IN THE CROWN OF LIFE

As well as the promises of rewards at the end of each letter, sometimes other rewards appear for faithfulness and steadfastness in the conditions that prevail in each church. This is the first of such rewards, The crown of life. There appears to be five crowns in the N.T. as follows

1. The evangelist's crown, called by Paul a crown of rejoicing in 1 Thess. 2:19
2. The shepherd's crown, referred to by Peter as a crown of glory 1 Peter 5:4
3. A crown for those who love the Lord's appearing, the vindication of the Lord, called a crown of righteousness in 2 Tim. 4:8
4. A victors crown for the consistent Christian in 1 Cor. 9:25 called there an incorruptible crown.
5. Finally, the crown of life, this is the only one that is mentioned twice, for the loss sustained faithfully in James 1:12 and here for loss of life in tribulation.

These crowns are within the reach of all believers, none of them are for gift or ability or success, but for faithfulness or service where the will of God has placed the believer.

Note "I will give thee", the Lord Himself will present the reward, it will not done by an angel or any other heavenly dignitary, just as the Lord Himself commends, so He personally rewards with the trophy.

The Lord rewards in four different ways at the Judgment Seat.

1. By crowns as in Smyrna
2. With Garments as in Sardis (Rev. 3:4 and 19:8)
3. Speaking commendation, "well Done good and faithful servant" (Matt. 25:23)
4. Authority given as in Luke 19:17 "be thou over ten cities". The authority was according to the degree of faithful service rendered on earth by the servant

Out of all this it is certain that the Lord is no man's debtor, the beloved believer serves out of gratitude for salvation, and the Lord rewards accordingly in these various ways, so we are always debtors to His grace.

THE APPEAL AND REWARD

The Spirit speaking, the importance of the Word, not the Jews nor the synagogue nor Satan but the Spirit is the authority, and this is ours by the Written Word, the Scriptures of truth.

The promise here is very important, it helps to determine what is exactly meant by the "overcomer". It is a fact that the second death is for unbelievers only as clearly taught in chapter 20 of this book, therefore this promise concerns every believing child of God, they shall not be hurt of the second death. From this the pattern will emerge that every true believer is an overcomer. To this would agree the passage in 1st. John 5:5 "Who is he that overcometh the world, but he that believeth that Jesus is the Son of God", all true Christians believe this, so all are overcomers. The overcomer in these letters are not some super celebrated victorious Christians, but simple believers who hold fast to their trust in God right through all experiences to the end.

How fitting this promise is then to persecuted Smyrna, facing physical death at any moment, that death issues in glory, to be with the Lord and eventually glorified and like Him, but the second death is eternal darkness, never to be reprieved. Paul teaches that even death is for us, we get gain out of it as in all other things. "All things are yours, Whether Paul or Apollos or Cephas or the world or life or DEATH or things present or things to come, all are yours"(1 Cor. 4:21-22), that is for our profit.

Israel in Egypt were saved by the blood, and the angel of death, which was a figure of this second death could not enter the house where the blood stood witness. This along with the other points was bound to greatly lift up the downcast in Smyrna.

A few words in conclusion. This was a poor rich church whereas Laodicea was a rich poor church.

Myrrh with the gold and frankincense was associated with the Lord coming into this world of sorrows, but in His return to reign, Gold and frankincense will be gifts given Him, but no myrrh (Isa. 60:6), He comes to reign and not suffer. It will be so with the dear believers of Smyrna.

CHAPTER ELEVEN

The Letter to Pergamos

These notes have not been so much concerned with the prophetic panoramic view of the churches, rather seeking to apply "What the Spirit says unto the churches", for today. However, in the panoramic view of things this letter is important as being the fusion of the church with the State. We can compare this with the days of Constantine, the Western and Eastern armies of Rome were in conflict, Constantine pledged that if victory was his, he would become a Christian, and he did. This made Christianity popular, instead of sackcloth there was silk, instead of persecution there was popularity. The heathen honoured Constanine in temples, the Christian honoured him in the churches. All was compromise, such is the burden of this letter.

During those times many errors in teaching arose, for example it seems the last rites sprang from baptism, the common belief was that it put away sins, therefore by waiting until their deathbed they could be sure of the removal of all sins.

The meaning of Pergamos is Marriage, thus signifying the union of church and state.

Pergamos was a capital city, a commercial centre, the seat of learning, boasting of a library of half a million books. It was also the centre of medical training, and the symbol of the crooked serpent belonged to this institution. Last but not least, Emperor worship was very much to the fore in this city, and was the early cause of much persecution as the believers refused to burn incense to the Caesar. In all this the city was much taken over by the powers of darkness, and therefore the Lord speaks of the throne of Satan in this letter.

There was much for the MIND of man in the books, much for the BODY in the medical field, but much to indulge the lust of the flesh also, such is man in his wisdom without God (1 Cor. 1:21).

Pergamos was patterned upon the city which Cain built (Gen. 4), both were cities of progress, entertainment, seeking to make living comfortable, but all without God. Here in such a city, the Living God planted an assembly, a church shining as a lampstand in the midst of such darkness.

SPECIAL FEATURES IN LETTER

1) The Lord presents one single aspect of Himself, "He which hath the sharp sword with two edges".
2) Doctrines promoting evil appear for the first time in these seven letters.
3) Satan's throne is mentioned.
4) Believers are mentioned by name only in this letter of the seven, Antipas, and O.T. characters as well, Balaam and Balac.
5) The value put upon Secret things, Hidden Manna, a Name written upon a stone which no man knoweth saving he that received it.
6) A series of pairs are mentioned throughout the epistle.

The sword mentioned twice	—— Two edged sword.
Balaam and Balac	—— Antipas, witness, faithful
Idolatry and fornication	—— Doctrine Balaam, Nicolaitanes
Double promise	—— Two eatings, Meats and Manna

These double features are to bring home the importance of the contents to the readers, things are in a serious condition, the warnings must be heeded.

THE OLD TESTAMENT BACKGROUND

This is easily found in the letter, the mention of Manna, Balaam etc. sends the mind of the reader right back to the people of Israel in the wilderness, and especially to the Book of Numbers. These references are as follows.

1) The sword in the mouth of the Lord would remind one of the Law from the mouth of God in Ex. 20. This signifies the holiness of the God with whom they have to deal and the sure penalty for breaking the law. Pergamos was to know the same principle, the Lord was about to fight against them with the sword of his mouth (Ch. 2:16).

2) Balaam and Balac referred to in the letter, the religious represented in Balaam and the political in Balac. The history concerning these is found in Numbers chapters 22-25.

3) Balaam was slain with the sword, how fitting this remark should be made in that history. "Balaam also the son of Beor they slew with the sword" (Num. 31:8)

4) The word "fight" in verse 16 should be rendered "War" and is suggestive of the war with Midian and the happenings at Baalpeor in Numbers 25, the compromise with Moab and the ensuing civil war in Israel.

5) The doctrine of the Nicolaitanes is suggestive of the Korah affair, when he tried to take over the people and be their master (Num. 16). This was the doctrine of the Nicolaitanes, to subject the people to their ways and rulership, they were self appointed as was Korah.

6) The reference to the manna of course was well known, this sustained the people throughout the wilderness journey. The hidden manna was that which was put in a golden pot and placed in the Ark of the Covenant in the presence of the Lord.

7) The reference to the stone is bound to be part of this pattern in the wilderness. Perhaps it is a reference to the stones on the breastplate with the names of the tribes of Israel inscribed thereupon. Again it could refer to the stone that Moses sat on with his hands raised to heaven in Ex. 17 coming in after the manna of ch. 16.

8) The word "dwelling" is also significant, the word the Lord used as to the tabernacle, "Let them make me a tabernacle that I might DWELL among them" (Ex. 25). The word is used twice in this letter, the assembly dwelling in Pergamos and Satan counterfeiting this and dwelling also.

The wilderness history finally ends with Joshua taking the people across the Jordan and the eating of the old corn of the land. So different from the eating of meats etc., associated with idolatry with the doctrine of Balaam.

WHY THIS WILDERNESS BACKGROUND?

As with Israel so with the Christian, they both leave the Egypt of the world and upon conversion find themselves in the wilderness. Exodus 16-17 is the provision for the wilderness, the Manna and the water from the rock, signifying the provision of the Holy Spirit. Then came Amalek, the flesh (Ex. 17) it is the flesh which is the trouble in Pergamos, the sword of Joshua and the stone of Moses go into action, and the restoration is accomplished. The supply of the Spirit, the Word and the intercessor were much needed and were undoubtedly greatly used.

Again, rebellion against the truth is seen in the affair of Korah, these same doctrines had gained foothold in this church.

The reference to discipline of a severe kind by the sword out of the Lord's mouth is in keeping with the sore discipline they experienced in the wilderness at that time. Balaam was killed with the sword.

The whole idea is that while in the wilderness of the world there is ample provision to keep the believer, and if he compromises he may face sore discipline as they were about to experience in Pergamos.

THE CATCH PHRASE, HOLD AND CAST

A few remarks are needed on the contrasting words, HOLD and CAST.

Certain doctrines were held, "Them that hold the doctrine of Balaam", and again others held a different doctrine "Them that hold the doctrine of the Nicolaitanes". In contrast to these Antipas and other held fast to the Name of the Lord, "Thou holdest fast my Name" (Verse 13) even in a place where Satan's throne was found. So the idea of "holding" appears three times in the letter. People were holding different things, some good and some bad, doctrine is important, as a man believeth so he is. The doctrine of Balaam had an adverse effect on the church as had also the doctrine of the Nicolaitanes, the holding of the doctrine of the Name of Christ had kept some in the midst of terrible opposition, the others compromised.

In contrast to the word "hold" is the thought of "casting", the opposite. To cast a stumbling block before the saints, what they held was really a casting down of themselves, all was to their detriment, they thought it profitable, in reality they were being mislead, the outcome being   loss of testimony and spiritual enjoyment, and a means of stumbling to the weaker members of the church. The catch phrase is very important, one can be deceived, the truth from the mouth of the Lord is the answer to all erroneous teaching .

THE TITLE OF THE TWO EDGED SWORD

The sword speaks of many things in Scripture, for instance, the sign of authority in Romans 13:4, the wearing of the sword by officials who represent the government. Previously it has been suggested that the angel figures the ruling element in each church, if that is so, the elders evidently failed to manifest authority in this church.

The sword also speaks of the Word of God and this is made clear in Heb. 4:12. Note the sword is found not in His hand but in the mouth, speaking of His Word in power. The reason for this is because doctrine was to the fore, the answer to the false teaching is the truth of the Word from the mouth of God. The government of the church failed to deal with the situation so the Lord comes in with severe judgment, He discerns and Has the power to discipline with a view to setting things on the right path.

The sword is two edged showing that no mercy will be forth coming. The blunt edge of the sword was placed upon the neck to signify mercy to the one conquered. No mercy was shown to Amalek or Balaam or Adoni-Bezek of Agag, Samuel hacked Agag to pieces with the sword. To Pergamos room is left for repentance, but if not, the sword was sure in its sweeping judgment.

There are four references to the sword in Revelation, three are with reference to the Lord, chapter 1, 2, and 19, and one with reference to the impostor of the Lord, the counterfeit that is to come in 6:4.

This then is how the Lord introduces Himself to those who compromise in this church, the symbol of the sword speaking of His Word which can oppose and set right the wrong, and discipline those who promote it. All this mingled with encouragement to those who remain faithful, and unaffected by the various doctrines that were seeking a foothold in the Pergamos church. This shall be the substance of the next chapter.

CHAPTER TWELVE

The Lord's Message to Pergamos

The previous chapter examined the background details of this letter, and the way in which the Lord is introduced with the sword out of His mouth.

Now, consideration of the contents of the letter itself to this compromising church will no doubt prove profitable.

THEIR COMMENDATION

It declares the grace and power of God in the Gospel when a company of sinners, saved by grace, can be such that they are commended by Christ, while they live in unholy surroundings as this city of which the Lord says, "Where Satan's throne is", meaning where Satan dwells.

Like a Daniel in Babylon.

Like an Ezekiel in a prisoner of war camp.

And unlike a Lot in Sodom, who failed, and compromised with the city of his dwelling.

Dwelling means residence, and Satan was at home in Pergamos dwelling in the midst of his deceived followers even as God dwelt in the midst of His enlightened people. Consequently the full category of evil was manifest in that city of Pergamos.

1. Falsehood was seen in the idolatry, the false instead of the true God.
2. Corruption appeared in the fornication.
3. Violence showed its ugly head in the slaying of Antipas.

All evil comes under one of these three headings, and when all three appear together, then there is a full manifestation of evil. In the days of Noah the Lord saw that the earth was full of violence and corruption, later after the flood the falsehood of idolatry came into public view. The full manifestation of evil is seen in personages later on in this Book of Revelation. The falsehood comes out in the false prophet of ch. 13. The corruption appears in the scarlet woman of ch. 17, and the violence is spread abroad by the beast of ch. 13, who, chiefly by violence amongst other things, rises to the utmost position of authority in the coming Empire.

Now the ten commandments of the law of God are in direct opposition to these, and also fall into three groups.

Commandments 1-4 declare the true God, and are in contrast to all that is imitation and untrue. When one leaves the Nature, Being and ways of God, then falsehood comes in to take its place.

Commandments 5-6 are honouring authority in parents and the sanctity of life, to depart from these leads to violence.

Commandments 7-10 are the opposite of corruption, and to protect a person's rights, his wife, possessions, good name and well being. To go against these principles is to give way to the lust of the flesh. Committing adultery, possessing wrongfully by stealing, corrupting a person's good name by false witness and covetousness, all come under the heading of corruption.

Yet in such a lawless, sinful city controlled by Satan, the little group of believers are commended by the Lord.

1) They had held fast to the Name of the Lord. This is significant when one remembers that Pergamos was the centre of the cult of emperor worship. The Lord and not Caesar, was their cry of loyalty, and the opposite of that angry mob who, on the eve of crucifixion cried out, "We have no king but Caesar" (John 19:15). These believers refused the worship of Caesar at terrible cost.

2) "Thou hast not denied my faith", "My Faith" is a further commendation by the Lord. "The Faith" often stands for the body of doctrine that

came to light by the coming and work of Christ, the high noon of the revelation of God, "Who in these last days has spoken unto us by (His) Son" (Heb. 1:2). There in the midst of the seat of learning, surrounded by the wisdom of this world, they held fast to the doctrines concerning the Christ. Today young Christians are faced with the same inducement, especially in the schools and universities, it is commendable when the young believer holds fast to the Name and doctrines of the Lord in what they do, and what they believe.

3) Their testing was not easy, strong forces were against them backed up by the ruling powers insomuch some of them had faced and succumbed to death. Antipas is mentioned by name, who according to church history met a horrible and painful death, and in the midst of such threats and suffering he refused to deny the Name of the Lord. He is commended by the Lord after his death in a twofold way. He was faithful, that would be to the person of Christ and His Name. He was also a martyr, this word means "witness" and no doubt his witness was to things so surely believed among the Christians. He neither denied the Name or the faith. Again it could be suggested that he was faithful in Walk, and witnessed in Words, just like his Lord before him (Acts 1:1).

Balaam is mentioned further on in this letter also by name and a striking contrast exists between the two men.

Antipas lived for Christ and Balaam lived for self.

The first was rejected by men and accepted by God, Balaam was accepted by men but rejected by God.

There was absolutely no compromise with Antipas, however compromise was the philosophy of Balaam's life and became the doctrine that he taught. He tried to keep in with Moab, Balac and God all at the same time.

Antipas met his death by the hand of man and Satan was no doubt behind this. Balaam also was killed by the hand of man but the authority of God was behind the sword that ended his life.

It is important to see here that all the believers were not put to death , Satan's throne was there but a greater and higher power was present, all was controlled by the throne of God. In all this there exists a good lesson on the Fear of God.

REBUKE, A FEW THINGS V 14

The Lord had a twofold charge against the church. the doctrines that were held by some, and the practice that issued out of those doctrines. The point is doctrine does not stand alone, practice is the result of what a person believes. Some well meaning Christians say "it matters not what one believes as long as the life is right". This is not the case, both stand together the second being the outcome of the first. The Lord speaks firstly of the doctrine of Balaam. Now this was the teaching of Balaam to the young girls of Moab; to join themselves to the young men of Israel and so to cause them to worship their gods, thus seducing them away from the God of Israel. They would say, "our gods are not as austere as your God, we have freedom", and freedom would be the cry of the day. It worked, the unholy alliance was made and the judgment of God fell upon Israel as recorded in Numbers ch. 25. Some in Pergamos held this idea saying, "Go in a little with what goes on in the city, a little Emperor worship, a little incense to an idol here and so on, the Lord knows our sincere hearts that we do not believe these things, we know they are just nonsense but it would be more favourable to profess before men a little of what is believed abroad, and so lighten our burden. Besides it gives an opportunity to do the service of God unhindered." These ideas were not taught publicly, rather held and spoken of in a more private atmosphere. One often hears the remark "they only hold this sort of teaching but do not speak of it publicly", however what a man holds he will find means to make it known to others.

What was merely deeds in Ephesus has become a doctrine in Pergamos, the deeds of the Nicolaitanes now becomes the doctrine of the Nicolaitanes, what is held soon becomes the accepted doctrine. It must be challenged with the truth,and the truth must be passed on (2 Tim.2:2). Paul taught publicly from house to house (Acts 20:20), he declared all the counsel of God (Acts 20:27). If a person cannot publicly teach what he holds, it is then most likely that it is wrong.

THE DOCTRINES THAT WERE HELD

The doctrine of Balaam affected practice without, it was to mix and compromise with any opposition. The doctrine of the Nicolaitanes had an inward effect, the laity and the clergy, the position of lording it over

God's heritage. Some are of the opinion that the Nicolaitane doctrine was more in a Gnostic strain, and was the promoting of the lust of the flesh without any fear of recompense from God. However their teachers also lorded it over their followers.

The truth enabled the believers to withstand persecution as they held fast the Name of the Lord, the error resulted in idolatry and uncleanness.

BALAAM AS SEEN IN O.T.

He was a Midianite, in the Scripture national names are used to convey certain principles and truths for the people of God. Moab speaks of the flesh, and Egypt speaks of the world to name a few. Midian has more than one thought behind it.

1) Midian speaks of the unequal yoke, the mingling of saved and unsaved in any connection. The first mention of Midian was the result of the marriage of Abraham to Keturah, and the fourth son that was born was called Midian in Gen. 25. Nothing else is recorded of Abraham after his marriage to Keturah although he lived about fifty years after that. Also Isaac was made separate from the sons of Keturah, including Midian, as if to suggest Abraham had seen his mistake in the union with Keturah. It was this very idea that made up the doctrine of Balaam in mixing by marriage etc. resulting with Israel lowering the standards that God had prescribed for His people in the law.

2) Midian means "strife", and this strife comes out of the unequal yoke either in marriage or business or any other form. It is interesting to see that Midian and strife go hand in hand very often in Scripture. Jethro was a Midianite, and Moses was fighting with the shepherds at the well which led to his introduction to Jethro. Jethro seems to approve of the fighting spirit of Moses and gave him hospitality and one of his daughters to be his wife (Exod. 3). Also Jethro the Midianite took a great interest in the strife and differences among the people of Israel in Ex. 18.

Long before the affair of Jethro was that of Joseph and his envious brethren, who among other things sold Joseph to the passing Midianites who in turn sold him into Egypt.

In the history of Gideon he engaged in warfare with the Midianites. Conditions in Israel at the time were not good, there was strife in the household of Gideon's father, and an undercurrent of strife was beneath the surface among the tribes. This came to the fore at the close of the campaign with Midian when civil war almost erupted between the children of Ephraim and the rest of the nation. It was only the peaceable spirit of Gideon and his wise words of wisdom that saved the day.

In all this a pattern follows, wherever Midian is found, trouble and strife is at hand. The doctrine of Balaam was by compromise to cause strife between brother and brother and between the nation and God. It worked. Israel worshipped the gods of Moab, and 24000 fell by the plague from the Lord. On top of this, many fell by the sword of those faithful to the Lord. Balaam taught the people the wisdom of the world, idolatry is the worship of the world, and all instituted by Satan to take the affections of people off God and unto other things. Fornication is the lust that is characteristic of the man of the world.

As with Midian so with Moab, God attaches great significance to his name. Moab was born of Lot and his daughters when he was in a drunken state (Gen. 19). Therefore, Moab came out of the indulgence of the flesh, drunkenness and corruption, and is consequently a picture of the Lusts of the Flesh in Scripture. A further use of the name of Moab is the "Flesh at ease" always seeking a way out rather than to fight, such is the world today. King Eglon in Judges 3 is a case in point, he was a lazy sort of man as well as indulgent with his summer parlours etc.. He met his death while sitting at ease. Balac was the same, he sought by the means of Balaam the destruction of Israel by a curse rather than to fight them, he was looking for an easier way out. This slothful character can be summed up in the words of Jeremiah, "Moab hath been at ease from his youth and he has settled on his lees". (Jer.48:11)

In conclusion, the doctrine of Balaam was compromise to that which opposed from without, to find an easier path in the city where Satan had his dwelling place. It could be said that the Hebrew children in Daniel ch. 3 refused the doctrine of Balaam in not seeking to save their lives by bowing to the image that the king had set up. Matthew Henry in his commentary stated that they could have found quite a number of reasons why they should obey the king and bow.

1.   Their fathers did it in the past and sought after idolatry.
2.   They were not in the land of Israel but in Babylon, and it was the norm there.
3.   They were without a temple and had to worship something.
4.   Others were doing it that were from the captivity.
5.   They must obey the king, the powers that be.
6.   They could still worship God in their hearts.
7.   Their lives would be saved and they would then be a blessing to others, one cannot serve his fellow man when dead.

However, over against all this was the first two commandments of the Decalogue, they must obey God rather than men. This was the spirit of Antipas and others in Pergamos. King Saul lost his kingdom because of compromise, and Lot lost everything he had because of the same snare, his fatal compromise with Sodom.

DOCTRINE OF THE NICOLAITANES

It perhaps could be said that Judaism was a form of this, Christianity came out of a Jewish setting, howbeit it was not an extension of Judaism rather it was a new movement altogether making Judaism obsolete. Being ignorant of this principle many Jews with a hankering after Judaism and the law in the Christian church, sought to lord it over Gentiles believers. This would be the deeds of the Nicolaitanes referred to in the letter to Ephesus. This state of things soon developed as is usually the case, there were always those willing to take a place of prominence among the saints and many others willing that they should do so. Clergy sprang from the priestly caste and later the garments were borrowed from the heathen. The outcome was a situation similar to the character of Balac, ease for the congregation, no exercise or development. To maintain a fashionable church with a good gifted man in control, and to be accepted by the community at large became the desired concept of the day. The prototype of this was the rebellion of Korah Dathan and Abiram, who tried to take over the people of God without a call from God, and they met a horrible end by the judgment of Jehovah. This doctrine may benefit those who are set up in position but it is detrimental to the congregation of believers.

1. This practice produces weakness and immaturity in the company that assemble
2. It exalts man and not the Lord
3. Such a practice ignores the Spirit of God and His sovereign will to raise up as it pleaseth Him.
4. The outcome is that a lot of needed teaching is not available.
5. Last but not least, it curbs a lot of gift from developing.

It takes a variety of gifted believers to bring a variety of truth before the people, the truth is too great for any one man to handle it all, hence the plurality of elders and teachers in the N.T. churches.

Now one must admit that in many churches today great and godly men are solely in charge, and they administer a grand service, however the things already pointed out will be lacking in the congregation.

The design of Satan towards Pergamos is seen in the bringing together of both of these doctrines in the same place. The doctrine of Balaam affects the members of the body causing them to miss out in sanctification by compromise and mingling with that which is without. The doctrine of the Nicolaitanes affects the Head itself, even Christ by taking authority and position out of His hands thus leaving the people in spiritual poverty. Both these ideas appear in the Colossian epistle, not holding the head, and the members of the body engaged in asceticism and worship of angels etc..

Summing up, the doctrine of Balaam is license to do as one feels, and the doctrine of the Nicolaitanes is legalism, to bind in and to bring into bondage. The first is the abuse of Christian liberty and the other is the removal altogether of Christian liberty. Both these attitudes are encroaching in many churches today, and no doubt Satan is still at work in his old Serpent ways.

THE DISCIPLINE OF THE LORD

"Repent or else" is the Lord's challenge, He is still in control, all must be unto Him. Neither Satan or any man can take His position of control from Him, He has the last word. Howbeit, the Lord gives them a space to show repentance and to set things right themselves, and if not He will discipline in some way with the sword of His mouth. Note the change in verse 16 from "thee" to "them". THEE is the angel, or the governmental element in the church, who had not been seduced by the evil, but had allowed it to persist. They have the responsibility to bring about the state of repentance, and if not, the Lord will come quickly unto this government represented by the angel with some severe form of discipline. Stronger language is used for the THEM, the holders of the said doctrines, the Lord will war with them with the sword out of His mouth. Now the sword is in the mouth of the Lord in ch. 19:15 and will be used to smite the nations at Armageddon and will bring about terrible destruction hitherto unequalled in history. The judgment then to those who held the erroneous and harmful doctrines must have been very severe, perhaps to their removal altogether.

THE APPEAL CH. 2:17

This is the last time the appeal comes before the promise. All are expected to be overcomers in the first three churches as profession is not anticipated, all are considered genuine. From Thyatira on, profession without reality is very much the burden of these last four letters, hence the appeal and promise is reversed in these. The appeal is important and is the same to all the churches, but is of special import here. In the place where such unsound teachings abound one must be careful "to hear what the Spirit says to the churches", this is the answer to all evil teaching, and can save from error (1 Tim. 4:16). Such a word for every Christian today. Read the Scriptures, devour them, get them into the heart and into the head and outworking in every department of daily life. Listen to the ministry of others, get the best out of it, much excellent ministry like the Manna is spread abroad upon this wilderness ground, and like the Manna so few gather it in the container of the mind. Much good teaching falls to the ground because of the lack of ears to hear.

THE PROMISE

The promise is twofold, the Manna and the stone. The first is undoubtedly Ex. 16 and the latter could well be a reference to Exodus 17, Moses siting on the stone, it was all for him, but affected others. Both of these speak of intimacy with God in eating or communion with Him and intercession.

Eating of the hidden Manna is in contrast to the eating of things sacrificed to idols in verse 14. Here are two tables, that of the false and that of the true. One cannot eat of both, the Corinthians sought to do so, some went into the temple of idols and ate with idolaters, then sat later at the table of the Lord (1 Cor. 8 and 10). Paul challenges them, "Ye cannot eat of the Lord's table and the table of demons" they are incompatible, either one or the other. The promise here is when one separates from the doctrine of Balaam, the Lord will make it all up to him most abundantly, by the wonderful intimacy with Himself. Eating is similar to that of John 6 when the Lord refers to the eating of His flesh, meaning feeding upon the Christ of God.

The hidden Manna was in a golden pot placed in the ark of the covenant in the presence of God within the veil, this typifying the close communion in His presence, which is becoming rare to most believers because of the busy days which characterize the times.

The white stone would speak of victory, such as Moses had in his intercession while sitting on his stone, Joshua prevailed over Amalek. Perhaps also the stone may be a reference to the breastplate. The breastplate was upon the priest when he went daily into the holy place to burn the incense of intercession. The names of the tribes were written upon the stones of the breastplate, each tribe being in the place foreordained by God, and these overcomers were in the place God would have them. The last stone was the Jasper, a clear stone representing Napthali, which means wrestling. Again the thought of intercession and intimacy is suggested.

The idea of "no man knowing" is similar to the New Song known only to themselves, sung by the 144000 in ch. 14, this speaks of personal experience. Each believer ought to have private experiences with God, such belong to themselves and cannot be shared with others. The lesson is, that if believers in a church such as Pergamos separate themselves from the prevailing doctrines being held by some, the Lord will reward them with much of His presence in the secret place with spiritual experience and power that will endure into eternity.

CHAPTER THIRTEEN

The Church at Thyatira

This letter, the longest of the seven is both interesting and instructive. The city itself is also extremely interesting. Thyatira was founded by Alexander the Great, and soon became popular as a place of industry and commerce. Because of the great industry carried on many guilds soon arose and the guild that would be best known by the Christians would be that of the famous Dyers Guild. Lydia likely belonged to this, being a maker of purple, used largely in the uniforms of the Roman army and so on. Her conversion story is found in Acts 16, she was also the first to be saved in the wonderful work of the Lord at Philippi.

The suggestion has often been made that Lydia after conversion went back to Thyatira and founded the church in that city. Really there is no proof of this, but it is an attractive thought just the same.

There was also a large Jewish settlement in Thyatira, and undoubtedly this greatly influenced the church in some way as is the case with many churches, Antioch, Corinth etc. suffered adversity from the Jewish influence.

Jezebel, also a woman is mention in this letter and so two women are associated with Thyatira, one good, namely Lydia, and the other evil, Jezebel.

SPECIAL FEATURES IN THIS LETTER

1) As already stated this is the longest letter of the seven, it is also the middle letter having three on either side. In the chiasm this letter has no equal, and therefore stands alone. Ephesus is parallel with Laodicea and so on but nothing compares with Thyatira. Because of this, the letter is of the utmost importance, and the message it contains was very vital to the church then, and to the churches of today.

2) "The Son of God" is peculiar to this letter, in fact this is the only reference to the title Son of God in the whole of the book of Revelation. This bears great significance in the interpretation of the letter.

3) Here is the mention of the first of four women who appear in the pages of Revelation. Jezebel likely represents a company of people as do the other women, that is, the woman in ch. 12 the Scarlet woman in ch. 17 and the Bride in ch. 19, each of them represent many people.

4) The terrible calamity of Division is seen here for the first time in these messages. This church was a divided church and more than two factions existed, likely as many as four different groups are referred to in the letter.

5) In spite of all these short comings, love to each other existed, this was absent in Ephesus, for if they leave the love of Christ they also leave the love of the brethren. None of the other churches so far were commended for their love.

6) The coming of the Lord for the first time is seen in these churches. "Hold fast until I come" (3:25) and the promise progresses into the Millennial reign of Christ, power over the nations given to the saints who reign with Christ.

7) The appeal comes after the promise for the first time, and hereafter this is the pattern followed.

8) The discipline promised will be a lesson to other churches "all the churches shall know" verse 23. This is the only reference in the seven letters to others churches apart from the appeal by the Spirit.

9) The remnant is seen as distinct from the others for the first time. "But unto you I say and unto the rest in Thyatira" verse 24. Here a clear demarkation exists of one group from the other.

10) "The depth of Satan" appears only here as a climax to the activities of Satan. Previously there was the synagogue of Satan, the Devil and Satan at work in Smyrna now coming to a culmination in the depths of Satan.

These single features make the message to Thyatira very weighty and far reaching in outcome.

THE OLD TESTAMENT BACKGROUND

This is easily observed, the mention of Jezebel places the background in the times of king Ahab and his wife Jezebel. Those were troubled times in Israel and the features that then existed follow the same pattern that prevailed at Thyatira. Smyrna had the background of Israel in Egypt, and Pergamos brought them into the wilderness, now Thyatira features them in the Land and under their kings. The history of Israel is being followed in these separate backgrounds.

Note the parallels with the times of Ahab and Jezebel.

1) The Son of God, this is in direct contrast to the worship of Baal that predominated in Ahab's time. Baal means Master, and Elijah represented the true and living God, the great struggle of the true and the false.

2) The "Eyes of fire" and the "feet as burning in a furnace" are reminders of the ministry of Elijah, he was the prophet of fire. He called fire out of heaven to consume men, he called fire down from heaven to consume his sacrifice. Fire was brought before him as he sheltered in a cave, and finally there appeared a chariot of fire and horses of fire as he was caught up to heaven by a whirlwind.
Fire, speaks of God's consuming judgment and this was the burden of the ministry of Elijah, and the contents of the letter to Thyatira.

3) The feet of brass also speak of judgment as the fiery prophet was unto Israel, they were trampled under the feet of judgment. The miracles of Elijah all featured consuming judgment with the exception of two.

4) Jezebel is mentioned by name, it was she who introduced the worship of Baal into Israel, she originated in Tyre and Sidon, the stronghold of Baal worship.

5) The reference to killing her children with death is suggestive of the slaying of the 400 prophets of Baal because of the victory of Elijah on mount Carmel, and the tribulation referred to could be a parallel with the terrible famine that lasted for three and a half years during the reign of Ahab.

6) The remnant reference, the "rest" in Thyatira is a reminder of the 7000 in Israel that had not bowed to Baal. Elijah thought he alone was left, the Lord informs him of "the rest" in Israel, all were not Baal worshippers, a remnant existed.

7) The reference to the reign of Christ and the believers in the promise is the true kingdom contrasted with that of Ahab. He was not of the dynasty of David, being king of the divided Israel when they split into two tribes under the family of David, and the ten tribes often referred to as Ephraim, or the Northern Kingdom. How fitting this is when one remembers that Thyatira was a divided church just as Israel was divided.

This is the O. T. background, it is sure because of the reference to Jezebel, and all the other features fall into place. This is not conjecture, rather all put there by the design of the Spirit for the edification and warning to believers both then and now.

WHY THIS BACKGROUND?

Idolatry is really the depth of Satan, and through Jezebel and the worship of Baal Satan had taken over Israel. The Devil is the enemy of the Word of God always, and Jezebel killed the prophets of Jehovah, the prophet was the channel of the Word of God to Israel. The Devil always seeks to take away the good seed of the Word of God, without this the believers will become weak, failing and soon subdued.

But when something is taken away a substitute must take its place, hence the teaching of Jezebel replaced the Word of God, and the worship of Baal took over from the worship of Jehovah. This in a similar way was taking place in the church at Thyatira. Paul makes reference to the incoming of evil in his day by identifying the "Seducing spirits and the doctrines of demons", the seducing spirit takes away from the truth, the doctrine of the demon takes its place (1 Tim. 4:1). A little leaven leavens the whole lump, the influence of the Jezebel group was far reaching, and the Lord was about to step in with judgment before all was lost.

Division is the way of men, to allow such is to follow the way of men and not that of the Lord, such was the development in Corinth

THE THREEFOLD PRESENTATION OF CHRIST

THE SON OF GOD v 18 is the embodiment of all truth as in Hebrews ch. 1, "God has in these last days spoken in (His) Son", the full revelation of God.

As Son of David the Lord has rights to Israel and Israel's throne.

As Son of Abraham, the Lord has rights to the church, the seed of promise as seen in the heavenly Isaac.

As Son of Man the Lord has rights to the earth, and in the Millennium He will subdue all under his feet bearing the title of the Son of Man.

As the Son of God, He is the heir to all things in heaven and earth, and has rights to all things, He is the designer of all, by Him all was created and exists, and all is unto Him, again this to be realized in the millennium.

The doctrines taught in Thyatira and the evil that prevailed was contrary to the revelation of the Son of God, similar to Corinth, His principles were being set aside.

1) A woman was out of place, such was the case at Corinth seemingly by the apostle's correction in ch. 11 and 14. A woman's name is prominent in Thyatira; whether a company or an actual woman who led a party, the fact is the same, a woman was out of her God given place in the church.

2) Gifts abused, again the sad reflection of Corinth, hence chapter 12 to 14. This party had the ability to teach as stated in verse 20, "to teach and seduce my servants" it was a case of gift and ability being misused to draw attention to self instead of to the blessing of others and the glory of the Lord.

3) Discipline was set aside also. At Corinth there was unjudged sin in the midst, a man who committed a terrible immoral act was still in the full fellowship of the saints in their priestly functions (1 Cor. 5). The governing element in Thyatira had failed to judge the Jezebel party, they had suffered the error and had failed to exercise any form of discipline whatsoever.

4) Because of divisions, unity cannot prevail. Corinth was the best example of this, the divisions are referred to in chapters 1 to 4 and again in chapter 11 of 1 Cor. So with this church, as already pointed out, different parties exist together, indeed anything but unity.

5) Separation was set aside. Corinthian believers went into the temple of idols (Chapter 8), they were found sitting at the table of idols (Chapter 10), therefore the ideal separation from evil certainly did not predominate there. The same can be said of this church, the fornication and the eating of things sacrificed to idols were condemned by the Lord of the churches.

6) Sanctification therefore could not be experienced because of the uncleanness being practised by so many of those in the church fellowship, both in Corinth and Thyatira. The morning star would no doubt speak of intimacy with the Lord as well as other things, this intimacy can only be realized when the life is clean and sanctified.

In all this a similarity between the churches at Corinth and Thyatira really existed. Evil often comes in different guises but is the same in kind.

Further links to Corinth can be seen in the "Depth of Satan" in verse 24 and the "Deep things of God" in 1 Cor. 2:10, another case of the common occurrence in Scripture of the imitations of God by Satan. Also the reference to "Love" is in keeping with the great chapter of love in 1 Cor. 13. A third further link may be the reference to the Judgment Seat "I will give to each one of you according to your works" (Verse 23), and the many references to the Judgment Seat in the Corinthian epistle such as chapter 3. 4. 6. 15. which all bring in the great time of testing of every man's work.

THE EYES AS A FLAME OF FIRE

By this symbol the thought is conveyed of the omniscience of the Lord, He sees all and nothing is hidden from Him. He is chief in the principle of discernment. The Lord can discern that good men were present in Thyatira in verse 24, and that all the church were not led astray by the seduction of the Jezebel party. In the same way it could be said that the Lord was aware that the stage had been reached by some that recovery was now impossible in verses 22-23. Some well meaning believers may try with much exercise before the Lord to bring about recovery to many in this church, not knowing that the space for repentance is now past. This is not the case with the Lord, He sees and knows.

The eyes of fire also convey the thought of consuming righteous judgment, similar to the statements in verse 23, "I Am He which searches the reins and hearts" and to judge accordingly. Such a solemn thought that the One who has the right to judge the churches does so with all knowledge of the conditions, motives etc. and judges with the fire of His righteous ruling.

THE FEET LIKE FINE BRASS

Brass or bronze speak of resurrection ground in Scripture, this can be seen from chapter one where the Lord is risen from the dead and His feet are like unto brass. The same idea is displayed in the pillars of the tabernacle, they are seen around the court standing in sockets of brass, a clear picture of the believers standing in testimony to the world outside, but in the power of resurrection.

Again, feet speak of judgment as seen so often in the victor putting the victim beneath his feet. The Lord Jesus being addressed as God in Heb 1:8 has the promise that all enemies will be subdued beneath His feet, in fact this is what the book of Revelation is all about. The feet in judgment also appear in chapter 14:20 where the winepress was trodden outside the city, all speaking of the fierce judgment of God.

In putting these two points together, the eyes as flame of fire and the feet like unto fine brass as if they burned in a furnace, the complete work of judgment is seen, the Lord sees the evil and condition, and has the power to judge the same. Many leaders in churches have the eyes to see the evils and errors that creep in among the saints, but have not the power to judge what they so clearly see. Perhaps their judgment is curtailed by a poor testimony, or the mouth is stopped by some indiscretion in the past. However, the Lord has the ability to see and rightly discern all, and has also the righteous ability to judge all. Such is the picture of Christ that is presented to Thyatira.

All this is significant when it is recalled that the background is that of the days of Ahab and Jezebel, and of course the ministry of Elijah the prophet of fire. He had the eyes to really discern Israel in his day, he also had the feet to bring about the righteous judgment that was needed. Such was his dealing with the false prophets of Baal at Carmel, he was able to call fire from heaven to consume his sacrifice unto the Lord, then to consume the false prophets with the sword. The fiery treatment of the mocking captain and his fifty men was also a demonstration of the principles here, again repeated with another captain and his men. The third captain saw the judgment and its source from God himself, repented and saved both himself and his men. Space was given to many in this church to repent like the third captain, but the time had run out, now the eyes and feet must do their work.

CHAPTER FOURTEEN

The Lord's Message to Thyatira

The presentation of Christ to this church and the Old Testament background has been considered, now for the details of the letter itself. This being the longest letter of the seven and also placed in the middle would indicate that the contents are most important to every church in every generation from then until now.

THE COMMENDATION

The commendation of verse 19 begins and ends with works, this is peculiar to this letter, the others mention works only once with the exception of Smyrna and Pergamos, where the word does not really occur. It would seem therefore that much was going on in Thyatira in the way of service and progress that was approved by the Lord. How wonderful, that in spite of many drawbacks, this church should produce services that were a testimony to the working of God in them, and manifesting development. The contrasting words would come in here, "The last to be more than the first" (verse 19). This commended progress against such a background of disorder, is a lesson to all churches, there is no excuse for the lack of progress in the things of God, there is always opportunity to shine for God, the darker the background the brighter the testimony ought to be.

Love is mentioned and this no doubt was the mainspring for the progressive works commended. The word for love is the strong word "Agape" which was lacking in Ephesus in verse 4. These are the only occurrences of the word in the Revelation. As in 1 Cor. 13 everything issues out of love, this was the situation in Thyatira, the love produced the service referred to and is the foundation for the increasing works.

Faith also commended by the Lord, was likely responsible for the patience commended in verse 19. It would seem that love produced the service, which is the proper motive for all service, and that faith produced the patience, as is always the case. This church had what Ephesus had not, accordingly no threat of removal is present in spite of the need to deal with other things.

THE CHIEF FAILURE

There were also things that must be condemned in Thyatira and the chiefest is the Jezebel company. "Thou suffferest that woman Jezebel which calleth herself a prophetess to teach and to seduce my servants to commit fornication and to eat things sacrificed unto idols" (Verse 20). The use of the Name Jezebel would suggest different schools of thought. First, that the name suggests a party of several people with the character of Jezebel, being one of the different divisions in the church in Thyatira. Another suggestion is that a woman was the leader of the party, and therefore completely out of place, as was Jezebel, perhaps the truth is a combination of both of these ideas. However, the result of the so called party is evident, let us consider the outcome.

1) The teaching was false, it was not according to the Word, this can be seen by the fruits it produced, fornication and idolatry. "By their fruits ye shall know them", was spoken by the Lord concerning false prophets (Matt. 7:20), meaning, one may not be able to detect the falsehood taught, but the results can be examined, and a true conclusion reached. The evil tree produces evil fruits, so with these, the fruits of fornication and idolatry manifested that the teaching was unsound.

2) The teaching was public, not merely held as in Pergamos but taught in the public meetings, in the days of Jezebel in Israel the teaching and worship of Baal was public, and became the accepted thing.

3) As stated already, the teaching was most damaging, true servants were influenced and seduced into committing evil. Note the two things fornication and eating things sacrificed unto idols, the order is reversed from that in Pergamos (verse 14). There the emphasis is on the idolatry and that which stemmed from it by the doctrine of Balaam, here the emphasis is on the uncleanness which would disqualify the true servants from handling holy things. The loss of sanctification Godward and the loss of testimony manward would inevitably lead to idolatry.

4) A distinct company were of this persuasion in Thyatira, not all of the assembly, as the Lord singles out some who were not so affected in verse 24. This company is placed under the name of Jezebel, the reason being that the same features which predominated in the days and rule of Jezebel were again apparent.

5) The saddest point of all is that the angel representing the governing body in the church was aware of the destructive teaching and did nothing to prevent it; all was tolerated instead of being judged at its first appearance. Likely in the early stages not too much attention was paid to the company and their teaching, and eventually the sect became so strong that the leaders were powerless when the realization was apparent that something ought to have been done, rather too late as is often the case.

6) The greatest evil produced by the teaching was the divisions that weakened the church as is inevitable; Satan is not divided. Different companies can be identified as follows:-

(1) The Jezebel party who were the prime movers in the false teaching, including those who commit adultery with her.

(2) Her children. These would be of the same persuasion but not just entirely joined to the Jezebel party, their judgment in verse 23 is distinct and different from Jezebel.

(3) The true servants that were seduced, these may be the same as "Those who committed adultery with her" in verse 22.

(4) The rest of the company referred to in verse 24 who have not known the doctrine, that is they were not attracted to it and did not embrace it.

However many different companies can de identified, division was evidently there and it is a serious and weakening malady.

In previous pages it was noticed that a close similarity existed between Thyatira and Corinth, the divisions are another feature in the comparison. Divisions were destroying Corinth and the Apostle Paul condemned this in many chapters in the first Epistle. In doing so he uses different words that would indicate the progression of such evils leading to division.

(1) Contentions, meaning strife and rivalry. (1 Cor. 1:11)
(2) Divisions, factions or parties (1 Cor. 3:3. 11:18)
(3) Divisions, different word from previous meaning scisms, or to rent a garment. (1 Cor. 1:10)
(4) Heresies, meaning separate companies. (1 Cor. 11:19).

These different progressive words could be illustrated by considering an orchestra.

Some grumble about others that they do not practice enough and are slightly out of tune; all perhaps out of envy. This is the first word, Strife and rivalry.

The discussion then turns to the renewing of the musical instruments, some are for it and some against, a petition is drawn up and signed, but not by all. This is the second word, different parties but in the same company.

The drummers are behaving badly and some refuse to play alongside them, others take the side of the drummers. Now this is a scism, like rending a garment in two pieces.

The so called offended party hive off and form another orchestra. This is then a sect, a heresy, which means a clear cut division, meeting in separate places and having no dealing with the former company.

THE JEZEBEL OF THE OLD TESTAMENT

Jezebel is a notorious name in Scripture, she is associated with everything that is contrary to God and the testimony. A few remarks about her character would be helpful.

She was brought into the nation of Israel by marriage, being the daughter of the king of Tyre and by union with king Ahab, a stranger therefore was brought into Israel.

It was through her the worship of Baal was established in Israel, as her father king Ethbaal was an ardent follower of Baal. Ahab raised up an altar for Baal in the house of Baal (1 Kings 16:32), when the king goes astray, all is lost as most go with him.

In her days Jericho was rebuilt, scorning the curse of God, and the Word of God was disregarded. However all was fulfilled according to the Word of the Lord. (1 kings 16:34).

Jezebel slew the prophets of the Lord with the sword.

She was the instigation of the stoning of the righteous Naboth, a man who upheld the Word of God as regards inheritance.

In all this there is a pattern, she was against the word of God, and sought to cut it off from the people, and to displace Christ with Baal.

Add to this, the painted face, for which she is best remembered, which was to make the flesh attractive and to deceive Jehu, which did not work, she was slain.

JEZEBEL TEACHING IN THYATIRA

The teaching prevailing in Thyatira had many characteristics of which we forever need to be aware, the same features adorn all false doctrines which are abroad today.

1) Attracts to self, she called HERSELF a prophetess. The ways of God are that the man is hidden and the Lord fills the place, such was the attitude of the sincere man John the Baptist, his words are most spiritual, "He must increase and I must decrease".
   Again the frame of mind of the apostles is found in 2 Cor. 4:5 "We preach not ourselves but Christ Jesus the Lord".

2) The teaching was of a seductive nature, taking away from the truth, when this is the case, the simple are waylaid as were some of the true servants of the Lord in verse 20.

3) Obviously there was an ability to teach, but it was wrongly directed; the motive was wrong, it was all for the presentation of self. Such was the case with Balaam, the same could be said about Samson who used his God given strength in a wrong way to the pleasing of self, and not to the glory of God.

THE SUCCESS OF THE FALSE TEACHING

False teaching is ever successful, it is always easier to follow error than truth. The main reason for this is the error generally allows more freedom to sin and to do one's own will, thus the teaching becomes attractive to the flesh.

1) True servants were seduced, they left the truth to embrace the error.
2) Fornication was the outcome. As has been already noted, in verse 20 fornication and idolatry is reversed from verse 14. The doctrine of Balaam was to lead away from the true God to idolatry, hence it comes first, but in the Jezebel teaching the attraction of the flesh was the bait and so the fornication comes first. This fornication was likely literal as in Corinth, but perhaps a spiritual adultery is the thought in verse 22.
3) This all catered to self will, the things that are appealing to the natural man, bringing to the fore the old nature which manifests itself in the indulgence of the flesh.
4) In churches today the flesh can still operate, things are treated as idols, possessions take the place of Christ and eternal virtues in the heart. Alas, also as to the uncleanness, the world is such a defiling place today that many of the true believers as in Thyatira are ensnared with the same immorality.

THE SAD RESULT IN THYATIRA

First, with such conditions as the apparent fellowship with idolaters etc., there was no real separation from the world which their profession of Christ demanded. Therefore conditions were similar to Corinth, there the believers frequented the temple of idols and became the means of stumbling weaker brethren, such behaviour was firmly condemned by the apostle Paul (1 Cor. 8).

Again, how could there be much spiritual food in such an atmosphere, ministry would be curtailed lest the different parties would be offended. It is a sad condition when some ministry has to be held back because of the attitude of some to the truths that ought to be taught. Happy is that church that has the privilege of the opening of all the Word of God in its hearing. "Faith cometh by hearing and hearing by the Word of God" (Rom. 10:17).

Much of what was practised and tolerated was really to increase numbers. This really is a vexation when many truths are laid aside in order to increase the congregation. What do numbers mean to the Lord ? A few faithful believers gathered together in harmony are more to the preference of the Spirit of God. The Lord often spoke to the few after the fickleness of the crowds was apparent, the four men who listened to the Olivet discourse: the eleven men that listened to the upper room discourse; the three disciples Peter, James and John often taken aside from the rest.

Luke wrote his Gospel for one man, not knowing of course that millions would read and study it. He wrote the book of Acts for the same man, in all he wrote fifty two chapters for the benefit of one man. While good numbers at any meeting is a bonus, yet the heart must not be set on this, God often works with the few and accomplishes great things thereby.

Another outcome of the division was the pride in some believing themselves to be of superior knowledge to their other brethren, thus creating the situation as in Corinth of the knowledgable and so called weaker brethren. These according to verse 24 boasted in knowing the "depths of Satan", and it is always dangerous to dabble in things Satanic as they were doing. Pride is always abhorrent to God but much more that obnoxious spiritual pride in knowledge, and a "holier than thou" attitude.

The grievous condition of division here was also related to idolatry, and this is always evil. To make an idol of anything is dishonouring to the Lord, and here it would seem to be literal idolatry as in the case of Corinth. It is terrible when believers backslide and leave the Lord, how much more serious when the devil has put a value upon the false idols to displace the Lord. This state often brought the displeasure of the Lord upon Israel in the wilderness days, and through this they lost the promised land in the first place.

The worst outcome of all in the Jezebel problem in Thyatira was that the true servants were seduced. They were true servants, useful to the Lord, but they left their estate to serve uncleanness and idols, being seduced from the Lord, and carried away with error.

The Lord speaks of "My servants" alas, no longer loyal to Himself but serving that which is false.

These are the sad results of the Jezebel teaching in the church, bringing disapproval from the Lord, and serious loss to themselves.

THE CALL TO REPENTANCE

The opportunity to repent was past, this letter goes beyond the others in this respect, the time of repentance is gone and judgment must then be faced. Three cases of judgment are noted.

First the Jezebel party, space was given to make all right before the Lord, but this was refused, hence the judgment is now announced. " Behold, she shall be cast into a bed", likely a bed of sickness, tribulation is also mentioned in verse 22. Terrible trouble was swiftly descending upon the Jezebel company, nothing could alter this, the time of repentance was past, no place could be found now as was the case with Esau in Heb. 12:17.

Then those who committed adultery with her are next referred to, these likely being the true servants of verse 20. To them repentance is still available, a space is given to bring about a change of direction, to turn again to the Lord with loyalty.

After this, her children are dealt with in verse 23. These would be the ardent followers of Jezebel, blinded, deluded, fanatical, death is pronounced on them, this then becomes a case of sin unto death. The parallel of this in the history of Jezebel was the literal slaying of the prophets of Baal by the prophet Elijah at Mount Carmel.

Another section of the church is referred to in verse 24. "Unto you", being the angel, the leaders of the church, and the rest, those in the church preserved from the corrupting doctrine of Jezebel. There is always a remnant for God, these believers kept themselves pure from what was current in the church, and no further burden was placed upon them. This could mean that discipline was no longer their responsibility, the Lord Himself was taking all in hand. They were also exhorted to hold fast that which they had, it would be terrible at this stage to imbibe the erroneous teaching after holding out so long. They must add the contents of this letter to what they have, "he that hath to him it shall be given, and he shall have abundance, but whosoever hath not, from him shall be taken away even that he hath" (Matt. 13:12). The Lord's return is presented as an incentive, the time will not be long, love the teaching, soon the time of testimony will be over, the Lord is coming soon.

Note how each part of the church is judged, Jezebel, then those servants who committed adultery with her, then her children and finally the rest, of whom the Lord finds nothing to judge, but warns of the need to hold faithfully to the end. All this is according to the pattern of Genesis ch. 3, before the Lord the man blames the woman, the woman blames the serpent. God then judges the serpent, returns to the man and judges him, and finally to the woman with her judgment. Here one section was faithful, no judgment but a clear exhortation to continue faithfully, and to keep His works to the end.

THE PROMISE TO THE OVERCOMER

Humility now, leads to power in the coming Kingdom. Some took pride in position and knowledge etc. but those who shall be great are those who humble themselves, this is always a principle with God, the way up is down. Jezebel obviously had a lust for power, but power in the future kingdom shall be greater and more enduring. The rod of iron speaks of strength, strength indeed to smash vessels of the potter; this speaks of the wonderful position of authority in the Kingdom of our Lord and power to dispense discipline even as the Lord presently was with power disciplining the church at Thyatira.

However, a greater promise is spoken of, "I will give him the morning star". This no doubt speaks of Christ Himself as in chapter 22:16 "I am the root and the offspring of David, the bright and morning star". This to the spiritual believer would be more valuable that any authority whatsoever, such a present incentive, not to covet power in the church but to have intimacy with the Lord. As the morning star He is the new beginning, all the new creation as the old is in Him, through Him and unto Him. Another point also suggested is most practical, the morning star, start the day with the Lord, give the first place to Him.

THE SPIRIT TO THE CHURCHES

This appeal here is most important because the truth of the Word of God was at stake at Thyatira. To this might be added the words of our Lord in verse 23 "that all the churches may know". So the dealings of the Lord with Thyatira are very special, and other concurrent churches ought to take heed, and so much the moreso today when the baseness of the Jezebel teaching is asserting itself in many churches at the present time.

Such were the Lord's words to the church of Thyatira.

CHAPTER FIFTEEN

The Church at Sardis

In every day life, what goes on outside soon affects those inside, and this pattern is the same for churches as well as homes, families and all such. If the country is poor, then most people will be poor, and the same can be said of rich conditions and many more such things. The church at Sardis was affected this way, the situation and culture of the place where they were situated had a deep effect on the members assembled and on the running of the church. How Corinth was affected by the outside is well known, they were surrounded by idolatry and immorality and it is not surprising that such things leaked into the church. Titus was warned concerning the churches in Crete, because the character of the people in Crete at the time was described as "Evil beasts, slow bellies and liars" (Titus 1:12). These traits could be manifest in some of the believers with whom Titus had to contend.

Now Sardis was built on a high rock and was well protected because of this position. There was only one way into the city, and the accepted thing was that if that entrance was heavily guarded, then all was secure. However, the city was conquered because of a lack of watching the other sides, the dwellers of Sardis were deceived by the thought that no entrance from these directions was possible. Commentators on these churches refer to a time when the city was besieged by a large army, a soldier out for a walk by night saw an old woman coming down a secret path to gather some sticks, the soldier followed her and later led the invading army right into the city. Sardis was completely taken by surprise. Nor did they learn the lesson, the same thing occurred many years later with a different besieging force. Such is the history of Sardis, if only they had watched, they did not learn by past defeats, they should have watched. In those days before the fall of the city it could well have been said of them "This was a city living, but death was about to strike, yet they were careless and complacent".

This brings in the contrasting phrase in chapter 3:2, which is featured in the other churches. "Thou hast a name that thou livest and are dying". The assembly was not watching, and they were about to suffer for their lack of surveillance. The Lord charges the church with not watching.

DISTINCT FEATURES OF SARDIS

1) The reference to Christ's past ministry is a feature in this letter. The call to watch is akin to Matt. 24:42 "Watch therefore for ye know not the hour", again in Matt. 25:13 "Watch therefore", and the word "watch" is found four times in Mark's account of the Olivet discourse. Here again the Lord will caution a company concerning the necessity of watching. The reference to coming as a thief was at the first spoken by the Lord in Matt. 24:43.

The promise of confessing before the Father is reminiscent of Luke 12:8 "Whosoever shall confess me before men, him shall the Son of Man also confess before the angels of God". Closer still is the reference in Matt. 10:32 "I will also confess him before My Father which is in heaven". This is the only letter of the seven that refers so directly to the Lord's past ministry on earth.

2) A great emphasis is on the Name, and is intimated four times.

Thou hast a NAME, verse 1, meaning the name of testimony.

Thou hast a few NAMES in Sardis, verse 4, the names of the faithful. I will not blot out his NAME, verse 5. This carries the thought of the security of the believer.

Finally, I will confess his NAME in verse 5. Here is the coming reward to the faithful believer.

The first and last reference to NAME is their confession of Him, which ought to be, and His confession of them. The middle two references correspond in thought, their NAMES known to the Lord and therefore never to be erased.

3) The letter begins and ends with the Spirit of God, this is peculiar to this letter, all end with the reference to the Spirit but do not begin so. This of course is the answer to a dead church, the life of the Spirit of God.

4) The Lord condemns before he commends, and this is unusual. The deadness is condemned before others are commended. The condemnation was of the whole attitude, then a few are commended.

5) Another feature of this letter is that the material is placed out in triplets as follows.
   a) The condition — a name, living and dead
   b) The exhortation — Watch, strengthen, works incomplete
   c) Recovery is three words — Remember, Hold fast, Repent
   d) The few — not defiled, will walk with Him, and worthy
   e) The promise is threefold — clothed, not blotted out, and confessed.

THE OLD TESTAMENT BACKGROUND

The O.T. background is not as evident as in the former letters, however, it is bound to be there. If Thyatira is looking back to the days of Jezebel, and when Philadelphia is considered the O.T. reference will be seen to be the days of Hezekiah, the reference therefore in Sardis must be between these two periods. All point to the days of Joash as found in 2 Chron. 24. Consider these similarities:-

1) The seed royal because of the treachery of Athaliah was almost wiped out, but a little boy was saved. How fitting here to be addressed as living but dying.

2) Alive, Joash was seven when he began to reign, weakness, a babe but with great responsibility before God and men.

3) His works were not completed, only when Jehoiada was priest did he go on in a responsible way. When the high priest died, then he went to pieces, he needed to be propped up it would seem.

4) He was a picture of great weakness, Syria defeated him with a small army, and he was left sick in bed.

5) He was not watching, he was complacent, and was murdered while he was asleep in bed, if only he had been vigilant.

6) Joash started his reign when he was seven years old, and this letter is introduced with the seven Spirits of God.

7) Seven is complete, but Joash failed, he did not complete anything at all.

8) Repairs to the house of God were commenced in his reign, and again were not finished, all is left incomplete.

9) In the reign of Joash the Spirit of God came upon Zechariah the son of Jehoiada and he warned the people and was stoned to death for his endeavours in the house of the Lord. The Lord Jesus made reference to this stoning of Zechariah to the dying nation of Israel in Matt. 23:35. The nation under the reign of Joash was dying, he was dying in his bed from diseases, and all this forms the background for this letter.

CAN ONE DIAGNOSE A DYING CHURCH?

The first thing to look for is works that have ceased. Ministry meetings, gospel efforts and many other good works of the past now no longer existing.

Also the things that do remain are in a shaky position, about to cease, "ready to die" is very searching in verse 2.

The necessary item of teaching in every church was missing in Sardis. The Lord refers to the ministry they heard in the past, "Remember therefore how thou hast received and heard". All in the past tense. When the teaching of the Word is omitted in the church, that particular church is about to die. As human life cannot be maintained without food, no more can a church go on without spiritual food.

Asleep, not awake to the need. How sad a condition is this, and so prevalent in many churches of our day. The need is to "watch" as the apostle exhorted and warned the elders of the church of Ephesus on the shore of Miletus. Elders must be aware of the spiritual need of the young, and what they face in this modern world. Shepherd care is essential in every church.

The absence of public confession, one can gather this factor was missing in the way the Lord encourages public confession in the promise. (Verse 5). The magnificent church at Antioch was started by public confession, and the Lord blessed the work abundantly to the establishing of one of the greatest churches in apostolic days.

Watch out for formality, this is the disease that threatened Ephesus, and in Sardis bore witness to a dying state, withal not seen by the believers themselves.

Of all these conditions, the most serious is the fact of sleeping when danger lurks without.

a) In the parable of the tares and wheat the Lord warns of this, "while men slept, the enemy came by night and sowed the tares".

b) Again in the parable of the ten virgins, they all slept, and the call of the arrival of the Bridegroom took them all unawares. Fortunately for some, they had oil in their lamps, others were left undone. This parable is one of many that divides the Olivet discourse into two parts. The Lord speaks of events leading to His return, pauses to speak some parables all with the theme of WATCHING and then proceeds with the prophecy.

c) In Gethsemane while the Lord was praying in deep distress, the disciples were sleeping, the Lord asks of them "could you not watch with me one hour"?

d) In 1 Thess. 5 the writer exhorts, "Let us not sleep as do others, but let us watch and be sober". A watching attitude should be paramount in the churches of today.

THE CAUSES OF DEADNESS IN CHURCHES

1) The first underlying cause of deadness is to be content with past ministry, one cannot exist on the food of the past, present conditions need suitable ministry to strengthen and fortify the believers to meet all things. When this is lacking, then failure, weakness and consequent deadness will be the result.

2) If there is no teaching, the appetite for the Word will soon be lost. This was the case in Corinth, they were as babes, they had lost any appetite they had in the past for the Word.

3) If there is no room for the Spirit to manifest the mind of God by Bible teaching, all will be done in the energy of the flesh.
Christians walking on earth, and not in the enjoyment of the heavenlies. Walking with men and not with the Lord.

4) With conditions like these, there will be no sense of expectancy as in Acts 4, how they prayed with eyes looking to the Lord for His intervention, and so it came with power.

All these and more would indicate causes that lead to deadness.

The great lesson to the Nazarite in Numbers 6 would be valuable here. He was not to be defiled by the dead, he was not to touch any dead body or go to funerals or touch a bone etc.. Death is corruption, and there is no place in the services of God for anything that savours of corruption, hence the seven Spirits of God.

THE LORD'S INTRODUCTORY TITLES VERSE 1

In the twofold introduction the number seven occurs in both parts, the seven Spirits and the seven stars. Seven is the number of completeness in Scripture, so this is emphatic here to a church which did not complete things.

The Holy Spirit came with a commission, to finish the Word of God, and the believers today have the complete inspired Word of God, nothing is to be added to it.

The Holy Spirit also will complete the church, the whole building is being "builded together for an habitation of God through the Spirit" (Eph. 2:22). This could have a double meaning, that God dwells in the church in the person of the Spirit, and that the Spirit is the power through whom the building will be formed and completed.

The Spirit of life in Romans 8:2 is likely what is indicated here, the Spirit being the answer to a dying church. This is a vital truth all should keep before them, "Not by might nor by power but by my Spirit saith the Lord" (Zech. 4:6).

While the Spirit refers to One who is Divine, the stars would speak of human channels. The Spirit invariably uses men. In Old Testament days, the Spirit is described as "clothing" men, and in the New Testament He seals, fills and endues with gift and ability in this time of grace. The stars are the responsible leading company in each church, so the answer to weakness and a dying condition is the same to every such church, the Spirit in life and power operating in dedicated believers.

The sevenfold quality of the Spirit. The believer could do nothing apart from the Spirit of God, in every department of the Christian life, all depends upon the Spirit.

a)   The Spirit of life in Christ Jesus (Romans 8:20)

b)   The body without the Spirit is dead (James 2:26). While James is speaking about a human body, yet the principle remains for churches also, there is no life in any church apart from the Spirit of God.

c)   Paul speaks of being strengthened by His Spirit in the inner man (Eph. 3:16).

d)   The Spirit brought all things to remembrance to the apostles in the writing of the Word (John 14:26). By the same Spirit the Scriptures can be known in depth today.

e)   Ministry, teaching is only by the Spirit in 1 Cor. 2.

f)   All gift and ability comes through the Spirit and can only be used in the Spirit's power in 1 Cor. 12.

g)   Even confession comes by the Spirit, "the Holy Ghost shall teach you in that hour what ye should speak" (Matt. 10:19-20).

The stars. Stars are to give light and guidance, and this is the calling of the elders whom the angel represents. Leaders are not to be so in name only, such is deadness, but in living vitality with a dominant care for the flock. Note "He that hath the seven stars", they are still owned by the Lord and He is ready to use them if they could shake off the deadness. The authority of the leading element is still recognized, as Matt. 18:18 "Whatsoever you shall bind on earth shall be bound in heaven".

BACK TO THE KINGS

The nation prior to the days of Joash was low, Athaliah reigned, really it was the flesh in control. The seed royal was all wiped out with the exception of a baby boy named Joash, saved by the wife of Jehoiada the priest. The boy was hidden in a chamber of the temple and was not found, this speaks of how little the temple was used. The King's son was presented to the nation, all went well until the death of the priest. After this, all went to pieces, weakness set in. Prophets were sent by the Lord, the people did not listen, the Word from the Lord was not wanted, that is likely how the dying state began in Sardis. Out of it all, Jehoiada shone, he was the successful one, and he was honoured by being buried with the kings, Joash was not. The successful overcomer shall walk with the Lord in white, such an honour, walking with the true King.

CHAPTER SIXTEEN

The Lord's Message to Sardis

The letter to Sardis is short by comparison with some of the others, but nevertheless contains a much needed message that carries weight in every generation, that is "the call to WATCH".

In this church, activities and exercises mostly were gone, the remaining ones were beginning to cease. The contrasting phrase is "living and dying", the man wounded in the parable of the good Samaritan is a good illustration of this condition. The man robbed on the Jericho road was left half dead, not half alive, that would imply that life was winning, but half dead means that the principle of death is at work; if help does not come soon, the victim will die. The man needed the good Samaritan who turns out to be the Lord. This church needs the Lord, He pours in the oil and wine, oil that speaks of the Spirit, and the seven Spirits of God are mentioned here, wine speaks of joy, and no greater joy than recovery, the stars speaking of government must operate here. The Spirit of life and the stars of light are indicated in the way the Lord introduces Himself, In Him was life and the life was the light of men (John 1:4).

THINGS NOT COMPLETE BEFORE GOD

A spiritual believer is grieved in looking upon deadness in any church, how much more is it so with Him who was the true Nazarite, who abhorred the defilement of deadness.

The works of this church were not perfect before God, which means "incomplete" not finished. How often Scripture warns against this condition.

a) The parable of the Fig Tree in Luke 13 has this in mind, all was as it should be, the best of soil as the tree was planted in a vineyard, yet no fruit was forthcoming. The fruitlessness was repeated in the second and third year, the process was not complete, fruit is the reason for the fig tree in the first place.
b) Another parable in Luke 14 has the same idea, the man who started to build a tower and was not able to finish it, the result was that he became a laughing stock before the people.
c) In the story of the kings of Israel many started well and ended badly, they did not complete their purpose in rule. The same could be said about Noah, Gideon, Samson and many others who did not finish well.
d) King Saul began well with good works worthy of praise, and ended badly, He was removed by God.

How different with our Lord, He finishes and completes all that was given Him to do. " I have finished the work which thou givest me to do" (John 17:4).

"It is finished" were His triumphant words from the cross.

When He washed the feet of the disciples he did not leave them wet, He finished the work and dried their feet Himself.

When he raised the widow's son from the dead, He delivered him to his mother for care, He finished the work, not only resurrection but reunion as well (Luke 7).

WORKS BEFORE GOD'S SCRUTINY

When He says "before my God", Christ is speaking as Man, and in this title He judges all. He uses the title "Father" in verse 5, and this presents Him as the Divine Son. The words "before my God" are searching, for whom does the believer labour ? The true motive for all labour is unto the Lord, alas, much labour can be done before the eyes of men, as pleasing men, such were the Pharisees, and the Lord severely condemned this practice.   The table of showbread in the tabernacle was before the face of God, for His pleasure, He was feasting upon it in a spiritual way for six days, then the priests ate of that bread. God's pleasure comes first, often what pleases God is not so acceptable to man unless he is spiritually minded.

As already noted, the Lord takes the place of the Son of Man, this is seen in the words "before my God" and therefore is the one who has the right to judge, and judgment begins at the house of God, the assembly.

WHAT THE LORD SEES

A Name, this church was living in the past, Samson did just this and went out as at other times thinking that the Lord was with him, alas, he was alone and ended in chains. Servants of God can live in the past, and to some extent loose out in their present service in their own generation.

Verse one states "This church was living", validity was there but so as by fire, there was very little to bring glory to the Lord in this dying church.

Dying, the process of death was at work, and time would take its toll, unless something is done soon the death will be complete, the church will cease to exist. Contrast the apostles in 2 Cor. 6:9, " As dying and behold we live", that was of course to the world, they were constantly facing death in their service, but the inner life was prospering.

THE LORD'S FOURFOLD EXHORTATION

1) The first of these exhortations was to WATCH. In the Olivet Discourse the Lord broke the prophetic outline to insert five parables and then continued with the discourse. The five parables were all of the one theme, exhortations to watch

The fig tree	—— Watch the times
The goodman and thief	—— Watch the house
The slave	—— Watch for the Master
The virgins	—— Watch for the provision, oil
The talents	—— Watch our stewardship.

In the goodman and the virgins sleep was the problem, and in the fig tree the slave and the talents, carelessness was the problem.

Vigilant watching is needed for both these hindrances.

2) The second exhortation was "To strengthen the things that remain which were ready to die". It would seem that full recovery to first

things was now impossible, but the things that remain must not expire as the former things.   Many exercises and services were a thing of the past.   People who often talk about the need of revival are seldom at prayer meetings !   The eye must be on the present works in any church that all are kept alive.   Old fashioned tenacity is needed today.

3) "Remember past teaching".   This is the third exhortation to this dying church.   This is the reason the past ministry of our Lord is prominent in this letter, there was a famine of the Word of God, in their services teaching was a thing of the past. When teaching for different reasons is absent from churches, responsibility remains for that which has been heard in the past.   When the Word of God is read and expounded, then all that hear are from henceforth held responsible by God, light brings answerability.   "How they had received" would likely refer to the delight they had in the teaching when it was first given, but such delights can fade if the teaching is not being maintained.   As suggested already, full recovery is impossible, and the Lord brings in the past teaching to meet the present need.

4) The last exhortation is very searching, "hold fast and repent".   The holding fast is to the present works, see that they do not meet the fate of the other good works and exercises.   The repentance is an awakening to the present dying condition, they need to be aware of the terrible failure and some endeavour must be made to set things right as far as possible.

It has often been pointed out that recovery is in three steps in this letter, Remember, Repent, Hold fast. Remembrance and Repentance are relative to the past failure, hold fast is relative to the present condition.

THE OTHER ALTERNATIVE

The Lord then warns of the only alternative if the repentance is not forthcoming. "If therefore thou shalt not watch I will come on thee as a thief" (Rev. 3:3).   In many books on the Revelation this sentence is interpreted as the Coming of the Lord, but this does not appear to be so, it could be a reference to some form of unexpected chastisement.   This is an alternative, if they "watch" then He will not come in chastisement, if they watch not, then the Lord will come in some form of judgment as in 1 Cor. 11 etc..

However, there may be a veiled reference to the Coming of the Lord as well, generally speaking the metaphor of the thief is a feature of the Lord's return. This warning is good for the church, to know that the Lord is not pleased with the company is bound to have a sanctifying effect to the good of all.

THE COMMENDATION FROM THE LORD

There are some that the Lord commends in this church as in Thyatira, profession is in view from the fourth letter, hence the "rest" in Thyatira, and the "few" here. It would seem that the reality is getting lesser with each letter, until practically the whole is spewed out in Laodicea. Their names are known to the Lord, sometimes in large congregations all are not known to each other, not so with the Lord, the Names of all His own are remembered. The Shepherd knows His sheep and calls them by Name (John 10:3). The Lord knoweth them that are His (2 Tim 2:19).

The Lord refers to the fact that this remnant was not defiled, a very appropriate word to use as deadness is defiling. Recall the Nazarite, he was not to be defiled by the dead, and of course the dead were to be buried out of sight. Note also that there is no command whatsoever that this remnant should leave this defiled gathering and start another church elsewhere. Rather they are exhorted to strengthen the things that remain.

There is a conditional reward to the few who have not defiled their garments. At the close of each letter there are unconditional rewards or promises, to the overcomers, which includes every true believer, therefore the promise is unconditional. Nonetheless there are several conditional promises in these letters also.

The crown of life to Smyrna
Walk with me in white, Sardis
Enemies to bow in Philadelphia
Keep from the hour, in Philadelphia
Sup with me in Laodicea

These promises have mostly to do with the present time, to enter into the good of these promises the believer must be clean. Enoch walked with God, to do so he was undefiled for the scripture says "Can two walk together except they be agreed" (Amos 3:3).

Walk carries the thought of fellowship, this can be seen from the first mention of walk in the Bible. The Lord God walked in the garden in the cool of the day, this obviously was to have communion with the man whom He had created.

This promise of verse 4 is threefold.

1) Walk with Me — is fellowship with the Lord, to walk with Him is to be like Him, and in the direction of His will.

2) Walk in WHITE, the colour of joy in the Bible, "Let thy garments be always white ... Live joyfully with the wife of thy youth" (Ecc. 9:8-9). White also is the colour of purity, and this would of course be necessary to walk with the Lord. Again, white is the colour of victory, as seen in the victorious Lord on a white horse in Rev. 19:11. The garments of the Lord when transfigured where white as snow that no fuller on earth could whiten them, this conditional reward makes the believer to be Christ-like undoubtedly.

3) They are worthy. Such a statement to be made by the Lord. We call Him worthy and so He is by virtue of who He is and what He has done and where He is, but for this exalted One to refer to His feeble people as worthy is commendation indeed.

THE PROMISE AND APPEAL VERSE 5

The unconditional promise is similar to verse 4. The overcomer shall be clothed in white raiment, this would speak of the righteous acts of saints and is so interpreted in ch. 19:8. There is bound to be the manifestation of practical righteousness in every truly born again believer, life must be apparent and God rewards that which His grace has produced.

Absolute security is seen in the expression "I will not blot out his name out of the book of life". This does not mean that believers can be blotted out, rather the secure consolation that this can never be.

The third section of the promise is the confession of the name of the overcomer before My Father. This looks at the Person of Christ as a Divine Person, just as verse 2 looks upon Him as human. There the Son of Man, here the Son of God, although not expressed like that here. The confessing of the name by the Lord Jesus before His Father is no doubt the bringing into the joy of the relationship with Divine Persons, this relationship was forged by faith in Christ.

In summing up, not the deadness but rather the manifestation of life in righteous acts.

The name not blotted out, rather the continuing in testimony; not dying as the rest of the church.

The confession is a reference to works that were completed, the confession of his name brings in turn the confession of the believer before the Father, this is the principle of sowing and reaping.

CHAPTER SEVENTEEN

The Church at Philadelphia

This is the most appealing of all the letters to the churches and it must have given the Lord much pleasure to dictate it, and for John to write it. In spite of this there was little to applaud in the eyes of the natural man, weakness was there, they were few in number and had little gift. This condition can be derived from the Lord's words of verse 8 " Thou hast a little power" or strength, and they were exhorted to hold fast to what little they had in verse 10. This is a common condition with many churches today, the lack of numbers, activity, and the want of gift. Therefore this letter is very much up to date in the present day.

The contrasting words are "Open" and "Shut" which would indicate that numbers are not everything, neither is gift nor strength, but the pleasure of the Lord in the company and His purpose to bless with an open door. Paul and his companions had learnt early in their experience that the servants are nothing, but God that giveth the increase is the vital factor in all service (1 Cor. 3:7). Laodicea likely had plenty as regards numbers, gift and money yet the Lord was outside that church altogether, they had not put before the Lord an open door, they rather presented to the Lord a closed door (Verse 20).

The open door would be opportunity for blessing that has been appointed by the Lord Himself, and can come from no other source.

The apostles were in the upper room with the door closed for fear of the Jews, the Lord appeared and gave them the great commission, that is He placed before them an open door, the literal door was closed but the Lord opened a spiritual door. The Lord commissioned them with the words " As the Father hath sent me so send I you, receive ye the Holy Ghost", then He talks about the power to remit sins, that is by their Gospel preaching (John 20:21-2), this indeed is an open door.

The great lesson that comes from this encouraging letter is that "Increase comes from God and no other source".

THE SPECIAL FEATURES IN THE LETTER

Although weakness was there this church was special to Christ and the special features indicate that this is so.

1) Here is the longest opening introduction, the Lord presents Himself in a fivefold way, and in each title is uncovered a source of grace and power, just what this company needed.
2) In keeping with the introduction there is the longest promise. This promise is again fivefold as if to say " Weakness does not deprive of future glory, or of the presence and nearness of the Lord while on earth". These two alone, the introduction and the promise declare a great Christ for the present and a great glory for the future. Note how in the promise the Lord speaks of pillars which indicate strength, there will be no weakness in the future state.
3) The "Word" is only mentioned in this letter. One would have thought this to have been the case with Ephesus the well taught church, but no, this is mentioned with a church in weakness. The Word is mentioned in verses 8 and 10 although there may be a difference in the two ideas. It was the Word that kept this company going in spite of weakness as is often the case.
4) Worship is only mentioned with this church (Verse 9), this is most amazing as one would think that worship would be expressed by the stronger churches of the seven. In fact this is reasonable as worship comes out of a sense of weakness and the superior power, majesty, and grace of God.
5) It is not therefore unusual to see that the Lord's love for the saints is expressed for the first time in these letters, "To know that I have

loved thee" (Verse 9). How comforting is this, the Lord loves His own not because of great virtues in them, or any spiritual capacity, but just because we are His own. He loves the dear believer in spite of weakness and failure.

6) Another great feature of this letter is the emphasis of the Lord possessing things, the word MY is seen many times.

My Word in verse 8.

My Name in verse 8.

The Word of My patience in verse 10.

The Temple of My God in verse 12.

The Name of My God in verse 12.

Finally, the city of My God in verse 12.

He possesses all, and He loves us, it is pleasant when One so rich favours and loves us, happy that believer that basks in this glorious fact. God has shared His Son with us, this no doubt is the meaning of "Heirs of God and joint heirs with Christ" (Rom. 8:17).

COMPARISON WITH SMYRNA

These letters follow a certain pattern as has already been pointed out, being in the form of inverted parallels. This being the second letter from the end it therefore corresponds with the second from the beginning, namely Smyrna. Note the following:-

1. There is nothing condemned in either church; that does not mean there was nothing to condemn, perhaps lesser things existed, but the building up of the churches was paramount to the Lord, the correction would come later.

2. The Synagogue of Satan is mentioned in both, indicating that the opposition to both churches was mainly from Judaism, the fanatical teachers that represented the Jews.

3. It follows then that both the churches suffered from a religious quarter, and not so much from imperial powers.

4. Crowns are part of the reward in both letters, to one the crown of life is promised, and a warning to the second, "let no man take thy crown".

5. Both letters contain a time factor, ten days is mentioned to Smyrna, and the hour of temptation is referred to in the letter to Philadelphia; in both cases the time of trial is controlled by heaven, and is therefore limited.

6. Christ in resurrection authority is presented in both letters, this is such an encouraging feature to both a suffering church and a weak church. As always, Christ is the answer.

WHY THIS LIKENESS ?

Because of need, although different in each case yet extreme need is there. One is suffering and the other is in great weakness, but what is common to both is discouragement. To Smyrna the word is "fear none of those things which thou shalt suffer", and to Philadelphia who likely bemoaned their weakness the word is "hold fast that which thou hast", the Lord recognized the weakness and did not therefore ask great things.

Again the resurrection is paramount in both letters as being fundamental; to Smyrna the next life is sure, such a glorious hope; to Philadelphia the Millennium is prominent and the place of the believer in it, again offers a magnificent hope.

Note that Smyrna presents the Lamb, the One who was dead and alive again, the First and the Last, and Philadelphia is taken up with the temple. Israel started with the Lamb and came to full glory with the temple of Solomon. Even so the Revelation itself starts with "The first and the last" in chapter one, and ends with the Temple of God in chapter twenty one. No doubt there are many other comparisons and reasons for the comparisons in these two letters that would be noticed if one would patiently consider.

THE OLD TESTAMENT BACKGROUND

The background of the days of Hezekiah is evident from the reference in verse 7 to Isa. 22. There a man called Shebna is referred to as being over the household of the king. He did not believe the word of the prophets concerning the coming captivity and had appointed a burial place for himself in Israel. The Lord then speaks of calling another man to be over the household, Eliakim, he would be clothed with the robe and girdle that belonged to Shebna. Then the Scripture speaks of him in this way " And the key of David will I lay upon his shoulder, so he shall open and none shall shut and he shall shut and none shall open" (Isa. 22:22). This is the reference here in verse seven of our chapter. Now both these men are mentioned in 2 Kings 18:18, these with others came to Hezekiah with the news of the Syrian ultimatum, and this was in the fourteenth year of the reign of Hezekiah. Therefore the O.T. background is obviously the reign of Hezekiah. Note these facts:-

1) The worship of Jehovah was lost in the previous reign of King Ahaz, he made an altar, the copy of that used by the heathen around him, and also remodelled much of the furniture of the temple, thus losing its significance. The temple worship was restored in the first year of Hezekiah, he opened the doors of the temple that had been shut and repaired them (2 Chron. 29:3). The forefathers had shut the doors (2 Chron. 29:7). Hence the references to the temple in this letter and the open and shut doors.

2) Hezekiah then proceeded to cleanse the temple according to the Word of God, and the Word of God is prominent in this Philadelphian church.

3) However weakness was there, in the invasion of Sennacherib Hezekiah was discouraged and sent word to the priests saying "This day is a day of trouble and of rebuke and of blasphemy, for the children are come to the birth and there is no strength to bring forth" (Isa. 37:3). The Lord then opened a door of victory, the enemies were destroyed by the power of God without lifting a weapon. The angel of the Lord destroyed 185000 of the army of Syria. As in this letter, the enemies bowed to the dust.

4) Hezekiah was sick unto death and was recovered by the Word of the Lord. How fitting, for that was the condition of this church and the recovery was by the Word that the Spirit said unto the church.

5) Hezekiah again is tested and comes out in weakness in the affair of the visit from Babylon, he let them see what was in his house. His house was no place for the enemies of God's people, yet he showed all that was in his house, was there a sense of pride here? In a way he lost his crown, the Lord spoke of his displeasure at the action of the opening of his house, this is one door that ought to have been closed, especially to the enemies of the Lord.

WHY THIS LIKENESS TO HEZEKIAH ?

Conditions are the same, "weakness" but the chief point is the power of the risen Christ, the power to subdue the enemy, the power of worship and the beauty of the sanctuary. Weakness and power are seen at the same time in the days of Hezekiah and in the experience of this church. When I am weak then am I strong; (2 Cor. 12:10).

All must be to God's pleasure, it is godliness that the Lord looks for and this can be present in spite of weakness. The pleasure of the Lord was seen in both cases in the prominence of the temple, Hezekiah brought it to the fore again, God is pleased, and to this church is promised a part in the temple of which the Lord speaks metaphorically.

THE FIVEFOLD INTRODUCTION OF THE LORD

Now to consider the way the Lord presents Himself to this church, He does so in a fivefold way, more than to any of the other churches.

Five is the number of weakness as stamped upon man in creation, the five fingers of the hand and the five toes of the foot are marks of weakness. This can also be seen in the five porches of John chapter five, there the people with infirmity are found around the pool which had five porches. Five is also the number of grace in the Scriptures, the Lord then came in with grace and healed the man who had an infirmity for thirty eight years, this is grace indeed.

These are royal titles, they are linked with the great king David. Power is needed in this church and where the word of a king is, there is power. On resurrection ground the Lord said, "All power is given unto me in heaven and in earth" (Matt. 28:18)

The titles fall into two parts, Who He is, and What He does. This is similar to the public confession of the blind man, "A man that is called Jesus" this was identification, "made clay and anointed mine eyes and said unto me, Go to the pool of Siloam and wash, and I went and washed and I received my sight" (John 9:11), this is what He did. The same twofold representation is found in the epistle to Colossians, chapter one expounds who Christ is in wonderful language, and chapter two rejoices in what He has done for the souls of men. This twin concept is a frequent occurrence in Scriptures, for instance the Song of Hannah in 1 Samuel also looks upon God in this twofold way.

CONSIDER WHAT HE IS

Being Holy would suggest the Priest. Being holy, He has the right to assess everything, all must be in keeping with this nature, He is the holy One of God, even demons recognize this.

As being "true" would suggest the Prophet. He was the true prophet, the one greater than Moses and clearly prophesied of in Deut. 18. Prophets were true men in contrast to false prophets, and true as embodying the Word of God. Then as having the key of David would make Him a king, here then is that threefold designation of the Lord that often occurs in Scripture, the Prophet, Priest and King. As Priest He brings the character of God, as Prophet He brings forth the Word of God, and as King He brings forth the power of God. Such was His testimony to God in the days of His flesh.

The Key of David would suggest resurrection power, He has the keys of death and hell, He will establish the Kingdom as being the lineage of David and on resurrection ground. Isa. 22 links the government with the earth, here it is an assembly upon the earth in testimony to the living God.

WHAT HE DOES

He opens and no man shuts, that is He opened the way of opportunity to all who will enter. He opened the door of blessing in the gospel, He opens the door of spirituality to every convert, they can go on to know Him who is the Life. In this letter it seems that the door is something that is going to open in the way of assembly blessing and fruitfulness.

The door then brings responsibility to those before whom it is opened. The crown shall be the reward of entrance, but neglect of entering is to let someone else take that crown. Some seek to open what He closes; a case in point would be the people of Israel at the border of the land, they refused to enter the land and the Lord closed the door. However, later they sought to enter in and many of them were destroyed for this act of disobedience (Numbers 14). Again Herod in Acts 12 sought to close a door which the Lord had opened, namely the Word of grace to the people, the door of the prison was opened to Peter and the door of the life of Herod was closed in a horrible way. One cannot meddle with the open and shut doors that the Lord sets up.

Paul speaks of open doors in his service for the Lord. He requests prayer for the Lord to open a door for utterance, that is ministry of the Word in Col. 4:3, as in 1 Cor. 16:9 he speaks of an opened door in the gospel, he speaks again of such a door in 2 Cor. 2:12. The first missionaries told with joy of the door of grace and faith opened to Gentiles in

Acts 14:27. One should always be thankful to the Lord for the open doors of opportunity in His service upon the earth.

In a wonderful way the Lord fulfilled all this in His ministry upon the earth. In the world that looked upon Him as a failure He walked in holiness and truth, the Holy One of God and the true bread, the true vine and many other such like describe Him. He had the key of David, the people marvelled at His authority, He was not like the scribes who always fell back upon the authority of another. Not so the Lord, His authority in the Word, the laws of nature in His miracles of healing, even the elements such as storm and calm were completely in His control. He opened the doors of teaching, never man spake like this man, and the door of spiritual experience for men the like of which was never before.

Well He could make this fivefold claim to this church at Philadelphia.

A sad little point comes out here, the Lord in His goodness sets before the believers open doors a plenty, but many like those of Laodicea present to the Lord a closed door, there is no room in their hearts for the Man of Sorrows, yet He was full of grace and truth (3:20).

CHAPTER EIGHTEEN

The Lord's Message to Philadelphia

It has been suggested in the previous chapter that the church at Phila-delphia was small numerically, and with little gift. This condition is not to be despised, in a small company many good merits emerge. For instance, the believers will all know each other, and this cannot be said of very large congregations where the personal touch is absent in most cases. Again, those in a small company have more opportunity for service and thus achieve greater development. Another point is that such a company will be cast upon the Lord in a greater way, and this is most precious to the Lord. Again a small company is not always look-ing for great things and are thankful for small mercies from the Lord.

When the remnant of Israel returned from the exile they were small in comparison to the huge number that remained in Babylon. When the work was started in the rebuilding of the temple, there was some dis-couragement from an unlikely source, namely the older men, and the work of the temple then ceased for over twenty years. Later, when the work was again started through the instrumentality of the prophets Haggai and Zechariah, the Word came from the Lord that "They despise not the day of small things" (Zech. 4:10). God had great things in mind in the seemingly small recovery, to wit the coming into the world of the Messiah, the Son of the living God. To this weak company the Lord was opening a door of blessing and opportunity as seen in the letter.

THERE IS MUCH TO COMMEND

1) "I know thy works", or deeds (Verse 8). Good works were present, perhaps not to the same degree as in Ephesus but they were of better quality, works done with the right motive. The works are not itemized as in some of the other letters, this is the most spiritual church and these works are for the pleasure of the Lord alone. So great was the pleasure of God in this that He was minded to bless them with an open door. No doubt the Lord kept the door open, taking into consideration their weakness and lack of power.

2) The pleasure and the opened door is also proffered because of their faithfulness to the Word of God. "Thou ... hast keep my Word" there was place for the teaching of Scripture in their meetings, and they sought to obey what they had learnt by that channel of the Holy Spirit. How unlike Sardis, where there was little or no place for the teaching of the word insomuch the Lord had to refer them to past teaching.

3) They did not deny the Name of the Lord, verse 8. To represent that Glorious Name demands Christian ethics, and also the willingness to suffer reproach from a world that puts no value upon the revelation of the Christ of God. There was no sign of compromise as with the church at Pergamos.

4) "Thou hast kept the word of my patience" (Verse 10). This is different from the word in verse 8, here it is the attitude of Christ when suffering rejection. The reference in 2 Thess. 3:5 is a help here. "The Lord direct your hearts into the love of God and the patient waiting for Christ". The word "waiting" should really be omitted and is so in the Revised Version and other translations, this makes the passage read "of entering into the love of God and the patience of Christ". This means that in suffering, the Lord as a man did not despair, but rested in the love of God for Him, and therefore patiently waited for the mind and vindication of God to be manifested. Such is the idea here, under pressure for the Name of the Lord they waited patiently as did the Lord before them for the display of God's pleasure in them. This vindication is seen in the latter part of verse 9, those of the synagogue of Satan would come and worship before their feet, and would know assuredly that the Lord loved the believers of Philadelphia.

THEY HAD NOT AN EASY PATH

This church kept the Word and the Name of Christ, not in a congenial society but in a hostile one. They suffered for righteousness sake and for the sake of Christ, and their enemies were many. The foremost of these enemies were the so called Jews who were of the synagogue of Satan, that is the religious Jews who were deceived into thinking they were doing service to God in the persecution of the Christians. Behind all this was the hiss of the serpent, the devil himself.

Satan is behind many troubles of the churches both internal and external. Consider this subject as it appears in 2 Corinthians:-

Chapter 2 the devices of Satan, the thoughts of Satan that copy God's thoughts and are thus counterfeit.

Chapter 4 his methods, one is to blind the minds of those who believe not.

Chapter 6 his subtlety, to mingle wrong with right so that the right will loose its separation and identity, righteousness with unrighteousness: light with darkness: Christ with Belial: he that believeth and an infidel, and the temple of God with idols.

Chapter 11 his design is to corrupt the purity of the assembly which is espoused as a virgin to Christ.

Chapter 12 his deception, even changing into an angel of light so as to deceive the unwary.

Chapter 12 his object, that is to hinder the servant of the Lord by buffeting and in many other ways.

It is noteworthy that while much evil is condemned in the first letter to Corinth, Satan is not mentioned in any way except by implication in the temple of idols, but so much is written of the enemy in 2 Corinthians as above. It would seem that in the second letter Paul is identifying the real source of the trouble in that church.

The answer to all this is the Word, so it was with the Lord in confronting the devil, and evidently with this church at Philadelphia also. In severe temptation they had not denied the Name of the One whom they served. Weakness yes, but strength and power in the Lord by the Word.

BLESSING ABOUT TO BE EXPERIENCED

The promise of the open door seemed to be blessing of some sort, and bringing responsibility with it. The open door perhaps could be seen in several ways.

First, as having victory over the enemies, they shall bow at the feet of the believers of Philadelphia. The word "worship" means to crouch or prostrate one's self and this word is used entirely throughout the book of Revelation.

Second, there are crowns to be gained, this brings in the responsibility, and the warning comes with it that others could take the crown if one is not responsive.

The great blessing of all would be the "being kept from the hour of trial". This may have had an application in the day this church existed, but has greater repercussions in the line of prophecy. Here it would be peace in a scene of unrest.

Whatever the open door indicated, one thing was sure, no man could shut it. Those of the synagogue of Satan would no doubt try to do so but would find it impossible, just as in the ministry of our Lord the porter opened, namely John the Baptist, and none could hinder Him finishing the work He was given to do by the Father. In the same way, none can hinder what God had in mind for these believers, only themselves, failing to gain the crown.

THE HOUR OF TRIAL UPON ALL THE EARTH

One must remember that there is a prophetic panoramic design in these letters covering this present church period. It is in this direction especially that this reference to the hour of trial is understood. Philadelphia is seen as being the time towards the end of the church period, with the threat of the Great Tribulation looming ahead. Even today one who carefully studies the Word and is familiar with the affairs in the political realms of this world can see great things emerging. However a few facts concerning that Tribulation are found here.

1) The time shall be short, looked upon as an hour, intense but short, the actual time will be three and a half years.

2) Also it will be universal, it shall come upon ALL THE WORLD, no geographical area shall escape its terrors.

3) The people largely involved are the earth dwellers, those who live for earth, time, materialism and that which appeals to the natural man, and who put no value whatsoever on the spiritual.

4) The purpose of the Tribulation in the first place is to try the earth dwellers, in the present time the world is being tried by the truth of the gospel, in the Tribulation they shall be tried by the lie of the serpent (2 Thess. 2). Believers in Christ have already passed that test.

5) The chief character of the times then shall be "Trial" it will not be easy either for those who reject the truth and believe the lie, nor shall it be easy for those who embrace the truth in the testimony of Christ. The world then shall go through a time of testing the like of which was never before experienced.

6) The church as represented in this Philadelphian company shall be kept from this hour of trial. This of course is in keeping with the tenor of Scripture, seen even in type with Enoch being caught up to God before the event of the terrible destruction of the flood. The trial is upon the world, and the believer is not of the world (John 15:19) and is taken out of the world (John 17:6).

THE LORD'S LOVE FOR HIS PEOPLE

Why should the Lord so bless this company, and the rest of the saints for that matter ? Because they are the recipients of His unmerited love. This love the Lord wants to be publicized, "I will make them to come and worship before thy feet and to know that I have loved thee" (Ch. 3:9). The believers expressed their love for the Lord in obedience to His commands, and He proves His love to them by the blessing of the open door. To such His Return would be most precious, and the word of consolation comes from the Lord to this church in the saying "Behold I come quickly".

With this promise of His coming there is an exhortation, "hold that fast which thou hast" (Verse 11). Hold fast, do not give up the bearing of the Name, and the keeping of the Word, as well as the patience of Christ in time of trial. Let no man take thy crown is no doubt relative to the open door. As in John 10 the "I am the door, if any man enter in", an open door is surely an invitation to enter in, but neglecting to enter would be to forfeit the crown. Such an exhortation, so many open doors of service and opportunity are set before the people of God, and each one brings with it grave responsibility.

If one refuses to take advantage of the open door someone else will get that same opportunity, and will do what the first was supposed to do. Samuel replaced Samson, they were both Nazarites from birth and no doubt the calling was to anoint the king. Samson failed, but Samuel was successful in his Nazarite vow and anointed David to be king. In the same state John the Baptist a Nazarite from birth, in a sense anointed the Lord by the baptism in water, then the Spirit as a dove anointed the Lord.

THE FIVEFOLD PROMISE

There is a wonderful prophetic sequence in this letter. First, Christ risen, and having the key of David, He has not come into this as yet, but all enemies in due course shall become His footstool and He shall reign. In the meantime, He is a king without an earthly kingdom. This is followed by the church age, the testimony of this assembly as being outside all religious pretensions that claim to be the mouthpiece of God. The passage referring to the Great Tribulation comes next, and the believer is kept from it, the coming of the Lord in verse 11 is the hope of the church, it must be occupied with Him, and look for Him. The Judgment Seat of Christ is then noticed in the rewards, namely the crown, and in the final promise to the overcomer the Millennium is set up. Here indeed is a remarkable panoramic outline of the times from the resurrection of the Lord until the final Kingdom is set up.

A few remarks on the fivefold promise is necessary.

1) As stated already, the titles of Christ in the introduction of this letter are fivefold and the promise at the end is also fivefold. A Great Christ for the present, and a wonderful assurance for the future.

2) To be a pillar is not literal of course, rather position and ornamentation. A pillar in Scripture speaks of the ability to carry responsibility, to uphold things. This can be seen in the description of James, Cephas and John by Paul when he first met them, his judgment was that they seemed to be pillars in the company. Pillars also are viewed

as ornamentation, the lovely character of a believer adorning the doctrines revealed in this time of grace. Both these ideas are in this promise, in the Millennium the overcomer shall have the place of great responsibility and of glory. These Christians were thought nothing of on earth, especially from the Jewish synagogue and such like, but they are accepted gloriously by heaven and that is what really matters.

3) The temple would speak of nearness, purity and worship, such will be the glory of the people of God in the coming kingdom.

4) He shall go no more out, on earth they suffered rejection and perhaps had to flee to the wastes for shelter from persecution, all that will be at an end. Safe and happy in the presence of God.

5) "I will write upon him the name of my God". Writing speaks of something enduring, and no doubt brings in the favour of God that shall never fail. The name of the city is added to this and the name of the Lord Himself.

6) The threefold name.
   The name of God would be the seal, as belonging to God.
   The name of the city would suggest citizenship, something
   similar to the passage in Heb. 12 that speaks of the
   blessing the Christian has come into.
   The Name of Christ would suggest union as being in
   authority with Him, we shall reign with Him (2 Tim. 2:12).

7) The most important feature of this extended promise is the intimacy with Christ, He shares all with us, His God, His city His Name etc.. Five times the word MY appears.

This no doubt is the Millennium and is proved to be so by the coming down of the New Jerusalem from heaven in verse 12. Now the same thing will happen at the beginning of the eternal state, and it is the teaching of Scripture, that features of blessing begun in the Millennium will continue into the Day of God which is eternity.

In summing up, this company was evidently rejected on earth, yet they held fast not to that which was accepted by the religious world, but the Word of Christ and the name of Christ. In such a condition the Lord finds great pleasure in them as He Himself was in the same position, His greatest enemies were the professors of a religion that had become empty before God. In such circumstances the Lord kept and declared the

Word and the Name of the Father. The coming kingdom would be a time of vindication for both Christ and His own, in the figurative language of the temple their position and favour eternally before God is made clear.

CHAPTER NINETEEN

The Church at Laodicea

The final epistle is tragic. No matter how God accords man with responsibility, man inevitably ends in failure and blindness. The final judge Samson behaved in such a way that his eyes were put out. Eli the Priest ended with dim eyes and could not see. This closed the great role the priest had to play; after him the prophet held the place of communication from God. The Pharisee, who had a long history of the return from exile was condemned by the Lord Himself as being blind. Now the closing church is spoken of as being blind. When the panoramic view is taken of this series of letters, Laodicea would speak of the last state of profession in the world before the Lord comes; but from a moral point of view this church is perhaps the most important of the seven. It manifests how a company that represents God can easily lose ground, and get away from the principles that gathered them in the first place; ending with glory to themselves and the Lord outside it all.

THE CITY OF LAODICEA

This remarkable city was well known in the old days. It was famous for many things including the clothing industry and that of banking. Also it seems some sort of eye salve was manufactured in Laodicea that was known far and abroad, added to this were the tepid pools which attracted many people for health reasons. The Lord made use of these things and others in His address to this church, as in the Gospels the Lord was the master of illustration. In Matt. 13 for instance He uses fields, birds, grounds, tares, wheat, a woman baking, men fishing, a man discovering treasure, a merchantman seeking pearls, and many other such things. All these were common everyday things from which all could learn.

Many of the saints that composed the assembly at Laodicea no doubt worked in these industries and were comfortably well off as seen in the letter. There is nothing wrong with being rich except that it can become a great test, Luke sees this danger and tells many stories of rich men in his Gospel. The Lord often spoke of the deceitfulness of riches as in Matt. 6, Luke 12, and especially in Matt. 19:23 "A rich man shall hardly enter into the kingdom of Heaven". This does not mean that a rich man cannot be saved, rather riches may hinder the man thinking of God in the first place. Riches seem to be the stumbling stone in this church.

THE SPECIAL FEATURES OF THIS LETTER

1) This is the only church of the seven that is not commended some way by the Lord, this no doubt was intended to make them feel ashamed.
2) Besides the lack of commendation from the Lord, this is the only church that commends itself, now that is surely a poor occupation and not according to the principles of spirituality that would seek to hide self.
3) The example of Christ Himself is placed before this church in verse 21, "even as He overcame and is set down".
4) The remarks go further back than any other letter, right back to the beginning of the creation.
5) Christ is outside this assembly, and seeks admission to the closed hearts of the believers. This is a sorrowful state for any believer to be in, since Christ should be all, in the life of an ordinary Christian.
6) They were obviously wretched, miserable, blind, naked; yet no ministering brother had the backbone to tell them so, this was left to the Lord Himself. They must have been visited by teachers having itching ears (according to Paul in 2 Tim. 4:3) who told them what they wanted to hear and not the truth exposing their terrible state.

7) The material is set out in a series of "triplets".

Three titles of our Lord, the Amen, the True Witness and the beginning of the creation of God.

There are three statements in verse 15. I know thy works, Neither cold nor hot, I would thou were cold or hot.

Cold and hot is found three times in the letter.

There is a threefold counsel in verse 18, the buying of the gold, raiment and eye salve.

Love, rebuke, and chasten are three actions of the Lord to this church. (Verse 19).

The Lord is doing three things in verse 20, Standing, knocking, willing to come in and sup.

Again in verse 20 the threefold response, hear, open, and to sup with the Lord.

They took pride in three things in verse 17.   Riches, increase, and need of nothing.

The Trinity is in the closing verses 21-22.

THE OLD TESTAMENT BACKGROUND

This is not as clear as in the other letters, but as they all are written in a chronological order this must follow that line. Ephesus spoke of Genesis and Smyrna of Exodus. Pergamos continued into the wilderness books and Thyatira leads into the books of the kings, seeing Israel then in the promised land. Sardis and Philadelphia continued with the land and some kings, so to complete the picture Laodicea must speak of the captivity. However the reference is not to the end of 2 Kings or 2 Chronicles but rather to a less familiar passage in Lev. 18. There the Lord warns Israel of how they are to behave when they receive the land. The nations that occupied the land before them were steeped in idolatry and uncleanness and for this cause the land was about to spew them out. Accordingly the land would spew Israel out if they behaved in like manner. They did so and they were spewed out, that is, they were carried into captivity.

A remarkable thing about Lev. 18 is the 24 references to NAKEDNESS, the Lord uses that word to describe this church in verse 17 "they were naked" and challenges them to buy of Him white raiment that the shame of their NAKEDNESS does not appear in verse 18. Then of course there is the reference to the spewing out of the mouth of the Lord, in similar fashion, Israel were spewed out of the land for idolatry, but here the church, because of riches, which really are a form of idolatry. The affections were towards their riches rather than the Christ of God. The Lord had been displaced. In the church at Ephesus He had been replaced by "church activity", here He was replaced by riches.

An arresting reference is found in Ezek. chapters 9 to 11, it speaks of Israel's condition just prior to the captivity. The glory was departing, first to the threshold of the temple (Ezek. 9:3) then departing the threshold for the gate of the court (Ezek. 10:19), after that from the midst of the city to the mountain and was gone in ch. 11. The Lord had not the position of being in the midst of this church, rather He was outside, and therefore outside the lives of the believers that composed that church, and was about to leave them by the spewing out of His mouth. Such a sad condition for any church to be in.

Such is the Old Testament background.

THE BACKGROUND ALSO OF COLOSSIANS

There is another background to be considered to this church and that is the epistle to the Colossians. Paul wrote an epistle to the first and last of these churches, one to Ephesus which was likely a circular letter and received by Laodicea also. He wrote an epistle to Colosse as well. Now the believers at Colosse were exhorted to read the letter to Laodicea and in like manner those of Laodicea were to read that to Colosse (Col. 4:16). Therefore one can conclude that this assembly was familiar with the epistle to the Colossians. This of course is known by the Lord, and reference is made indirectly to this letter.

1) Colossians chapter one is renowned for its wonderful outline of the Lord Jesus as the Creator, similarly here He is presented as the Beginning of the Creation of God.

2) "I counsel thee", this is very like Col. chapter 2 where the counsel is to beware of men and to consider the fullness of the Christ, the riches that are found in Him, so that each believer may enjoy being complete in Him.

3) Christ is found seated on the right hand of God in Col. 3:1 and this letter closes with a reference to just that, He is sat on His Father's throne in verse 21.

There are many other such parallels but enough has been given to point out the similarity of the two letters, that to Colosse and that to Laodicea.

WHY ALL THIS LIKENESS?

Israel could gain or lose the land by their behaviour and the value they placed upon Divine obedience. Colosse was in danger of losing out spiritually in the same way and Laodicea had got their priorities wrong and were in danger of losing out in spiritual experience and testimony. They put value upon the wrong things, they were living for time, and not for Christ and eternity. Several times in the Gospels the Lord speaks of gaining the life or losing it, such is the thought here.

They speak of their accomplishments, rich and increased with goods, needing nothing, but the Lord gives a fivefold portrayal of their real condition before God as being wretched, miserable, poor, blind, and naked, this is the losing of the life. When the Lord said "I counsel thee to buy of me gold tried in the fire, white raiment, and eye salve", this is a call to the gaining of the life. These dear believers taken up with timely and natural things were losing the real purpose of life. Paul in Phil. 3 talks about the losing of all things here that he might know Christ; this is the true goal in this life for those who believe. The communion stated in verse 20 is the real joy in life and must be pursued by all true Christians.

The example is seen in Israel, God took them out of the bondage of Egypt not so much to bring them to a promised land but to bring them to Himself (Exod. 19:4). This was the true purpose in their release from Egypt, and the same goes for the believers, God has redeemed them with a view to delighting in their worship and communion. This was lacking at Laodicea.

THE THREEFOLD TITLE OF THE LORD

The CREATOR would be primarily a reference to the past, although the future is in mind also. The true WITNESS would be present at the time, He was witnessing against them with the truth. The AMEN is mostly to do with the future. There is much gold to be mined in the different ways the Lord presents Himself to each church, and this one is not behind the rest.

THE TITLE, THE AMEN

When the Christian says "Amen" he means "May it be so" but when the Lord says, or is, the "Amen" it means it SHALL BE SO. The real meaning to the Amen is found in 2 Cor. 1:20. "For all the promise of God in Him are yea, and in Him Amen, unto the glory of God through us". That is to say, that God will only work through Christ, and all promises and prophecies are fulfilled through Him, by the "we" Paul means all that are saved by grace, all believers have a great part in that fulfilment. The point is, God will only work through Christ and this is seen very clearly in this letter. Consider how often the work is through Christ and Him alone.

1/ I counsel thee.
2/ Buy of ME
3/ I love, I rebuke.
4/ I stand at the door.
5/ I knock.
6/ I will sup with him and he with ME.
7/ The overcomer shall sit with ME on MY throne.
8/ I am sat on MY Father's throne.

In all this the Lord Himself is the channel, the prime mover in all activity, He is the Amen. In this "Amen" of Christ, is found the greater things in life, precisely what these saints were missing. The believer saved out of the world is really in the wilderness in God's estimation, and can only be happy in wilderness conditions with the presence of the Lord, and the joy of communion with Him.

THE FAITHFUL AND TRUE WITNESS

The Lord was the faithful witness in His earthly ministry, the True witness would be the substance of His ministry, the Faithful witness would be the manner and energy of His handling of that Truth, His relation to His Father and so forth, this line is especially in the Gospel of John.

Notwithstanding, He is still the witness as in this letter. No doubt this assembly was visited by many ministering brethren besides what gift they had in their own ranks, but all failed to tell them the truth regarding the real condition that existed. These were teachers having itching ears (as already suggested), but the Lord will tell them the truth as in this letter, here again is the faithful witness. He continues to witness in the heart of every believer by the channel of His Word and the conviction through the Holy Spirit.

In "being faithful", there is neither favour nor frown in His discipline, He morally judges all according to righteousness.

This must have shamed the first readers of this epistle, how they had been occupied with the material things of this life and had failed miserably to be faithful witnesses to the future eternity, and the refuge that is found in Christ alone.

THE BEGINNING OF THE CREATION OF GOD

Why this title? No doubt the material creation, and the new creation are in view here, and the reason for this title is most promising. The Lord was able to bring order out of chaos as in the first chapter of the Bible, and in the New Creation to bring souls out of darkness to light etc., in the same way He can bring direction and order to this disorderly church.

Another reason for this description is that in the creation, either old or new, all must be unto Him, He is the reason for the creation in the first place. Yet the Lord is outside this assembly.

The New Creation ought to have been displayed with power in the lives of these saints, alas this was not the case. Although unfaithful, they had part in the New Creation only because Christ is the beginning of it, and the foundation of all God's work. It is well that God looks for no merit to favour with salvation.

Nevertheless, there is still room for this church to enjoy their inheritance in Christ, a new beginning is possible with them. The Lord challenges them to:-

A New Trade in verse 18.

A New Company in verse 20.

A New Incentive in verse 20.

Yes, a new beginning was within reach of this church, or the only other alternative was to be rejected in testimony by the Lord spewing them out of His mouth.

It would be fitting to close this chapter with a practical view from these three titles.

If He is the Amen, His will ought to be done, alas in verse 20 He is outside the life of the believer.

If He is the Faithful and True Witness, He is their example, and they ought to emulate Him.

If He is the beginning of the creation of God, then all should be unto Him, and not unto themselves. These practical points of course have a bearing on all believers in Christ today.

CHAPTER TWENTY

The Lord's Message to Laodicea

The spiritual condition of this church was far from commendable, in fact it was deplorable. There was a want of teaching, humility and power in their service, but more than this, there was no affection in the heart for Christ as there ought to have been. Some of the other churches had little in the way of service, but at least they loved the Lord, and this was accepted as an offering before the face of God. There is nothing like that here, hence the appeal to the individual if perchance there would be a response and a heart that would open to Him. The great lesson that emerges is, that a church with gift and riches can function apart from the Lord, howbeit without His presence and blessing. Nevertheless, while the assembly still existed the Lord will move in grace towards them if happily they may experience restoration.

WITNESS TO THEIR CONDITION

A church that has departed from the Lord and first principles will not get by without some indication from God of their sad condition, such is the case with Laodicea. The Lord witnesses to this church in a threefold way.

1) By Illustration. The tepid pools with which they were familiar, are used by the Lord to bring home to them their offensive condition. To bathe in the pools was believed to be good for the health, and many

people did so as a form of therapy. To try to drink the water was another matter, it was lukewarm, and would have caused nausea and vomiting, the best thing if one got a mouthful of this water was to spew it out of the mouth. The normal Christian feeds upon Christ as in John 6 etc. but the Lord also feeds upon His people. This point is well illustrated in the showbread in the tabernacle, it was called the bread of faces because the Lord continually looked upon the bread as symbolizing the people in their order and sanctification. The Lord would love to have been partaking of the saints of Laodicea in this way, sad to say He could not do so, rather like to the water of the tepid pools, He would spew them out of His mouth. This is rejection in strong terms, rejection of their worship, service and every church activity.

2) They were also condemned by their own words, "Thou Sayest". There is a great warning in this direction in the First Epistle of John, three times in chapter one he refers to "If we say", and four times in chapter two the words are found "He that saith". The self boasting in John's Epistle is profession without possession, or reality, here in this letter it is possession (of the material of this world) without a true profession of Christ before the world. In this way they condemned themselves by their own mouth.

3) Finally, the condemnation by the Lord Himself with five words that would make one shudder, wretched, miserable, poor blind, and naked.

Wretched instead of the peace of the Divine security.
Miserable instead of being joyful in the Lord.
Poor instead of the experience of the riches in Christ.
Blind instead of joy in the revelation of Christ.
Naked instead of being clothed with Christian character.
In this fivefold way they stand condemned before the Lord.

THE FIVE CONDEMNING WORDS

The five words used by the Lord to describe this church demand a little more attention. They are used elsewhere in the N. T. and the consideration of them in a little measure is bound to reap profit.

1) Wretched is only used one other place in the N.T. and that is

Romans 7:24 "O wretched man that I am, who shall deliver me from the body of this death". The word carries the idea of enduring great toil and difficulty, the state of mind that arises out of the hopelessness of the task. Such is the predicament in Rom. 7 with a man under law striving to please God, the terrible painful yoke, and the fruitlessness of the task.

To be used of the Laodiceans is so fitting, they were really misled that material prosperity was spirituality, and really they were groaning under this delusion, the state produced was wretchedness. The man under law in Rom. 7, and the Laodiceans under prosperity were both being tested, and found wanting.

2) The word "miserable" is used by Paul when reasoning of the state of believers if there was no resurrection of the dead. "If in this life only we have hope in Christ, we are of all men most miserable", (1 Cor. 15:19). Really believers are to be commiserated with, pitied if life in Christ affects believers for time only, this is what Paul is driving at. The word "miserable" there means to be pitied, and the same word is used by our Lord to convey the state of affairs of this church, they ought to be the objects of pity, they are missing the mark.

3) Poor is the third word and used often in the N.T. writings, and used mostly concerning material poverty, and so describes poor people that followed the Lord in the Gospels. The word carries the thought of extreme poverty, and results in seeking alms and begging. This church boasted in its possessions and were rich, alas they had not the true riches, their riches were not reckoned by heaven. Really they were beggars and that is the way the Lord speaks of them in the next verse.

4) The forth word is "Blind" and is frequently used in the N.T., especially in the gospels. It is used of blind persons in a literal way, but the Lord used the word five times in a moral way in Matt. 23 to describe the spiritual blindness of the religious Pharisees. It is moral blindness that is implied by the word in this letter, the people were blind to all their great rich inheritance in Christ, and consequently were not rejoicing in soul and spirit.

5) The final word is "Naked" and again it is used extensively of literal nakedness in the N.T.. Here the Lord as with the previous words uses it in a moral way. They were naked before Him. That is, there was the lack of character and dignity of which garments speak in

Scripture. The word is used twice more in the Revelation in this moral sense, first as to a warning to watch, "Blessed is he that watcheth, and keepeth his garments, lest he walk naked and they see his shame" (Rev. 16:15). The other reference is in ch. 17:16 where in the judgment of the scarlet woman, she shall among other things be made naked, implying the loss of everything in which she gloried. The five words could be summed up in the following way.

Wretched, as Romans 7.	If no Spirit then no power
Miserable, 1 Cor. 15	If no resurrection then no joy
Poor, as ungodly,	If no Saviour then no riches
Blind, as Pharisees.	If no illumination then no light
Naked, as Adam.	If no righteousness then no character

The last two are most important, blindness was how Samson ended, such a gifted man, and that gift largely lost.

Naked is the way Noah ended after such a useful, obedient and fruitful life (Gen. 9:21).

THE COUNSEL OF THE LORD

"I counsel thee", Christ is the answer as always. Then the Lord challenges them to buy, what does the Lord mean in using the word BUY ? When this exhortation is used in Scripture it means there is a price to be paid, but not with material things. Generally it means to "experience", as in Isaiah 55:1 where the prophet preaches and urges the hearers to buy wine and milk, without money and without price. Material money could not buy that of which the wine and milk speaks, nor could a price in earthly values be put upon these, it means to pay the price by experience. The experience may be costly in hardships and self discipline, but the gain could not be weighed by earthly values.

This would be called "The school of God", and the Lord had this in mind when reasoning here with this backsliding church.

The three things the Lord counsels the believers to buy of Him are most instructive, here are the true riches which heaven acknowledges.

1) Gold is the first spiritual commodity offered by the Lord, and not only gold, but gold tried in the fire. Now gold in Scripture speaks of that which is glorious and Divine, often used of the ways, works and glory of God Himself. Tried in the fire means that it has been well

tested, and has been proved to make rich the many men of God in the past, who rejoiced in God and in the things not seen. This gold then would speak of the doctrines touching the Godhead, and the rich maturity that transpires out of, not only the learning of these doctrines, but in an experiential way making them reality in the life. "That thou mayest be rich" is a reference to the maturity to be gained of the buying by experience, that of which the gold speaks. Paul voices this sentiment by saying, "As poor yet making many rich; as having nothing, yet possessing all things" (2 Cor. 6:10).

2) Garments in Scripture speak of character, the Lord had this in mind in the second exhortation regarding white raiment that they may be clothed. Christian ethics should adorn every believer in Christ, Laodicea was wanting in this practical living before the world. The gold is what one would talk about, and the white raiment symbolizes the godly life which is seen by the world, the doing of good works, the very likeness of Christ Himself.

3) The Eye Salve that thou mayest see, comes last. Note the way the words are put "Anoint thine eyes with eye slave", the anointing would suggest the work of the Spirit in bringing discernment and understanding to the soul of the believer.

The Gold would be suggestive of the doctrines and experience of God Himself, the white raiment no doubt speaks of Christ, and the anointing is indicative of the Spirit. It would seem the Trinity is presented in the threefold exhortation.

Again, the three things are in an experiential order. The knowledge of the gold is bound to be effective in the life in an ethical way, and this experience in life would lead to the eyes being open to discern all things as the spiritual man.

The gold would be classed as edification, the raiment as the exhortation to be practical, and the eye slave would bring the comfort of discerning all things and knowing that God holds the future. All this corresponding to the edification, exhortation and comfort of 1 Cor. 14:3.

The story of the conversion of Zacchaeus would well illustrate the gold, he was was made rich by that which was better than the gold of earth, and willing to suffer loss because of it. The clothing would be similar to the man with the legion of demons, who was found clothed and in his right mind. The blind man of John 9 whose eyes were anointed with clay is illustrative of the anointing with the eye salve, he turned out to be most intelligent, he was able to see, and was commended by the Lord.

THE THREEFOLD STATEMENT OF VERSE 19

The Lord appeals to this church in two ways to bring them back to godly activity for Himself, first by the thought of discipline in verse 19, then by incentive in verse 20.

How amazing that the love of Christ for the saints is paramount in this letter. One could well expect this to Philadelphia as in verse 9 because of their devotion and zeal, but to this backsliding church to be assured of His love is grace indeed.

However, if a father loves his child, then he wishes the best for him, and discipline will be forthcoming to mature, and to build character, (Heb. 12:6). So with the Lord here, if love is there, one can expect chastening. The Lord sometimes works on two levels, first by rebuke, and if that is not heeded then by some form of chastening. The rebuke would be the contents of this letter, and if this is not regarded then chastening in some way is bound to follow. The chastening would be more severe than the rebuke.

The Lord of the churches expects a twofold response from the company at Laodicea, zeal and repentance. They were most zealous in business, and if they approached their Christian state with the same zeal, then repentance is bound to follow. Repentance would be a new beginning, the Lord is always willing to bring about recovery, and to welcome the prodigal back home.

THE APPEAL AND INCENTIVE TO THE INDIVIDUAL

The Lord is outside the church, Paul knew this experience when he first came to Jerusalem, but Barnabas discerned that he was genuine and introduced him to the church (Acts 9). How the Lord must have felt to be outside the company that He blessed so richly, and in His grace, gathered together. He had placed an open door before the saints of Philadelphia, and He does so continually with all believers, but the Laodiceans presented a closed door to Him (Verse 20).

This precious verse is often related to gospel presentation, but the appeal is to believers, and every word is most instructive.

a) "Behold", the words of John the Baptist at the beginning, "Behold the lamb of God", something great in the estimation of heaven, and displayed before the eyes of mankind for close scrutiny. The Lord would attract to Himself, and draw them away from the business and social life that occupied them. This appeal is to every believer today, who is caught up in the fast stream of modern living that leaves little time for His Things.

b) The door would speak of response, the responsibility to hear and open. the Lord leaves the choice to them, they can open and enjoy His blessing, or keep the door of their lives closed to Him and thus experience discipline, and loss.

c) He knocks, but speaks of hearing His voice rather than His knock, this signifying that restoration is by means of His Word. It is the Holy Scriptures that make wise unto salvation, and all recovery is likewise by the Word. The disobedience to the Word brought the fall in the garden of Eden, and the means of recovery came by the Word of Promise concerning the seed of the woman. Hence the need of ministry meetings and Bible readings where the Word is expounded, this often leads to recovery in those who are following afar off.

d) The promise of "Supping with them" is very precious. Here is one of the conditional promises that emerge in these letters. The supping would speak of fellowship as with a meal around the table. "I will sup with him", this would be the imparting from the Lord to the believer great light concerning Himself that can cause the heart to burn, the experience of the two on the road to Emmaus would be a case in point (Luke 24:32).

e) "He with me", would be the other side of the fellowship, the Lord's delight in the communion with His people. For this reason He saves in the first place, and with this in mind the creation of the first man was planned and carried out. The Lord spoke in a similar vein in John 14:21 saying "I will love him and manifest myself to him". No doubt in the glory the loved ones in Christ shall enjoy perfect communion with the Lord, but this promise has to do with time, the feasting upon Christ now. How precious is this verse, yet spoken to Christians in a backsliding condition.

THE PROMISE AND APPEAL

The letter ends with a wonderful thought, the throne above, in the
first letter He is seen walking upon earth, here seated with the Father
upon His throne. Such unity and intimacy is implied in this statement,
and a like intimacy is the promise to the overcomer. This is the most
condemning of all the letters, yet in spite of this, the fact of being in
Christ is everything.

Those who are spiritual long for closeness with Christ in this life,
how great the joy when this will wonderfully be effected eternally, not
because of spiritual capacity or victory, rather the glorious purpose of
Christ for His own.

Little need be said about the appeal, except if it was so important to
the other churches to heed that which was spoken by the Spirit, how
much more this poverty stricken church. No matter what the condition
of any church today, the Word is necessary, and always will be until the
Lord comes and church testimony shall cease.

A FEW FINAL WORDS ON THE CHURCHES

Each of the seven letters has an O.T. background, and all in chronological order, this interesting fact has been pointed out in the notes. In a
similar fashion, the way the Lord introduces Himself to each church
also suggests a sort of order in a chronological way.

To Ephesus He is walking, this is like the dispensation of "Inno-
cence" in the garden of Eden.

To Smyrna, life is spoken of, the promise of life was first made to
the Patriarchs in the seed of the woman etc..

To Pergamos the Sword in the mouth of the Lord could well be a
reference to the Law from the mouth of God, this corresponds to the
covenant to Israel at Mount Sinai, making them a nation before God.

To Thyatira, the Son of God is noticed. This would then go forward
to the incarnation and ministry of the Son of God upon the earth. "We
know that the Son of God is come" (1 John 5:20).

To Sardis the Holy Spirit is referred to, and this suggests the present
time, the dispensation of grace, the time of the Spirit who is sent from
heaven to form the church among other things.

To Philadelphia the Key of David is mentioned, and this advances the programme to the Millennium when the Lord shall reign as David's greater Son.

Finally, to Laodicea the Lord as Creator is seen, not only the old creation but the new, the creation of the new heavens and earth, the Day of God spoken of by Peter, and is eternity itself. On this final note the letters end. Thus the seven introductions cover all the time from Genesis to the close of the Revelation, all the book of God.

The seven promises at the close of each letter also are marvellously linked together. Life in Ephesus and deliverance from death in Smyrna, the positive and negative. Secret things in Pergamos and public reigning with Christ in Thyatira, going in and going out. Then the name not blotted out in Sardis and they shall go no "more out" in Philadelphia. These first three couples contain opposites, Loadica stands by itself, the eternal throne of Christ. Again, as stated in earlier notes, the last four are intimate, Received of MY Father in Thyatira, before MY Father in Sardis, Name of MY God in Philadelphia, and finally MY Father in Laodicea.

THE PANORAMIC PROGRAMME

The panoramic view is not the most important thing in these letters, rather the Words spoken by the Spirit to the churches. However, a few remarks just to show the main points of this theory will be necessary.

1. The apostolic period would be viewed in Ephesus, apostles are only mentioned in that particular letter.
2. The times of persecution under Imperial Rome follows with the letter to Smyrna.
3. The compromise with the church and state comes out in Pergamos, being the time of Constantine and after.
4. Thyatira covers the dark ages of 1000 years the time when Rome was in control, this is the longest letter.
5. Sardis moves forward to the Reformation.
6. Philadelphia to the great missionary enterprises of the last century.
7. Lastly, Laodicea prefigures the church as material and worldly in the final days before the Lord returns.

Perhaps a difference may be made in the last two, Philadelphia representing the Church in the final days, and Laodicea as Christendom spewed out of the mouth of the Lord by His taking His people out of the world by the rapture, thereby showing His rejection of the rest. Each one can be persuaded in his own mind to these things, but again, the most significant thing is the contents of the letters themselves, and their import for the churches of today.

CHAPTER TWENTY-ONE

The Throne of God in Rev. ch. 4-7

From the earlier pages it has been noted that Rev. chs. 4-7 are all one section, and concerns the opening of the seven seals. The material gathers round a theme, "The Throne", which is mentioned 24 times in the four chapters. This great section of Holy Scripture demands a twofold approach. First, the meaning of the passage, what God is really saying, because the four chapters contain a very solemn message which all should understand, especially Christians and Jews. The second approach must be of a practical and devotional nature. The latter is the way in which these chapters are usually considered. How often Rev. 4-5 is read among the Lord's people, and little aspects expressed that no doubt touch the hearts of the believers. All this is good, and is a ministry of comfort, howbeit the real theme of the section is largely ignored, and believers are left in ignorance instead of being edified. In these pages both these ideas shall be considered.

THE FOUR LIVING CREATURES

Now these four living creatures are the key to the understanding of the whole section. Consider how much space is given to them. Out of the eleven verses in ch. 4 six are given to the description of these heavenly beings, more than half the chapter.

They are again mentioned in ch. 5 verses 6, 8, 11, and 14. Also in ch. 6 they are mentioned in verses 1, 3, 5, 7, and finally in ch. 7 verse 11. Obviously they play a great part in the section and really are the key to the interpretation of the Throne and its reason for such prominence in the four chapters. The object now is to trace this and to see the beautiful structure that God has set forth, and its searching message.

John was in a very unique position in prophesying from heaven, all other prophets prophesied while upon the earth. Often they prophesied of heaven as seen from earth as did Ezekiel in his first chapter, and Daniel as in the 7th chapter of his book, but they did not visit heaven as John did here. While in heaven for this little time John heard something for the ears, and also saw something for the eyes. Perhaps in this experience he considered the words of the Lord Jesus "Blessed are your eyes for they see and your ears for they hear" (Matt. 13:16), although that was a reference to the ministry of Christ upon the earth, how much more blessed to be acquainted with the ministry of the Lord in heaven.

What he heard in ch. 4-5 was the four great expressions of praise and worship. The first two concern the earth, the creation of it for God's pleasure, and the saints reigning over it in the future. (4:11) (5:9-10). The next two concern the Lamb, the worth of the Lamb and the dominion of the Lamb (5:12-13). Now in the first three of these outbursts of worship, the living creatures lead the way. The final one concerns all that have breath, and so includes the living creatures. There is another outburst of praise in 7:10-11, making five in all, the number of grace, again the living creatures are involved. These five praise passages could be summarized like this, the first concerns creation, the second is a new song, the third is to do with the attributes of God, the fourth the Majesty of the throne, the final is salvation.

What he saw was most impressive, the throne and He that sat upon it, and he saw the elders, and most important, he saw the four living creatures.

WHO ARE THE LIVING CREATURES?

Some interpret these as merely symbols of the attributes and expressions of God, and they really do not exist. This explanation is doubtful when they are able to speak, and lead the praise and worship to God. Besides, the throne is literal as also the elders etc. therefore these must be of a very high order of angels. Paul speaks in Eph. 1 of the Lord being exalted high above principality, powers, might, and dominion, and again speaks of elect angels in 1 Tim. 5:21. From this one gathers there are several ranks of angels, and these living creatures would be classed very highly indeed. Their chief purpose seems to be to praise God, which shows how right and important it is to praise God. They seem to be similar to the Seraphim which Isaiah saw which were above the throne, they also praised the Lord saying "Holy Holy Holy is the Lord God of Hosts, the whole earth is full of His glory" (Isa. 6:3). This was before the captivity of Israel. During the captivity Ezekiel also saw the throne and its heavenly attendants, and this time below the throne and upon the earth, and lifted up from the earth (Ezek. 1). They appear again to Ezekiel and he identifies them as the Cherubim in Ezek. 10:20.

The living creatures in Rev. 4 have similar features as faces etc. but from the whole description they seem to be vastly different. The Seraphim and Cherubim have different responsibilities and relationships as easily seen in the context of their chapters, but here the living creatures are related to the throne, and to creation, hence the number four which speaks of that which is universal.

CONSIDER THE LIVING CREATURES

1) As already noted, they are four, the number in Scripture which is connected with that which is universal.
2) They have to do with creation, this is evident from verse 11 and the events of chapter 6 in which they play a great part.
3) Their chief function is to praise the Lord, and cease not from doing so day and night.
4) Each has a different face, that of a lion, a calf, a man, and a flying eagle, the cherubim of Ezekiel each had four faces, here one face each.
5) They had many eyes, full of eyes before and behind, it seems also that each of their wings are full of eyes. Eyes speak of "Intelligence" in Scripture, these then were most intelligent in the things of God, not only as to what God has done in the past, but also His wonderful doings in the future.
6) One of the most important features and seldom noticed, is the fact that they are numbered, and continually, throughout the chapters,

each carry their own number. The first is the one with the face of a lion. Number two has the face of the calf, number three has the face of a man, and of course the last called the fourth living creature has the face of a flying eagle. This factor may not seem to be important, but really it is the key to the understanding of the opening of the seals in chapter 6, and in fact all the section of chapters 4-7.

Chapters 4 and 5 cover a scene in heaven, and chapters 6-7 a scene upon the earth, the opening of the seals in heaven brings in accordingly the events upon the earth.

EVIL UPON THE EARTH

The seals of chapter 6 have often been spoken of as judgments, actually, they are more than judgments, they are EVENTS that include judgments, tremendous events that affect millions of people and a great part of the earth. The chapter speaks of the opening of six of the seals and the beginning of chapter 8 that of the final seal.

The plan of the book set forth in the earlier chapters of these notes on Rev. is based upon problems that especially perplex the people of God in times of suffering and persecution. These problems, seven in all make up the seven distinct sections of the Revelation. The first was "Must church doctrine and practice continue" ? The first three chapters dealt with this and make known the mind of the Lord that no matter what the conditions are within or without, the testimony must continue unto Himself.

Now the second problem is dealt with in chapters 4-7, and this time the problem that arises is "Why is there so much evil and trouble in the world" ? Consider wars, tribulation and such other things that result in hardship and suffering to the human race. It is not only believers that suffer in ch. 6-7 but humanity in general. One could answer, "because of sin and the fall", but the real cause is presented in these four chapters. The answer is in the Lamb in the midst of the throne, the sealed roll and the living creatures.

THE LAMB AND THE ROLL

John wept, the only case of anyone weeping in heaven, but there is a special reason for this unique experience of John. The throne of God is set up, and One sits on the throne, it is God Himself, described by the light and glory of precious stones, namely the jasper and sardine. There is a roll or scroll in His hand sealed with seven seals. The challenge goes out, "who is worthy to open the book and the loose the seals thereof" (5:2).

One of the elders instructs John saying "Weep not, behold the Lion of the tribe of Judah, the root of David hath prevailed to open the book and to loose the seven seals thereof" (Verse 5). Now it is obvious that these are royal titles and refer to the Lord as King, the Lion out of the kingly tribe of Judah and the root going back to the kingdom and dynasty of David. John of course looked for the Lion, and there in the midst of the throne and the living creatures he sees a Lamb and not a Lion. The Lion speaks of the sovereign but the Lamb speaks of the sacrifice, even the cross of our Lord. Although the Greek word for Lamb is different from that of John 1:29 and other such passages, however the death of Christ is maintained in the words "freshly slain". To put it very simply, the Lion, the King was presented to Israel and to the world and was rejected, He was crucified, hence the Lamb. This is the record of the four Gospels, the Lord presented to Israel as their rightful king with all the proper credentials was despised, rejected and crucified as the Lamb, Isa. 53 instead of Isa. 11.

Now if the Lord had been accepted by Israel, there would be no opening of the seals and the involvement of the living creatures.

The words of the Lord Himself best explain this concerning the coming of the Spirit "When He is come He will convict the world of sin, righteousness and judgment. Of sin because they believed not on Me, of righteousness because I go to the Father ..." The presence of the Spirit is a demonstration of these things; SIN, the world has been proved it is sinful in the rejection of Christ "if I had not come and spoken unto them they had no sin, but now they have no cloak for their sin" (John 15:22). The failure of the people to believe on Christ when He was upon the earth proves that sin is the condition of the people. "Of righteousness because I go to the Father", here in Rev. 5 is the Lamb in the midst of the throne, heaven and the throne have accepted Him, therefore He must have been righteous, and all His claims were true. The Lion is rejected, the kingdom of peace and prosperity was put aside by this rejection, if there is no king there cannot be a kingdom.

Peter talked about this in his sermon in Acts 3, saying "He shall send Jesus", and then he spoke of the times of refreshing and the restitution of all things, a reference to the Millennium no doubt. So instead of the Lion there was the Lamb, consequently, instead of the kingdom blessings there is the opening of the seals.

THE OPENING OF THE SEALS IN CH. 6

Now this is where the number of each living creature comes to the fore, and to miss this point is to miss the whole message of the section. One of the four living creatures is mentioned in Ch. 6:1, when the first seal is opened, the second living creature is linked with the second seal, the third with the third seal, and the fourth with the fourth seal. It is so simple, each living creature is numbered and opens that seal number accordingly. The real significance of this is found in Ch. 4:7, the first was like a lion, the second was like a calf, the third like a man and the fourth a flying eagle. Each of the four is numbered and retains that number. Now the fact that these four living creatures are involved in the first four seals which have to do with the earth, there must then be a connection between the face of each, and the outcome of the opening of each seal.

When the Lamb opened the first seal, there was a noise of thunder and one of the living creatures, being the first one of course, said "come", the two words "and see" ought to be omitted as in the R.V.. This means that the living creature is not telling John to come and see, rather a command for the event to take place. Here is where the importance of the likeness of each of the faces comes to the fore. The Lion is connected with the rider on the white horse who came forth conquering and to conquer in verse 2. This horseman is a counterfeit of the Lord as described in ch. 19:11 as sitting upon a white horse when He comes to rule. The meaning is so clear, the Lion of the tribe of Judah was rejected and the result will be that another king will come who is ambitious for himself, the man of lawlessness of 2 Thess. 2. He shall bring much misery to this world and to Israel especially. Now this has been the character of the world ever since the cross of our Lord, men of personal ambition in the political scene have sought to conquer right down the centuries to the latter times, one could think of Hitler, Stalin, and so many more of this infamy, moreover, all will culminate in the man of lawlessness as depicted in this first seal. The white horse speaks of victory, yet he is not satisfied and wants to conquer more, the bow would speak of warfare.

The people cried at the trial of the Lord Jesus "Not this man but Caesar", and Pilate delivered the Lord to the cross. The world has had its cruel, ruthless and ambitious Caesars ever since. The inscription over the cross was that of the rejected king, Jesus of Nazareth the king of the Jews, the Lion was denied and the Lamb was upon the cross. If Christ had been received, the kingdom and King would have been a reality, and the nation of Israel with all other nations of the world would have been spared much misery.

THE SECOND SEAL. v 3-4

The horse of the second rider is red and would stand for blood and slaughter, red is also the colour in the Rev. that depicts that which is Satanic, such as the red dragon of 12:3, and the scarlet woman of 17:4 and she is sitting upon a scarlet coloured beast in 17:3. The great sword would speak of the instruments of war, being great would indicate the modern technical weapons of the last days seen already in the Gulf War of a few years ago. The rider upon this red horse was given power to take peace from the earth, and to kill one another, war upon war. In the past 2000 years of world history it appears that if the times when war was absent from the earth, were totalled they would only come to a mere 200 years. Why is this ? Because the Prince of peace has been rejected. How fitting that the second living creature who is like a calf or an ox cries "come" to the events of war and woe down through the past 2000 years, and to terminate in the terrible wars of the last days such as prophesied in Ezek. 38-9 and especially the battle of Armageddon in ch. 16 and 19 of the Revelation.

The calf is a symbol of peace, but this was rejected when Christ was given a cross instead of a throne. The words of our Lord were mingled with tears when he cried "If thou hast known, even thou, at least in this thy day the things that belong to thy peace, but now they are hidden from thine eyes" (Luke 19:42). It has often been said "There shall be no peace upon the earth until the Prince of Peace shall come whose right it is to reign".

THE THIRD SEAL, FAMINE V 5-6

The third seal brings forth famine, the experience of millions of people in every generation and increased greatly of late in the severe famines of places in Africa etc. which have caused the loss of millions of lives, still, there is worse to come. Starvation and inflation are depicted in this third seal, a black horse and its rider appears when the seal is opened. Now black is the colour associated with famine in Lam. 5:10 "Our skin was black like an oven because of the terrible famine". Again speaking of famine, the Nazarites of Israel are described as "Their visage is blacker than coal, their skin cleaveth to their bones, it is withered, it is become like a stick" (Lam. 4:8). Inflation is seen here in the words "A measure of wheat for a penny, and three measures of barley for a penny". These are inflated prices according to the buying power of the penny then. Inflation has galloped these last years, and will be a feature of the last days. The rich can still buy and can afford the luxuries of the oil and the wine. However the real crisis in a famine is when money becomes useless, and has no buying power because of the fact that the material hardly exists. It would seem that the calamities that these seals speak of have always been present, especially since the crucifixion of the Lord, but down the centuries there has been a marked increase which will climax in the Tribulation of the last days. Famine is not a new occurrence, presently millions are perishing each year and worse is to come when the mystery of iniquity comes to the full head.

Now famine is the opposite of prosperity, and the greatest time of prosperity shall be in the Millennium. The little prophecy of Joel is interesting in this respect. Chapter one speaks of famine, the lack of many things, the words used are mighty in describing famine conditions. Chapter two is a great prophetic outline and brings in the Lord Jesus returning to the confused state of Israel and the then world. Chapter three completes the picture with the enemies judged and removed, and the prophecy ends with the wonderful prosperity of the Millennium. "And it shall come to pass in that day that the mountains shall drop down new wine, and the hills shall flow with milk and all the rivers of Judah shall flow with waters..." (Joel 3:18).

Man was linked with the earth and it's prosperity in Eden before the fall, and even after in Gen. 3. When the Perfect Man is come there shall be unique prosperity in the earth. The world to come is to be subjected to a Man according to the purposes of God as stated in Psalm 8, the same statement is made in Heb. 2 and issues in the Man, Jesus. He did come with all the promise of prosperity, He was cast out, the Son of Man had not where to lay His head, finally they gave Him the cross. Because of the rejection of the Man the world has experienced famine, scarcity and such like, which will come to an unprecedented head before and during the terrible Tribulation that is to come. No wonder the third living creature has the face of a man, the Man who could have reigned in righteousness would have caused the prosperity of the earth to burst forth. A lovely title used of the Lord's return is "The coming of the Son of Man" (Matt.16:27, 24:30). The third living creature with the face of a man is a great lesson to this old earth and all who dwell upon it.

THE FOURTH SEAL, DEATH AND HELL V 7-8

In the opening of the fourth seal, the fourth living creature, whose face is like a flying eagle says "Come", thus starting a chain of catastrophic events that have cost millions of lives down the passage of time, but as the other seals, this will come to a climax in the end times.

Four is the number of universal things in Scripture, so these calamities are not confined to any particular nation, but spread over the whole world with appalling loss of life in the final scenes of this earth as seen in this fourth seal.

The reason for this terrible loss of life is perceived in the fourth living creature who is like a flying eagle. This would speak of the One who has the power to lift the people up to the enjoyment of heavenly experiences. The Lord's ministry lifted up the people. Those cities in which the Lord ministered, and performed mighty works, but rejected Him, heard from His lips the heavy tidings of judgment, in the which He speaks of their "being exalted to heaven" (Matt. 11:23). The inhabitants of Capernaum etc. instead of tasting heavenly blessing they were to be brought down to hell. This is exactly what this seal brings forward in keeping with the living creature like a flying eagle.

Here a pale horse appears, and its rider is called "death", the only one of the horsemen that is named, and hell follows with him, thus making it clear that the scene concerns unsaved people. The awful outcome is that one fourth of the earth's population is slain with the sword, indicating war; hunger, speaking of famine; and pestilence, indicating disease etc.. The beasts of the earth are also mentioned as depleting the people of earth, this may be taken literally, but most likely a reference to the beast like dictators of Rev. 13. This fourth seal embraces the previous three seals, the beasts would be the conqueror of seal one, the sword looks back to the second horseman, the hunger mentioned in verse 8 corresponds with the famine of seal three.

This is a troubled world we live in and betterment is not to be, evil and its accompanying trouble will escalate to the final world judgment. All would have been so different if when Christ presented Himself to the people, they had received Him. Israel and the world rejected the majesty of the Lion, (Seal one) the Prince of Peace, (Seal two) the prosperity that would have come with God's perfect Man, (Seal three) and the heavenly One, (Seal four) as in the words of John the Baptist, "He that cometh from heaven is above all" (John 3:31).

Now it was in the councils and foreknowledge of God that the Lord would be rejected, and His death upon the cross is looked upon as a Divine Sacrifice for sin, which subject is dealt with in ch. 7, nevertheless the people are held responsible for the rejection of Him whom God had sent. Consequently, the world suffers the penalty under the governmental dealings of God with the nations of this world.

SEAL FIVE, MARTYRS. V 9-11

Is the world really that bad ? Was it so evil in the past to have rejected the Perfect One ? Yes, and the world is just the same, it has not changed and seal five makes this clear. Here are the martyrs that will be slain for the Word of God and for the testimony they hold. Obviously the world has no place today for either the Word of God or the testimony of Christ. There have been martyrs during the dark ages, and in numbers even to the present time, but worse is to come in the events that surround the Great Tribulation. The Word of God, is this rejected ? Yes, by the masses, it has been put out of the schools in some countries, and out of the homes and hearts of people in general. Churches have closed their doors because of lack of attendance. Again, numerous cults are abroad, who profess to accept the Word, but in doctrine and works, reject it; they refuse to bow to its clear teaching.

The Testimony mentioned in verse 9 is the Person of Christ and His gospel according to ch. 12:17. It is noteworthy that people will appear religiously to accept God, but give no place whatsoever to the Son of God, He is still despised and rejected of men. Most of the swearing that abounds in this world at present is in the form of taking the Name and titles of Christ in a blasphemous way. The world is bad, as bad as can be, and still in rebellion to the claims of Christ.

Verse 10 makes a reference to them that dwell upon the earth, this is one word in Greek meaning "earthdwellers", those who live only for this earth and its pursuits and pleasures, and have no interest in the eternal things of God.

There have been many martyrs, but according to verse 11 this is only the beginning, many are yet to follow especially in the final scenes of this Book of Revelation.

The world of today is still in the spirit of rejection and many suffer accordingly, this is the reason for wars, famines, hardships, refugees and many others things that fill the tabloids of today.

THE SIXTH SEAL, REV. 6:12-17

This seal brings forward events right up to the Coming of the Son of Man, and is in keeping with the description in Joel 2 and Matt. 24 and such like passages.

Some spiritualize the contents of this passage, but if this is the actual event of the Coming of the Lord as Son of Man then the contents must be taken literally. There is no attempt to spiritualize the events recorded either by Joel or Peter in Acts 2. The pouring out of the Spirit was literal as were the tongues and prophecies etc. so why not the happenings to the sun, moon and stars as well ? At the death of Christ there was a literal earthquake according to Matt. 27 and the sun was literally darkened when the Lord was passing through suffering upon the cross, why cannot these things be repeated when He returns ?

The passage deals with the Day of the Lord, and that day starts with His coming as the Son of Man and ends with the passing away of the heavens and the earth after the Millennium and subsequent events as described in chapters 20-21. Peter writes the classic passage on this, speaking of the passing away of the heavens and the earth which are now, and the words of verse 11 in this chapter are very similar to those of Peter (2 Peter 3:8-14).

Puny man appears to be great and important in the eyes of the world, yet if he is without God, he will not be accounted in the day of wrath (verses 15-16). The day of wrath in verse 17 includes the events at His coming and those at the conclusion which will close this earth's history

The question is asked in verse 17, "who is able to stand"?

The Lord stands, "they shall perish but thou remainest and they all shall wax old as doth a garment, and as a vesture shalt thou fold them up and they shall be changed, but thou art the same and thy years shall not fail" (Heb. 1:11-12). Many others shall stand as well, and some of these are the subject of chapter 7.

SALVATION TO OUR GOD REV. 7

This is a chapter that speaks of salvation, of which there are several in the Revelation. Truly this is a book about judgment, and the righteous government of God, yet He delights in mercy, hence the great salvation passages scattered throughout this book.

There is a clear distinction between the two companies that fill this chapter, the first is the Jew in verses 1-8 and then the Gentiles occupy verses 9-17. Now in the church which is His body no such distinction exists, but the time depicted in ch. 7 is beyond the time of the calling of the church and is clearly stated to be the Great Tribulation of which the prophets spoke in the O.T. and the Lord in Matt. 24. The tribes of Israel are mentioned, in no way could these be identified as the "Church" today. Again they are sealed in their foreheads, this is a distinction from the "Mark of the beast" in the foreheads of his followers in Ch. 13:16. Another point, these are seemingly preserved through the terrible times of the Tribulation, and appear on the other side in Ch. 14:1, hence the seal. They will not be hurt by the political upheavals as hinted in verses 1-3. There is no ground whatever in making the 144000 here to be different from the 144000 in Ch. 14:1. Some say that the company of ch. 14 is of Judah only, nothing in that chapter would indicate this, besides 12000 of Judah are sealed in this chapter (Verse 5). Now these are not all of Israel that shall experience salvation, but those who will be sealed. These will be preserved whereas many others shall be killed for their allegiance to Christ. The 144000 are called the "firstfruits" which would mean that a vast harvest of others would undoubtedly follow (14:4).

These sealed ones likely will do the preaching of the "Coming King-dom" in those days, however this is not explicitly stated.

The second company are Gentiles, and come out of the Great Tribulation, and again they must not be confounded with the church. For almost 2000 years God has been calling souls to Himself in the Gospel, such live their testimony for God, and depart to be with Christ after serving their generation. Millions lived in peaceful times and never experienced a Tribulation such as described by our Lord and the proph-ets before Him. However, there has been from time to time periods of persecution and trouble, but these did not end with the coming of Christ as does the Great Tribulation. Nevertheless, whether now or in Tribulation times, the salvation is the same, redemption by the blood of the Lamb, even the Lord Jesus.

The close link with ch. 6 is most beautiful. There the Lamb was rejected as was the Lion of Judah, here He is accepted as King, hence the throne which is mentioned 7 times in verses 9-17. They also ac-knowledge the Lamb, and the salvation found in Him in verse 10. They will not follow the impostor upon the white horse but will wait for Him that is True who will sit upon the white horse in Ch. 19:11. They will hunger no more, famine will be in the past for them, they did not reject the blessed Man, hence the blessing of verses 16-17. Wars are over, death is past, they live unto God, their condition is portrayed as "being led unto the living fountains of waters". God shall wipe away all tears from their eyes. These shall believe and receive the Man, Christ Jesus, hence the blessing.

The world of the past rejected the Lion, the Prince of Peace, and consequently the terrible calamities issuing from the seals has been their lot from then until the present day.

The section begins in ch. 4 with the throne and Him that sat on it, and ends with the blessings of the saved before the throne in ch. 7:17.

In conclusion, the living Creatures can been seen as indicating the reason why trouble and hardship are the common experiences of the people of the earth, as in the past, so in the present, and in greater meas-ure in the approaching last days. All is traced back to the rejection of the Lion, the Righteous Man, the Prince of Peace. Also the blessedness of the people who received Him as Saviour and Lord, in peace they are before the throne of God.

These two classes are summed up in "Seals that are broken" in ch. 6 speaking of man's doom, and "Seals that cannot be broken." in ch. 7 speaking of the eternal security of those in Christ.

CHAPTER TWENTY-TWO

Revelation ch.4 Viewed Practically

T he words and ways of God are not only for the enlightenment of the mind but also to draw out the heart in devotion to Himself.

Hence this remarkable passage with the next chapter have affected the most simple Christian, and at the same time most deeply affected the mature believer producing love and worship unto the Son of God's love. This often is succeeded by feet that are willing to follow the Lord, and hands fully dedicated unto the service of Him alone.

None was more practical than the Lord in the Gospels, and of course the Acts is the living out of the Apostolic doctrines and the reception of the Spirit, the forming of church testimony in many cities. Every epistle in the N.T. deals not only with doctrines, but the outworking of those doctrines in the lives of believers before God and men. The Revelation is not behind in this, it is a very practical book as well as being the prophetic book of the N.T. Any reader can see this straightway in the opening chapters containing the Words of our glorified Lord to the churches, letters of a most searching and practical nature, consequently this portion as the earlier chapters is full of sobering lessons and princi-ples that carry much weight. In fact, this is the purpose of the book in the first place as stated in 1:3, "Blessed is he that readeth and they that hear the words of this prophecy and KEEP those things which are writ-ten therein".

Chapters 4 and 5 go together, but the material of ch. 4 shall now be considered in this light.

THE APOSTLE JOHN

1) John, a most interesting man and worthy of practical consideration. First, he stands in a unique place, the only one to prophesy from heaven. Enoch and Elijah were caught up to heaven but no word from either of them ever came down from heaven. Ezekiel on earth saw heaven opened, he said "the heavens were opened and I saw visions of God" (Ezek. 1:1), however, he was still upon the earth and from earth viewed the heavenly visitors. John the Baptist saw the heaven opened, and the dove descend upon the Lord, but again from the standpoint of earth. Paul seemingly in 2 Cor. 12 was caught up to the third heaven, the paradise of God, however the words that he heard he was not allowed to utter. This experience was of God to develop his own maturity and was not therefore for others. Stephen saw the glory of God, Jesus on the right hand of God, again, speaking from the the platform of earth.

In contrast to all this John saw and heard and prophesies from heaven, and there must be a reason for this. John holds a solitary place in Scripture as being a figure of the church, he is the disciple whom Jesus loved, the one so close to His breast. His prefiguring the church is indicated by the words of the Lord concerning him, "If I will that he tarry till I come what is that to thee" (John 21:22). The church is indeed until He comes, the church awaits the rapture, the catching up of all believers at His return as clearly taught in 1 Thess. 4:13-18. Therefore it is not a coincidence that John here is caught up into heaven. Surely this is a picture of the rapture, and ought to touch the hearts of God's waiting people, such an experience John had, and such an experience awaits all believers in Christ, when He returns.

2) John saw and heard many things, but the first voice he heard was that of the Lord Himself, "the first voice which I heard was as it were of a trumpet", in this same way the voice of the Lord Jesus is identified in ch. 1:10. How wonderful at the rapture to hear the voices of loved ones, silent for many years, but the first voice will be that of the Lord Himself. "All that are in the graves shall hear His voice" (John 5:28). The living saints at His coming shall hear the voice also, as the Lord

shall descend with a SHOUT, all the church shall hear that call. How marvellous to hear the voice of the Blessed One we have been serving and seeking to know all through the years of testimony.

Some believers love a Red Letter Bible in order to highlight the words of Christ, in His ministry it was said that never man spake like this man. In post resurrection, Mary Magdalene heard the words of comfort, post glory, Saul of Tarsus heard the voice that led to his conversion and commission, but to hear the voice of the glorified Man call up to glory outshines all, what a day, more blessed than any in all the past spiritual experiences. The voice which John heard was as it were a trumpet, Complete authority is here as the warrior must obey the sound of the trumpet. Again, the two silver trumpets of Num. 10 were used to gather the people to the door of the Tabernacle, and the trumpet is used in the prophecy of Isaiah to gather those of Israel who are scattered abroad (Isaiah 27:13). If John is a picture of the church as suggested, then this "trumpet voice" indicates the great gathering of His beloved, the church. There is a close similarity between the wording here and that of 1 Thess. 4:13-18 which would confirm this idea.

3) Note also, when John is caught up a greater intelligence is experienced "Come up hither and I will show thee the things which must be hereafter", the rapture is something to look forward to, but such a prospect to be given the spiritual insight into Divine things that many devoted and inquiring saints have longed for during their lifetime.

4) How wonderful also to know from the reading of this chapter that The throne is in full control, "If God be for us, who can be against us" (Rom. 8:31). In the light of this, why should the child of God have anxieties when the Almighty is in control.

The effect upon John must have been marvellous.

He was rejected and banished by those on earth, but welcomed in heaven.

Alone perhaps on Patmos, now with the millions of heaven.

In the gospel he came in, now he goes up.

As a Daniel, he learns that heaven is in control and not Rome or any other great nation of earth.

He was in the Spirit, this phrase occurs four times in the book.

Ch. 1 to see the person of Christ.

Ch. 4 to see the heavenly Throne.

Ch. 17 to see the wilderness of this world.

Ch. 21 to see the city, the true bride in contrast to the false bride of ch. 17.

THE THRONE AND HE THAT SAT ON IT

One cannot fail to see that the THRONE is the key word in chapters 4-7 occurring no less that 24 times. The THRONE is the first of many things mentioned that John saw, but the section begins with God upon the Throne and ends with believers before the Throne in 7:15-17.

A throne speaks volumes to any man, it would present sovereignty, a King or a Queen sits upon a throne, one who has sovereign right. The throne also would intimate "Glory", at least it ought to, the person occupying the throne ought to have qualities in keeping with such a position. "Rule" is also another thought suggested by a throne, and perhaps the most important point about a throne, it is the centre of gathering, such is the case in chapter 4-5. To the believer, the throne of God is all these and more. The attitude to all this ought to be :-

a) Yielding, and loyalty to His rule.
b) Worshipping at His footstool.
c) Obedience to His commands.
d) Gathering unto Him, He the centre of all, as in the language of Ps. 16, "I have set the Lord always before me".

Two things about the throne are brought before John in this chapter, Him that sat on the throne, and the activities that were about the throne. These activities are described by five prepositions, ON in verse 2, ROUND in verse 4, OUT OF in verse 5, BEFORE in verse 5-6 and IN the midst in verse 6. It would be profitable to search these out further.

1) On the throne, v 2 the one who occupies the throne John really cannot see, but describes Him as the light of precious jewels. The jasper, which is a clear stone would speak of the purity and holiness of God, GOD IS HOLY, and this is seen in the worship of the living creatures in verse 8 Holy Holy Holy Lord God Almighty. Perhaps this scene reminded John of the experience on the Mount of Transfiguration called by Peter, "The Holy Mount" in 2 Pet. 1:18, the Lord then

appeared with His countenance as the sun and His garments as the light.

The sardine stone is red, and would speak of redemption, the provision of God to bring sinful man into His presence. This would indicate that "GOD IS LOVE", and again John could think back to Gethsemane, the Lord Jesus prostrate upon the ground, under the shadow of the cross one may say. This again comes out in the worship of 5:9, "Thou art worthy — for thou wast slain and hast redeemed us to God by thy blood".

2) Round ABOUT the Throne v 4. First, a rainbow in sight like unto an emerald, the colour of this green stone speaks of creation in Scripture. The bow indicates the faithfulness of God as made known to Noah in Gen. chapter 9, both these together present God as the FAITHFUL CREATOR (1 Pet. 4:19). John could well say in looking at this colour, "GOD IS LIFE". This as the others comes out in the worship, "Thou hast created all things and for thy pleasure they are, and were created" (Verse 11). So the typical teaching of the stones is in the passage itself, the Jasper is "Holy Holy holy", the Sardine is seen in "Thou hast redeemed us to God by thy blood", and the Emerald in the words "Thou hast created all things".

Also around the throne were 24 elders, who are they?

They cannot be angels.

a) Angels never sit on thrones.

b) Angels are never called elders.

c) They are never crowned in Scripture.

d) They never sing, except for an obscure passage in Job 38:7.

e) These are a distinct company from the angels throughout the Revelation.

If not angels, then they can only be believers in heaven.

If so, they cannot be those of Israel.

a) Israel is still on earth in the Book.

b) The sea of glass is empty here, full in ch. 15, and there no doubt Israel is in mind.

c) These lead the worship, and therefore cannot be Israel (Heb. 2:12).

d) Israel inherits the earth.

These elders can only be the church.

a) Elders are connected with the church in 1 Tim. 3 etc.

b) The elder is referred to in 2 and 3 John in the first verse of each epistle.

c) Elders speak of experience as in 1 Tim. 3.

d) These elders appear to be most intelligent in the Book.

e) The church will reign with Christ, and thrones are promised to the twelve apostles who are in the foundation of the church (Matt 19:28).

f) Garments are also spoken in connection with the church at Sardis and the Bride of Ch. 19

g) Crowns are promised to believers of this church period as for example in 2 Tim. 4:8, in fact five different crowns are promised, and two of them are mentioned in the letters to the churches of ch. 2-3.

h) Again, these are victor's crowns, and speak of experience.

j) They are golden crowns and this indicates the Divine nature of which Peter speaks in 2 Pet. 1:4.

It is worthy of note that the churches appear in ch. 1-3, the elders in ch. 4-19 and the bride in 19-22, and they never overlap. These are three views of the church, first in testimony on earth, then in heaven as the elders, finally in the glory as united to the Bridegroom, but the church throughout is seen in these different spheres.

Israel is still to be dealt with in the Revelation, and even in this section is seen on the earth in ch. 7. John would picture the church in the catching up, the elders represent the church as near to the throne of God, appositional.

Whether one takes them as Israel or the church, great lessons emerge in their description.

1. An elder would speak of experience unto maturity, and this was the aim of Paul in his ministry. (Col. 1:28)

2. White garments speak of purity and indicate victory as well, this colour then would carry the thought of "character", they had been overcomers, and had kept themselves unspotted from defilement.

3. Crowns would denote reward, service that was acceptable to the Lord and rewarded accordingly. Crowns also speak of authority and are victors crowns which is the meaning of the name "Stephen", those who suffer with Him shall also reign with Him.

4. The crowns were golden, speaking of Divine glory, this was also their motive, all was unto the Lord, and their position as around the throne would also indicate this attitude.

3) OUT of the throne. v 5. "Out of the throne proceeds lightening and thunders and voices". Different ideas are associated with these. The lightening would indicate the swift action of God, and generally is linked to the ways of God in Judgment. The Son of Man shall come as swift as the lightening, is the way His coming to judge the world is described (Matt. 24:27). Thunder also carries a similar thought, but also signifies God speaking as in the law from Mount Sinai, there the thunders precedes the lightening, His word must be kept, ere judgment fall. Here the lightening precedes the thunders because His coming in judgment is chiefly in view. The voice came out of the throne, God is speaking, and is still speaking today in many ways as in Job 33:14-21.

This threefold expression of God speaking especially in judgment occurs in three other places in the Revelation, 8:5, 11:19, and 16;18. The order is sometimes different, for example voices come first in ch. 8:5 and again an earthquake is added to the three passages. The main contrast is that the lightening, thunder and voices in ch. 4 are in heaven and out of the throne, whereas the others are on earth, hence the earthquake is added. The voices are important, this is communication, there is always a message for the people to hear, again voices in the plural would be a unity of thought, the agreement of heaven at the movement of God in judgment.

4) BEFORE the throne v 5-6. This time the thought of APPROACH is suggested in the preposition "before", to come before the throne of God, as in O.T. language to come before God. Elijah expressed this when he said "as the Lord God of Israel liveth before whom I stand", (1 Kings 17:1). In this saying he meant two things, he represented God as His spokesman on the earth, and also his constant need of His presence, Elijah was a man of prayer (James 5:17). It is wonderful that believers have the boldness or the right to stand before the throne of God. However, certain conditions are needed and these are noted in the seven Spirits and the sea of glass. Prayer must be in the Spirit, as in Eph. 2:18 "Through Him we have access by one Spirit unto the Father". The seven Spirits would speak of completeness, the Spirit also intercedes for us with groanings that cannot be uttered (Rom. 8:26). The reason for this is "we know not what we should pray for as we ought", however, if we are in the Spirit we are complete.

Again the Spirit is seen as seven lamps of fire burning, which of course speaks of purity, the burning away of all dross. Paul had this attitude in mind when he spoke of "lifting up holy hands" (I Tim. 2:8).

The sea of glass carries a similar thought, this is answerable to the laver in the Tabernacle at which the priests washed before going into the holy place to minister in the service of the Lord.

Sanctification is necessary in order to approach God, "Follow peace with all men and sanctification without which no man shall see the Lord" (Heb. 12:14).

5) Finally, in the MIDST of the throne v 6.   This brings forward the living creatures of which the greater part of the chapter speaks. These have a tremendous bearing in the government of the earth as already referred to in this book.

THE FOUR LIVING CREATURES

Their detailed description presents principles of a very vital nature as follows.

a) The most important feature is they have LIFE, they are called "living creatures". This is the great essential in any relationship with God, there must be life. Adam was first formed of the dust of the ground, but the breath of life was needed before he could obey, and be used of God. The new birth in John ch. 3 and the progression to the water of life in John ch. 4 indicates that eternal life is a fundamental requirement and is the prominent theme in the gospel of John. Each believer begins their relationship with God when dead in trespasses and sins, they hear the voice of the Son of God and live.

b) Eyes, these are symbolic of intelligence, insight into the deep things of God, and these were full of eyes before and behind. Such a lesson, to be intelligent to what the Lord has done in the past, "whatsoever things were written aforetime were written for our learning" (Rom. 15:4). Eyes before would indicate intelligence in what God is going to do. Peter has this in mind in writing "Beloved be not ignorant", and then he unfolds the future Day of the Lord, and the Day of God (2 Pet. 3:8-13).

Their wings also were full of eyes, now wings are used to mount up to the heavens (Isa. 40:31), this would suggest understanding in heavenly things as contained in the Prison Epistles. Nicodemus was taught by the Lord first in earthly things, then he advanced into the heavenly things (John 3:12).

c) Speaking of the wings, each living creature had six of them similar to the Seraphim of Isa. 6. There is no information as to how the wings of these living creatures were used, but a most interesting use is found in Isa. 6, with two wings they would cover their faces, implying that the identification of the worshipper is not to be seen. With two wings they covered their feet, again the service and walk of the worshipper must be hidden. With two wings they did fly, only a third of their energy was expended in the service of God, the rest of their power and energy was used in worship. Such a lesson, not self but the Lord, "Holy Holy Holy, the whole earth is full of His glory".

d) Their faces were that of the lion, the calf, the man and the eagle, these have often been linked with the different presentations of Christ in the Gospels, no doubt there is a link, all must take character from Him. The Lord Jesus is the model for every believer in every grace and activity. The lion would suggest dignity, none displayed dignity like the Son of Man. The calf denotes service, and the service of the Lord could not be surpassed in motive, energy and success. The Man speaks of wisdom and intelligence, and never Man spake like this Man. The flying eagle speaks of the heavenly experiences, and the Lord had such upon the mount of Transfiguration and the prayer of John 17 and many other cases. He was continually in the bosom of the Father.

e) Their praise is important in the proper use of divine titles, and a wonderful sense of the holiness of God. God is worthy of praise and perhaps there could be more of this when the Lord's people are in collective fellowship. The worship and praise here is collective, all four living creatures are engaged together in the praise to God. Note, they praise God first, who He is and what He is, and later praise Him for what He has done, creation and redemption.

f) They affect others in a positive way, "and when the living creatures give glory and honour and thanks to Him that sat on the throne, the four and twenty elders fall down before Him ... and cast their crowns before the throne" (verse 9-10). It is good to affect others in a positive way, the Lord when praying motivated a disciple to prayer, he waited until the Lord had ceased praying then said "Lord teach us to pray". (Luke 11:1). When Mary poured out the most precious ointment in John 12 the house was filled with the odour of the ointment, she was taken up with her Lord but the house was affected also. As the Scripture says "Let us consider one another to provoke unto love and to good works" (Heb. 10:24). None liveth unto himself, the believer in behaviour affects his Lord as in Rom. 14, and no doubt affects his brethren either for good or bad. It is good when others are affected in a profitable and spiritual way.

Moses affected Joshua, Joseph affected Pharaoh and all Egypt for good, and Paul affected Timothy. Elijah affected Elisha and Elisha in turn the sons of the prophets, the list could go on, how wonderful when people transform others and help to mould good character. Every believer should be like this.

Truly, this is a very practical chapter, and the lessons therein need to be be manifested in every believer.

CHAPTER TWENTY-THREE

The Lamb and the Book

S imilar to ch. 4, this chapter lends itself to Christian ethics, and as
the Lord Himself is presented, the lessons are bound to be per
fect, and the heart accordingly is motivated to bow in devotion
to Him.

Three things are prominent in this precious chapter, The Lamb in the
midst of the throne, His ability to open the seals thereof, and the wonderful outbursts of praise that succeed that action. "THE LAMB AND
THE LANGUAGE" would be an fitting title to this chapter. The three
great passages on worship occupy most of the chapter.

THE LAMB IN THE MIDST OF THE THRONE

A challenge goes out, "who is worthy to open the book", there is no
response, no one in heaven or on the earth or under the earth was able to
do so. John wept, probably the only one ever to weep in heaven, then
comes the announcement concerning the ability of the Lion of Judah to
open the book. Only a Divine Person could open the seals, just as John
the Baptist made clear that only a Divine Person could baptize in the
Holy Spirit. The meaning of this all important scene has already been
dealt with, but a few remarks need to be made about the Lord Jesus as
the Lamb in a practical and devotional way.

The Lord is here described in parabolic language for the second time in the Revelation. First, in ch. 1, as He stood in the midst of the lampstands, now as the Lamb He stands in the midst of the throne. The first vision is relative to the church, this second is relative to the whole earth. Consider as follows:-

1) He is in the midst of the throne and the living creatures and in the midst of the elders (Verse 6). What a glory God has given to Him, the cross is past forever, now He occupies the throne, His Father's throne (ch. 3:21), but at His return He will fill the throne of His glory (Matt. 25:31). In light of this, He ought to have the place of authority in the heart and life of every blood bought believer.

2) "As it had been slain". Heaven can never forget the sufferings and the great price that was paid by the Lord upon the cross. This burdened the heart of the Lord in the days of His flesh, He spoke of the baptism of suffering He had to be baptized with, and how He was straitened until it was accomplished (Luke 12:50). So now in the glory, can that baptism be forgotten ? The breaking of bread celebrated on Lord's Day by believers shows His death, and the continual preaching of the gospel is a reminder upon earth of that terrible suffering. Heaven also remembers. Four times in the Revelation it is stated that the Lamb was slain.

a) In verse 6 where He appears in the midst of the throne because He is God, in the midst of the 24 elders because He is the means of redemption.

b) Again the phrase appears in verse 9 as part of the praise, His ability to open the book and because He has redeemed to God by His blood.

c) Also in verse 12, and this time His worth is foremost to receive praise, riches, wisdom, strength, honour, glory and blessing.

d) The expression "the Lamb slain" occurs finally in ch. 13:8. There it is found in reference to the book of the Lamb slain from the foundation of the world, although this foundation of the world is perhaps a reference to the martyrs, now written in the Lamb's book of life, the record going back to the beginning of time. However, with these three references in ch. 5 how could we cease to love Him, the heart of the redeemed is bound to go out to Him more and more.

3) It must be understood that the Greek word for Lamb here and through the 28 references in the book of Revelation is a different word from

the other four mentions of the Lamb in the rest of the N.T. The other four are found in John 1:29, John 1:36, Acts 8:32, and 1 Peter 1:19. The word here indicates a little Lamb, a little Lamb in the midst of the throne, and also seen in wrath in ch. 6:16. What is this ? Surely it seems to teach that pride, loftiness and high-mindedness that accompany the natural man is not found in our Lord although He is King of kings and Lord of lords.

Isa. ch. 2 is important in this respect in the way God judges Israel and the nations, it is especially their pride that calls for the fiercest indignation. Mention is made of words such as lofty looks, haughtiness of men, proud and lofty, lifted up, ceders of Lebanon that are high and lifted up, high mountains and high towers, and so on (Isa 2:10-17). All perfection is seen in our Lord, pride and all such as would characterize the natural man is absent in Him although He inhabits eternity.

4) The Lamb has seven horns. Horns speak of power and authority, and are often viewed in Scripture as being symbolic of kings. Here is perfect power, first seen in the Gospels in all His marvellous works, then in the Acts as working with His sent apostles, now on the throne, the perfect ability to rule the world. No man ever had this, many tried to reach it and failed, the world to come is to be subjected to the rule of the perfect Man (Acts 17:31. Heb. 2:5-6).

5) The seven eyes express perfect wisdom and intelligence to direct that power. Some kings in the O.T. had excellent power but lacked wisdom to direct it aright. Solomon saw the necessity for wisdom to be added to the power he already had, his position of such authority demanded wisdom if it was to profit the nation. The Lord Jesus shall rule the world in righteousness, and the features that shall appear then, have already been displayed in that Perfect Man in the days of His flesh. No wonder Paul speaks of Christ being the power of God and the wisdom of God (1 Cor. 1:24).

6) The seven Spirits would suggest the full fellowship between the Lord and the Spirit of God. It was always so, "The Spirit of the Lord is upon Me", is what the Lord read in the synagogue at Nazareth. Peter preached this in the house of Cornelius, "How God anointed Jesus of Nazareth with the Holy Ghost and with power" (Acts 10:38). He cast out demons by the Spirit of God in Matt. 12:28, so in the coming kingdom the unity of power and wisdom will be evinced in the Perfect Ruler in fellowship with the Holy Spirit.

7) The Lamb had the power to open the seals, that is to order coming events, to the removal of all dross in preparation for His rule as the Lion of Judah, the root of David. The Lord Jesus shall rightly intervene in the governments of this world; make all the necessary adjustments; purge the nations; put down all enemies; regather Israel; remove the curse, in all bringing in perfection. He has the power and wisdom to do so.

8) The Lamb stood in the midst of the throne, there in readiness. The time will come when the Lord who is now seated at the right hand of God shall rise, first to descend to the air for His church, and later to come as the Son of Man to rule. Stephen saw the Lord Jesus standing on the right hand of God in Acts. 7. Either the Lord stood to receive the first martyr, or He had not yet sat down, perhaps symbolically standing waiting for the repentance of Israel. When Stephen was stoned, Israel's rejection was then complete, the Lord then sat down. This of course is only conjecture, but nevertheless is very attractive.

However, here in Revelation 5 the Lamb stands in order to set in motion the last great prophetic events.

THE LANGUAGE OF THE PRAISE

There are three tremendous outbursts of praise in this chapter, and all the result of the ability of the Lamb to open the seals. The praises are of a progressive order, increasing in volume and intensity as the passage unfolds. The first praise is by the four living creatures and the twenty four elders, and is called a "new song". The second is sounded out by the addition of ten thousand times ten thousand angels. To the third is added all that had breath in heaven, earth and under the earth.

The theme also is of an increasing nature. The first expression of praise is for redemption, the second is unto the Lamb Himself, and the third takes in all time, for ever and ever, and culminates in glory unto Him that sits upon the throne and to the Lamb. The first is what the Lord has done, the second is Who and What He is, and the last is unto His eternal glory. God is worthy to be praised and surely believers now could be more occupied in this worthy exercise.

THE FIRST GREAT PRAISE CH. 5:9-10

This first note of praise is for Redemption and is the worship of the four living creatures and the twenty four elders. It seems certain that the elders express the church, this is the only reasonable conclusion that can be arrived at as seen in previous pages. That being the case, the theme of redemption is most appropriate. Other saints are represented in the golden bowls of incense which is interpreted as the "prayers of the saints". When the church is raptured and glorified in heaven, other saints will continue in earthly testimony. These are seen in chapter 7, the sealed of Israel and the multitude of Gentiles in the Tribulation time. How wonderful that the suffering saints on the earth mingle their praise with those in heaven. They suffer terribly yet they are engaged in heavenly exercise and praise, "Thou art worthy". This first homage is also called "A new song". The first song in the Bible is found in Ex. 15, the song of Moses and is the pattern of the many Bible songs that follow such as that of Deborah, Hannah and so forth. One of the features of Bible songs is that they are based on experience, the intervention of God. So it was with Israel in Ex. 15, God had come in and delivered them from Egypt and Pharaoh. A new song is a further development in the way that God reveals Himself in the experience of the singers. This development is expressed in the words of this magnificent song.

There are seven things for which they sing praise and these cover a long space of time, from the death of Christ to the end of the Millennium, a period of about 3000 years.

a) They are occupied first with the worthiness of the Person, the Lamb. "Thou art worthy", Christ is all to them, it is so good to be occupied with Christ and the glorious worth of His Person.

b) They then advance to His death, "thou wast slain", this is the foundation of every blessing. By the obedience of Christ to the will of His Father even unto death, He has opened the floodgates of blessing to both Jew and Gentile. The rest of this song is the outcome of that death, rejoicing in what the cross has really accomplished.

c) "Thou didst purchase us unto God by thy blood" (Verse 9 R.V.). Unto God is first, the real purpose as with the Nazarite in Num. 6, eight times it speaks of "Unto", which means that attraction in towards God, all else fades away. A similar occurrence was with the conversion of the Thessalonians, they turned to God from idols (1 Thess. 1:9). This is always the case, the heart of God went out to His creatures, even fallen man, and has redeemed many UNTO Himself. By thy blood indicates sacrifice, the Lamb was slain, the death of Christ can be looked upon as a murder and in many other ways, but the chief thought is that it was a Divine sacrifice for sin. This precious aspect of the death of Christ is appreciated, "Thou hast redeemed us to God by thy blood".

d) Where they come from is next stated, "out of every kindred and tongue and people and nation". This fourfold description appears seven times in the Rev. and highlights the world wide aspect of the grace of God. Four is the universal number in the Bible, this goes beyond the bounds of Judaism, the Lamb of God was for the world (John 1:29). The Pascal Lamb in Egypt was for Israel only, types often fall short of the reality being only shadows of the good things to come.

e) With the thought of "Unto God" emerges the primary reason for salvation. People profess faith in Christ to escape judgment and to come into the wonderful blessing in Christ, but the important factor is that God saves for His own glory. A hint of this is seen in the expression "Kings and priests", or a kingdom of priests. Either way, God has something in which to display His eternal grace, and many are fitted by that grace to worship Him.

f) The O.T. priests were important, at certain times they were able to go into the presence of God in worship, however this is greater, the right to come before God continually because of redemption as in Heb. 10:19-22. These who sing this new song are doing just that.
The Revised Version of 1881 reads this as a "kingdom of priests". This would mean that every one in the kingdom would function as a priest, and not just one family as under the law. Every one in the church redeemed by the blood of the Lamb can and will function in priesthood. However, the fact of reigning like a king is also true. When Paul stated that the Corinthians were reigning as kings without the apostles, he meant that the time of reigning had not yet come, now is the time of reproach, the carnal Corinthians knew little about reproach (1 Cor. 4:8).

g) "We shall reign on the earth". This is the final statement. The kingdom of priests was in operation while they sang this song and the time to reign upon the earth would shortly come. Happy occupation worshipping as priests in heaven, and looking forward to reigning with Christ. With these thoughts the first great praise ends.

THE SECOND PRAISE V 11-12

In the second expression of homage the angels join the previous company of living creatures and elders, the number is vast, amounting to 100 million. This is likely representative of all the angels and simply means myriads of angels. John beheld this great sight, and all around the throne, such a widening circle. He also heard the voice of the vast company, they speak with a loud voice, each single angel speaks with a loud or great voice, and the aggregate must have been tremendous. This great praise is unto the Lamb, it is not called a song, nevertheless it has the same starting point, "Worthy is the Lamb". This is followed by a sevenfold praise, another one of the great sevens in the Book of Revelation. At first glance it would seem that the sevenfold expression of praise lacks order. Perhaps there is an order in keeping with the opening of the seven seals in the next chapters. There could be other structures seen in this praise, but the link to the seven seals is very genuine. Consider as follows:-

1) Power, this would be seal one. The rider of the white horse goes out to conquer, authority and power will be seen in the counterfeit man. The Lamb is all powerful, He shall destroy the man of lawlessness and all the host of his armies with the breath of His mouth. Power belongs unto the Lamb.
2) "Riches". This of course would include moral riches as well as material, but consider seal two which brings forth war. War makes poverty, wars are costly and have impoverished many nations. The Lamb shall make war, a war on moral grounds, nor shall He be depleted by the fierce conflict. His kingdom shall be rich in prosperity and righteousness.
3) "Wisdom". This is over against seal three which was famine. The wonderful thing about Joseph was his wisdom to provide for the time of famine. Pharaoh said of Joseph, "There is none so discreet and wise as thou art", and he made him minister of food in Egypt. The wise rule of our Lord shall bring in times of prosperity in the Millennium, but He shall wisely withhold the rain from places that do not

value the Righteous Kingdom nor its King (Zech. 14:18-19). Therefore wisdom can avoid the terrors of famine, if in the case of Joseph,
much more in Him of whom Joseph speaks.

4) "Strength", this would correspond with the fourth seal, death and
hell. It takes mighty strength to deliver from death and hell and that
strength or might is in the Lord Jesus. He has destroyed him that had
the power of death that is the devil. He is risen from the dead, death
had no strength to hold Him. How beautifully the Lord appears in
this way in ch. 1:18 "I am He that liveth and was dead and behold I
am alive for evermore, and have the keys of hell and of death". The
Lord Jesus was declared to be the Son of God with power by the
resurrection of dead ones (Rom. 1:4). All might and strength is His,
and shall be fully manifested when the Scripture will be fulfilled,
"He shall swallow up death in victory (Isa. 25:8).

5) "Honour". this is definitely linked with seal five, those under the
altar who were slain for the Word of God and for the testimony they
held (6:9-11). They wanted vindication, white robes were given unto
them, the time of their honouring was not yet come, the world despised them, God honours them. How much more with our blessed
Lord, the Man whom God delighted to honour. The obedient One
who suffered death according to the will of God in the days of His
flesh. The One who suffered death is now crowned with glory and
honour, and there is greater honour to come in the Day of His manifestation.

6) "Glory". The manifestation of His glory is in accordance with the
sixth seal. There the signs in heaven, the moon as blood, the sun
darkened and such forth are associated with the coming of the Son
of Man in Matt. 24 and Joel 2, it is the day of His glory a step further
on than the previous word Honour. The Lord is honoured now, seated
at the right hand of the throne of God, but the manifested glory is still
to come.

7) "Blessing". The final seal brings in silence in heaven and proceeds to
the final scenes of judgment that result in the purging of all things
and the bringing in of lasting blessing as at the closing chapters of
this prophetic book.

Such is the second outburst of praise, all is unto the Lamb, and the
worth of the Lamb is seen in the opening of the seals.

THE THIRD OUTBURST OF PRAISE V 13-15

In this final passage of worship every created thing which is in heaven and on the earth and under the earth join in. This corresponds with Phil. 2, "every knee shall bow ... of things in heaven and things on earth and things under the earth." Here in Rev. 5 is the addition of things such as are in the sea. Perhaps both these passages speak of all praising His Name, but not all at the same time, some when He comes, others at the Great White Throne judgment etc.. This universal praise could be the summing up of all praise howbeit at different stages.

The praise this time is fourfold, in keeping with the universal aspect. It begins where the last one ended, with blessing, speaking no doubt of the Millennial Kingdom. The mention of the throne would confirm this, and He that sitteth on the throne is the joint recipient of the praise along with the Lamb.

These four then present Millennial features.

1) "Blessing", once the curse is removed and the reign of righteousness begins, the result will be great blessing. This is what the whole creation groans and waits for in Rom. 8. A parallel is seen typically in the beginning of the reign of Solomon, peace and prosperity.

2) "Honour". This would suggest the Lord entering into His rightful place as figured in the ark having been brought into its permanent place in the temple and the staves for transportation removed. The ultimate is reached.

3) "Glory", this would point to the presence of God with His people, in the dedication of the temple by Solomon, the glory filled the place.

4) "Power" (R.V.) is again seen best in Solomon. No king before or since had such dominion, his kingdom extended greatly, he ruled with authority and wisdom. However, a contrast with Solomon is also here. His kingdom came to an end, his importance lay in his birth as the Son of David, and his reign is a type of that of Christ. Yet he failed morally as so many other kings and he was succeeded by a foolish son resulting in a divided kingdom. Here there is no failure, this kingdom is forever, He shall never give way to another, nor shall the land or people ever be divided. Here the great voice is not only praise but UNITY. The four living creatures say "Amen" as 2 Cor. 1:20. All the promises of God are in Him yea and Amen.

The twenty four elders fall down and worship Him that liveth unto the ages of the ages.

Such a magnificent chapter, and no doubt it sets the pattern for worship, the sincere believer who loves Christ, can learn many things about worship from this passage.

CHAPTER TWENTY-FOUR

Practical Lessons from ch. 6-7

In chapter 6 the scene is upon the earth; the outcome of the heavenly scene in ch. 4-5. It is most encouraging to faith to understand that what takes place in heaven has a bearing on earthly events. This could be stated more emphatically, earthly events are entirely planned and controlled by heaven, it is always so.

a) Consider in 1 Kings 22:19 where Micaiah the prophet spoke to king Ahab saying "I saw the Lord sitting on His throne and all the host of heaven standing by Him on His right hand and on His left". The story goes on to unfold the "lying spirit" in the mouths of the false prophets of Ahab to persuade him to go forth to battle and so to his death. The whole operation was ordered and carried out by heaven, and the result on earth seen in the death of the king.

b) Daniel had the same thought when he said "He changeth the times and the seasons, He removeth kings and setteth up kings, He giveth wisdom unto the wise" etc. (Dan. 2:21).

c) Also in Daniel ch. 7:13-14, he sees one like unto the Son of Man coming before the Ancient of Days and there was given unto Him dominion and glory and a kingdom, and all people nations and languages should serve Him ... and His kingdom, that which shall not be destroyed.

It must be kept in mind that Revelation 4-7 are dealing with one subject, a problem that is of great concern to many, why is there so much trouble on the earth, why do wars, disasters and many such things dog the steps of puny man ? The answer is that the Prince of Peace has been rejected. The terrible calamities of ch. 6 are therefore the lot of man, and are of his own doing.

The "seals" are events that are most fearful to read and will be dreadful to experience upon the earth. Nevertheless, these seals can be approached in a practical way as well as prophetic. Note the SEVERITY of God in ch. 6 and the GOODNESS of God in ch. 7. The great multitude experience salvation that comes from the same hand of God that judges so severely in the opening of the seals. Notwithstanding the most important lessons can be seen in the display of character in the world of fallen mankind in the 6th chapter. Such features as these should never surface in the life of a believer.

SEAL ONE presents "ambition" , not the ambition to be quiet as in 1 Thess. 4:11 "That you be ambitious to be quiet" (R.V.) but worldly ambition, going forth conquering and to conquer, this attitude has produced the like of Hitler, Stalin and others in more recent times. The spirit of discontent can be seen today in the political and business world and in most other things even affecting the least known of people of the present time.

The spirit of discontent is what Paul warns against in such passages as Phil. 4:11-12 and 1 Tim. 6:6. This is the mark of the natural man and ought not to be a feature in the life of any Christian.

SEAL TWO speaks of war of which the symbol is a great sword, and power is given unto the horseman to take peace from the earth. The world has been plagued with war since the early history of Gen. 14, strife, division, violence, and killing are common traits in the world of mankind, and again such a temperament ought to be absent from the believer. The Lord said "blessed are the peace-makers" (Matt. 5:9), Paul exhorts "be at peace among yourselves" (1 Thess. 5:13). "The fruit of righteousness is sown in peace of them which make peace", is the exhortation of James 3:18. There ought not to be hostilities or strife among those who have obtained the "peace with God through our Lord Jesus Christ". War is the opposite of unity and peace, peace and unity go beautifully together.

SEAL THREE brings forth famine and inflation, these are depicted by the black horse and the balances in the hand of the rider. Even the rich are afflicted, losing the luxuries of life in the oil and the wine. What lesson can be learnt from this ? First, that of wisdom as already noted, the wisdom of Joseph diverted the real tragedy of the famine in Egypt. However, the chief ethic in times of want is that those who have, share with those who have not. This was the case in the Gentile churches, they shared their goods, even in their own poverty with the poor saints of Judaea (2 Cor. 8:11-16) (Rom. 15:25-7). In 2 Cor. 8:15 Paul illustrates the principle of sharing with the Manna of old saying, "As it is written he that had gathered much had nothing over, and he that had gathered little had no lack". It is obvious what really happened was that the person who had gathered much was moved with compassion to him, who being weak had gathered little, and shared of his abundance. The miracle was not in the "omer" or measure, but in the heart. The principle of sharing runs throughout the Scriptures, the chief example is God himself who shared with us His well Beloved Son.

In **SEAL FOUR** death and hell were the result of the opening, the pale horse and its rider. Death needs no symbol as the bow to the first rider, the sword to the second and the balances to the third. The pale horse and its rider is enough to chill the strongest heart with its fear of death and hell. How different from those under the altar in the next verses and the great multitude in ch. 7. To them the sting of death is gone and hell shall not have them, hell has been robbed of its prey and the resurrection shall be the end of death. To the ungodly death is really death, God's just judgment upon sin, how wonderful to know Him that is "the resurrection and the life" who on the other side of death said, "I am He that liveth and was dead and behold I am alive for ever more Amen, and have the keys of death and hell" (Rev. 1:18). John fell at His feet as dead, but was told to arise, death is passed for him, a thankful heart should always be present in every believer for such great salvation.

A change is made with **SEAL FIVE**, not a horseman now but an altar, and the lives of those who figuratively were offered upon it. The martyrs are in the picture but they cry for vengeance. They are on the other side of death and await the resurrection, but even in this condition they have a great lesson to learn, that of "patience". If these are told to wait and to be patient, how much more those of earth who are seeking to do the will of God and the service of God. Such are tempted to act before God's time and have need of patience. Abraham was marked by failure in this respect, he sought to bring forward the promise of God concerning the seed in a fleshly way of his own, and Sarah's devices. The promise of God can only be fulfilled in God's own time and way. Joseph in prison, Moses seeking to deliver Israel by the slaying of the Egyptian, David's endeavour to build a house for God are all examples of the same thing. "Learn patience" is the message of seal five.

The **SIXTH SEAL** would guard against materialism and the snare of an earthbound attitude. Changes in the sun, moon and stars, every mountain and island moved out of its place would suggest there is no stability in the things of this world. It is better to trust in the "Rock of Ages" and to lay up treasure in heaven. The earthdwellers so often referred to in the Revelation have nothing secure beyond this earth, and one day all shall be taken from them as at the end of this chapter. From kings and leaders down to the bondman; all are levelled by the coming of the Lord and wish to be buried out of sight. How different is the attitude of the Christian to whom the apostle Peter exhorts with the word "looking" three times in his final chapter. Looking for the day of God, looking for a new heaven and a new earth and seeing we look for these things (2 Pet. 3:11-14). The new heavens and earth will be indestructible and therefore shall never pass away.

The lesson then is not to get earth-bound and not to develop a materialistic spirit as did the church at Laodicea. "Using this world but not abusing it for the fashion of this world passeth away" (1 Cor. 7:31).

The different states of people mentioned in the closing verses are interesting. There are seven classes mentioned, falling into three categories, the political, military and social are all calling upon the mountains and rocks to fall upon them to hide them from the face of the Lamb. Such a contrast to Calvary when the Lord was surrounded by such while upon the cross. The wrath of God fell upon Him, God was hidden from Him in the terrible forsaking that brought forth that agonizing cry "Why hast thou forsaken me". The Lord was able to endure withstanding all the suffering, coming out triumphant on the other side of death in resurrection power.

Such is the practical import of chapter 6.

THE TRIBES OF ISRAEL IN CH. 7

This is an amazing chapter, and above all manifests the grace and mercy of our God, first dealing with Israel then the nations of the Gentiles in blessing. Most searching lessons emerge from this chapter also and the first would be the opening statements concerning angelic movements. The mighty power and authority of angels is seen here in holding back the great forces of darkness.

Also, how they are one with God in intent and concern for those who are the saved on earth.

There is much material in these opening verses to keep prophetic students on their toes, however the most striking point is the power of the angels to hold back the movements of judgment until the elect are sealed. These have power to hurt the earth, sea and trees but all is withheld until the sealing is complete. The work of judgment must give way to the more important work of salvation. A similar thought is expressed by Paul in his teaching, that while the mystery of iniquity is at work yet all is hindered by the works of God at this time. Satan would endeavour to bring to the birth his wicked designs, even "last day conditions" before the appointed time, but the presence of the Holy Spirit and the forming of the church by God withstands his activity until the purpose of God for the church is fulfilled (2 Thess. 2:5-10).

Another sanctifying thought is the "sealing", seals which cannot be broken in contrast to the broken seals of the previous chapter. Christ is the One who can open and no man can shut, which is ch. 6, and shuts and no man can open which is ch. 7. There is always a seal, "the Lord knoweth them that are His" (2 Tim. 2:19). In the Ephesian epistle the seal seems to be the Spirit Himself "Grieve not the Holy Spirit of God whereby ye are sealed unto the day of redemption" (Eph. 4:30). The day of redemption is that of which Rom. 8:23 speaks, the changing of the body of the believer making salvation complete at the Lord's coming. The first coming of the Lord to die on the cross secures the redemption of the soul and spirit of the believer, the body is still in a corrupt state and awaits the resurrection. Then the body shall experience redemption at the second coming of the Lord.

The seal of the Spirit is spoken of in 2 Cor. 1:21-22 and is coupled with the other great operations of the Spirit, the "anointing" and the "earnest". The seal of the Spirit marks the Possession by God, the earnest is the Promise of God, the first payment of all that God has promised, and the anointing is the Placing by God, a position according to His order and grace. Priests were anointed, therefore placed as priests, they could not function in the Tabernacle without the anointing. Kings in Israel could not take the position to reign apart from the anointing.

The teaching concerning the Spirit and the believer is most encouraging. The sealing here in Rev. ch. 7 is sure and keeps secure the believer as every seal of God whether in salvation or in service as indicated here.

It is obvious that God has a future for Israel, the covenant with both Abraham and David await fulfilment, and this final book of the N.T. shows how and by what means the final purpose of God for Israel shall be accomplished. Therefore, believers should respect Israel as Paul reasons that many things that Gentile believers hold dear have come into being through Israel (Rom. 9:4-5). In fact Romans 9-11, that wonderful section takes up the promises to Israel which are yet to be fulfilled, and it would be reasonably impossible to say that in all this God had only the church in mind and not Israel. This book of the Revelation first deals with the church in ch.1-3, then Israel. The beautiful exhortation in Ps. 122:6 is worthy of obeying today, "Pray for the peace of Jerusalem, they shall prosper that love thee". Here the sealed tribes of Israel are marked out for preservation and blessing in a day that will soon come. Likely these sealed ones are the heralds of the gospel of the Kingdom in the last times, although this is not stated.

Another important point could be dealt with before leaving this Jewish section. It has been a wonder to many that the tribe of Dan is left out of the list of the tribes, and wonderful fanciful reasons have been given for this omission. The number of the tribes here is twelve and must be carefully compared with the many other listings of the twelve tribes of Israel. There is a pattern in all the other lists and that is, if it is the "historical" thought then Levi and Joseph appear. Further, when the "inheritance" is in mind then Levi is omitted and instead of Joseph, his two sons Ephraim and Manasseh are listed. Examples of this can be found in Ex. 1 where the twelve include Levi and Joseph because historically they came into Egypt. Contrast Ezek. 48 where the inheritance is finally divided out, Joseph and Levi are omitted and in their place are Ephraim and Manasseh. This is a consistent pattern throughout Scripture. Therefore in comparison with the names of the tribes in Rev. 7 Levi is brought in and so is Joseph (verses 7-8) but Manasseh is also mentioned, so where is Ephraim ? It is most likely that the mention of Manasseh in verse 6 should really be Dan, and the suggestion has been often made that this is a copyist error. Apparently Manasseh and Dan are quite like each other in Greek. Whether this is accepted or not, the omission of Dan is contrary to the pattern of all the other listings of the tribes in the Bible.

However, one great thing comes out of this section, "The faithfulness of God". Here the sealing is before the tribulation which is suggested by "hurt not the earth" of verse 3. In ch. 14 this company is seen after the tribulation on Mount Sion with the Lamb. There is no reason whatever to make the 144000 there to be a different company from the 144000 in this ch. 7, although some do make a difference. Being the same company therefore this is a manifestation of the faithfulness and the power of God, not one of the company failed to stand finally with the Lamb on Mount Sion in spite of the horrors of the Great Tribulation. Paul would agree with this and often in his epistles speaks of the faithfulness of God. "God is faithful by whom ye were called unto the fellowship of His Son Jesus Christ our Lord" (1 Cor. 1:9). This faithfulness began on earth and will continue unceasingly into eternity.

THE GREAT MULTITUDE OF GENTILES V 9-17

One sad thing comes out of this happy section and that is the failure of John to inquire concerning the great sight of an innumerable multitude of the saved of the Lord. God delights in the inquiry of His people and in the way they eagerly grasp the mind of God at any given time. John 16 shows the failure of the disciples to inquire concerning the Lord's words and the Lord expresses disappointment at their lack of interest: "But now I go my way to Him that sent me and none of you asketh me whither goest thou "? (John 16:5). Perhaps for this very reason Peter was always inquiring and asking questions that the Lord gave him a special commission with the "keys of the kingdom". John fails in this and no doubt the elder was waiting for an inquiry, and in fact had to put the words in the mouth of John saying "What are these and from whence came they"? The believer who is constantly inquiring about the Word and the Lord is bound to grow. One longs to see this feature in these closing days.

The passage is remarkable and is no doubt what Paul called "The fullness of the Gentiles" in Rom. 11:25. Many Gentiles have come into the blessing of the gospel from Pentecost until the present time and will be so until the rapture. However, God has more in mind and this great multitude coming out of the Great Tribulation answer to the sheep of Matt. 25. It would appear that this is the completion of the fullness of the Gentiles.

The gospel message is seen clearly in this section. God has only one way of salvation, and although the time will be different the message is still the same.

1) The grace of God is seen in the vast number, not a few but a great multitude which no man could number, which means no man could estimate. The heart of God is great towards the Gentiles.

2) The universal call is a manifestation that God is no respecter of persons, the same God is rich unto all that call upon Him. Seven times in Rev. mankind is summed up in four categories, verse 9 gives us the first reference; nations, kindreds, people and tongues. The number four is used of the universal view in Scripture as in the four points of the compass. The gospel is for all in this time of grace, as in Tribulation times.

3) They stood before the throne and before the Lamb. Such a position, the gospel message not only saves from judgment but brings unto God. They are saved from deserved wrath and brought into a position of glory, yet they had no claims, promises, or covenants as Israel had, for these are Gentiles. Before the throne would speak of service as in verse 15 "therefore are they before the throne of God and serve Him day and night in His temple". Standing (v 9 R.V.) is the attitude of a servant in readiness. Before salvation they served themselves, the world and the devil, now they are the servants of God.

4) They are clothed in white robes. "Robes" are one of the rewards for faithful servants in Scripture, but a further meaning is here, verse 14 explains the significance and will be dealt with at length.

5) They had palms in their hands. The palm in the Bible speaks of victory, and they were therefore overcomers. They trusted and followed the Lamb in spite of all threats of violence and death, and in an atmosphere of deception they believed the truth respecting the Lamb.

The palms were used in the feast of Tabernacles, the last of Israel's religious festivals which are also prophetic. The feast of Tabernacles will be fulfilled in the Millennium. These saved Gentiles shall enter into that kingdom, and after that into eternal blessing.

6) They all cry with a loud voice, "Salvation to our God which sitteth upon the throne and unto the Lamb". These saved of the Gentiles acknowledge that the source of salvation is God and the Lamb, and they do so with a loud voice. Although they were called upon to suffer terribly in the tribulation, they had remained faithful in the midst of much confusion and deception, yet they praise not themselves but the throne and the Lamb. No boasting is evident here, how glad they are that God has saved them, and all the glory is given to Him. It could be written over this passage "Not of works lest any man should boast" (Eph. 2:8-9).

In all this the triumphs of the gospel come out, Paul was proud of this message because of what it could do. It transformed the lives of people and brought them to glory which Judaism and philosophy etc. failed to do. "The gospel of Christ is the power of God unto salvation to every one that believeth" (Rom. 1:16). This message through God will gather millions unto salvation in the most distressing time of all, the Great Tribulation. Today salvation is so easy as opposition is not such that life and well-being is at stake, yet few go in for salvation. Still, God's purpose in the call of the church goes on in this time, and the principle remains that if believers live godly lives they shall suffer persecution (2 Tim. 3:12).

Verse 14 presents the foundations of the faith and interprets the meaning of the white robes. The blood of the Lamb is what saved them, not the position of the Lamb in the midst of the throne nor the horns or eyes that speak of the Divine qualities of the Lamb. It is the blood of the Lamb that brings peace, His death as a Divine sacrifice for sin. A parallel as in Egypt, it was essential that the Lamb without blemish was killed and its blood sprinkled ere the first-born could be delivered from the angel of death.

The statement that they washed their robes is instructive, this denotes human and personal responsibility, they washed their robes, is a way of saying they trusted and firmly believed that the sacrifice was of God, and sufficient to save them, and that there was no other way. They washed their robes, others rejected and believed the lie. The result of believing was the white robes, every blot of sin removed, the white robes indicate righteousness imputed as in Rom. 4:22 rather than the reward of righteousness as in Rev. 19:8.

THE BLESSING OF THE REDEEMED 15-17

This is perhaps the most beautiful passage in the Revelation, the blessedness and tranquillity of those redeemed by the blood of the Lamb. While the proper interpretation here is of the saved Gentiles coming out of the Great Tribulation, yet the blessings are verily true of all that belong to Christ.

All this blessedness and favour can be seen in a glance by a comparison with Israel in their Egypt to Canaan experience.

1) Out of the tribulation of Egypt and the terror of a cruel Pharaoh came the people of God into the wilderness. Delivered first from judgment by the blood of the Lamb, and from slavery to Pharaoh by the Red Sea. The pattern is the same, here are people saved from wrath and from the slavery of sin, standing on resurrection ground as in type through the Red Sea.

2) God then instructed Israel "let them make me a tabernacle that I may dwell among them" (Ex. 25:8). This next stage is seen in verse 15 "He that sitteth on the throne shall dwell among them".

3) They shall hunger no more is similar to the supply of Manna in the wilderness.

4) "Neither thirst any more" is comparable to the water out of the rock which was a wonderful picture of Christ giving the Spirit. The story of the Manna can be read in Ex. 16 and that of the water in Ex. 17, John had both these chapters in mind when he wrote of Christ the Manna in John 6 and the water of the Spirit in John 7.

5) The shelter from the sun and heat could be likened unto the pillar of cloud by day. It would seem it was in the form of an umbrella, a mushroom shape that shaded the whole camp and which gave the people comfort from the heat of the sun.

The whole wilderness journey is covered in these few points as all these blessings abode with them until the end of their pilgrimage. They came into the land by the crossing of the river Jordan which speaks of resurrection life, and is hinted here by the reference to the living waters of verse 17. Ephesians begins figuratively with Jordan; believers on resurrection ground seated with the Lord Jesus in the heavenlies. Romans on the other hand considers the coming out of the world of Egypt and into the wilderness by the Red Sea. Here both these ideas come together, the Lamb shall shepherd them, this would be the wilderness and all that it entailed, the living waters would be entering into the land.

God shall wipe away all tears, this is the end, all the trials and dangers are over, and they come into the goodness of the provision of God in the land.

This passage like so many others in the Revelation is based on an Old Testament background, and assures of a wonderful message, God in faithfulness will see all believers through unto the end, then eternal blessing.

THE GREAT TRIBULATION

While it is most certain that there is the wilderness background in this passage, yet the source of the people cannot be overlooked. In the tribulation they hungered, thirsted literally because of their faith, they were denied the necessities of life by the reigning powers. They no doubt will flee to the wilderness where they would be exposed to the hot rays of the sun and be without shelter. The end of their suffering is contemplated here, the Lamb shall lead them, in some miraculous way He will provide and sustain them as sheep in the wilderness. Finally He shall lead them to the living fountains of waters, into the fullness of life eternal. God shall wipe away all the tears of the past sorrow and suffering. The terrible past is over, they have proved the faithfulness of God. So it shall be to millions that shall come out of the Great Tribulation in the last days, the fullness of the Gentiles shall have then come in (Rom. 11:25).

CHAPTER TWENTY-FIVE

The Seven Trumpet Judgments

To obey God is costly, but to disobey Him is more costly. Therefore the believer, in love to His Lord who seeks to obey Him will meet with opposition and problems. This is augmented if the times are characterized by persecution from religious quarters or the ruling powers. Problems such as would arise under times of persecution is what this book of Revelation is all about. So far these notes have dealt with the problem of ch. 1-3 can church testimony continue in troubled times ? The answer is given in the seven letters to the churches, no matter what the affliction whether inside or outside, the church is able to continue, the Lord is a ready helper. The second section comprising of chapters 4-7 dealt with the problem "why is there so much trouble on the earth"? The throne of heaven is in complete control, and the presence of the Lamb in glory was the reason for the troubled earth, the Son of Man had been rejected hence the earth is responsible for its own troubles and tribulation. Now comes another problem and a very serious one at that, "why does the Lord not answer the prayers of suffering saints in troubled times when they need Him most" ? This is dealt with in ch. 8-11 which we now approach.

It has been noted that each section begins with something from the Jewish Tabernacle. The section on the churches began with lampstands, and the throne of God pictured in the ark of the covenant began the

second section. Here this third part in keeping with the tabernacle idea
starts with the "golden altar".

Now this altar has to do with prayer, "the prayers of all saints" in 8:3.
This theme continues to the end of chapter 11.

"Men ought always to pray and not to faint" (Luke 18:1) is one of the
Lords's many exhortations and encouragements to pray. The fact that
fainting is mentioned shows that the background of that exhortation is
"the passing through of affliction". Prayer is the only hope but the prayers
seemingly are not answered, God is silent. The parable that follows in
Luke 18 bears this out, the woman continues her request with importu-
nity to the unjust judge, then the Lord relates the parable to the last days,
even the days now under examination in the Revelation. How fitting
then that this section should commence with A SILENCE IN HEAVEN.
This is followed with the prayers of saints as if to suggest that heaven is
silent to their prayers. Many believers in their personal affliction have
passed through this valley besides those who suffered in terrible times
of persecution.

James in his little epistle would seek to answer this difficulty saying
that some prayers are not answered because they ask amiss. They ask
for the wrong things and not things according to the will of God and
certainly not to His glory, rather to consume upon their own lusts (James
4:3). Again in his first chapter he considers the case of the double minded
man praying, alas in vain for that man can receive nothing from the
Lord. In his final chapter he hints that the lack of righteousness in life
can be a hindrance to prayer, he gives the example of Elijah saying "The
effectual fervent prayer of a righteous man availeth much" (James 5:16).
However, in spite of these different hindrances to prayer that are based
upon lack of something in the life of the petitioner, there are times, especially in deep trouble when the spiritual soul having only hope in God
prays earnestly and nothing happens. This situation is often seen in the
Psalms.

Psalm 22 I cry in the daytime, thou hearest not.

Psalm 35 Keep not silent O Lord, be not far from me.

Psalm 81 Keep not silent O Lord.

Psalm 28 O Lord my rock, be not silent unto me.

The parable already referred to by the Lord carries the same problem, the widow appeals to the unjust judge but he refuses to do anything
about her trouble. This great section in Revelation has all this in mind,

and the encouragement to go on with the praying although it seems that heaven is silent. To trace this section then is most important, and to see all from the Lord's point of view.

THE SILENCE IS ONLY FOR A SHORT TIME

Note that the silence does not endure for ever, only a short time an half hour. This suggests that God may delay the answer but soon it will come, in the meantime the petitioners are not to faint. This whole section has already been anticipated in ch. 6:10 the souls of those slain upon the earth, and under the altar they cry " How long O Lord holy and true dost thou not judge and avenge our blood on the earthdwellers"? They are praying in heaven as well as on earth, yet unanswered. This section then is worthy of great scrutiny, the situation was so with the early apostolic church and will be the trying experience of believers in the coming Great Tribulation, besides a lesson to all who seek to pray.

THE SECTION AS A WHOLE

Much ground is covered in these four chapters but as can be expected of the book of Revelation, the structure of the material is in a most orderly fashion. The section falls into two main parts of two chapters each.

A. An angel is prominent in the beginning of ch. 8
B. Trumpets, judgments on sea and earth. 8
C. Havoc from the bottomless pit. 9
D. The effect, no repentance of works of hands. 9

The second pair of chapters follow the same order.

A. An angel is prominent in ch. 10
B. One foot on the sea the other on the earth. 10
C. The witnesses killed by the one from bottomless pit. 11
D. The reward for the works of the saints and prophets. 11

As can be seen the two pairs of chapters are a repetition of ideas that cover the working out of the councils of God, and with this the dear suffering believers must wait until the time comes. The exercise of patience is therefore the great lesson.

THE ANGEL AND THE INCENSE ALTAR 8:2-5

The "incense altar" from the Tabernacle is taken up by the Spirit to introduce this third section of the Revelation. The altar would speak of intercession and the incense of prayer.

This is the first word of consolation to the praying believers, the fact that heaven is aware of their prayers (Verse 3-4) and that all is really not in vain. The incense was given to the angel and it in turn was added to the prayers of all the saints.

The angel before the altar is interpreted by many as being Christ Himself, this may be so but is most unlikely, as already stated there are four great symbolic pictures of our Lord in this book of Revelation, to make this angel, or the one in chapter 10 to be the Lord would upset the pattern as indicated earlier in the book.

Again, the description of the angel suggests an angel indeed, but of a very high order; consider as follows:-

1) The incense was given to this angel, the Lord is incense in Himself, the sweet fragrance of the Son of Man, nothing can be added to His perfections.

2) This is an "another" angel, that is, of the same kind as those of verse 2. As often pointed out, there are two Greek words used often that are translated "another" in our Authorised Version. One means another of the same kind, (Allos) the other word means another of a different kind (Heteros) the first word (Allos) is used here which puts this angel in the same category as the seven of verse 2. To make this angel to be the Lord it would then be consistent to make the seven angels of verse 2 also the Lord !

3) This angel is before the throne, the Lord as the Lamb is in the midst of the throne. The angel here is acting as a servant to the Lord and to the saints, and besides, angels know how to worship in 5:11-12. Angels are often the go-between God and men as in the case of the law and even of this book of Revelation in the very first verse.

4) The ALTAR actually is a type of the Lord as the Great High Priest and must be taken as such here, again the incense that was given to

the angel is no doubt the intercession of Christ Himself and to this is added the prayers of the saints on the earth.

5) It might be profitable to know that when Christ is presented in the Revelation there is no doubt as to His identity even though the description may be in symbolic form such as in chapters 1, 5, 12 and 19.

The thought behind this passage is not so much as to whether the angel is Christ or no, but rather that all prayers of the saints are known and considered in heaven.

THE SEVEN TRUMPET JUDGMENTS

Why are these judgments seen in the form of seven trumpets ? As stated earlier in these writings, there seems to always be an Old Testament background to each passage, so where does one read of seven trumpets in the O.T. ? The answer is in Joshua 6 where seven priests blowing seven trumpets are seen walking around the city of Jericho before the fall thereof. Again, they circled the city seven days, and on the seventh day they circled the city seven times. Seven is therefore prominent in that chapter. What is it all about ?

Two reasons are before God in all this. The first, God will judge Jericho, the judgment is sure and the seven days is the respite between. The second thing is that the Lord would teach His people to learn patience, so the circling day by day and nothing happening would teach them to wait God's time. They were not to know all that God had in mind, their's was to obey and to wait. The enemy must have thought them foolish and failures as each day was the same, the walking around to no effect. However, the judgment came at last, and was sure and complete. A curse was laid upon the ruins that if any would seek to build again it would be to death in his family. So it was in the days of Jezebel and Ahab, Hiel the Beth-elite laid the foundation with the death of his first-born and set up the gates with the death of his youngest son Sequb (1 Kings 16:34).

How fitting all this is in this passage, the people are praying, heaven is silent, but the trumpets teach that in the first place the enemy shall be judged and destroyed. On the other hand the people must learn to wait, to be patient as those who encircled Jericho in that far off day.

Again in the case of Jericho, the Lord granted victory at their weakest point. The seventh day they walked round the city seven times, their energy was about gone, they must have been very weary, then came the crash of Jericho. So in this case, the saints in their suffering are weary, but then amidst such weakness the Lord answers prayer, victory belongs to the Lord and His people.

WORLD PUNISHED FOR THE CROSS OF CALVARY

These seven trumpet judgments are in a very special order, and contain a significant message to this guilty world that crucified our Lord.

1) Trees were the first to suffer with the sounding of the first trumpet, one is reminded that the blessed Lord was crucified upon a tree (1 Pet. 2:24). The cross was from a tree of course, and "cursed is everyone that hangeth upon a tree" (Gal. 3:13). This is a reminder to the world that heaven remembers and avenges that terrible miscarriage of justice.

2) With the second sounding the sea being turned to blood is another reminder of Calvary. The shedding of the innocent blood of the Lord Jesus, God made Him to be sin for us, nevertheless the world is guilty of His death, the shedding of His blood.

3) The sounding of the third trumpet brings into action a star called "Wormwood", waters are made bitter, the result of this would be terrible thirst. Our blessed Lord experienced thirst on the cross, in fact one of those heart rending cries from the cross was "I thirst". Again as with the others, Calvary with all its suffering is recalled.

4) The sun is affected with the forth trumpet. How appropriate, the sun was darkened at Calvary when the sinless One was made sin for us. Here the sun as well as the moon and stars are darkened by a third, men love darkness rather than light, so darkness is their portion.

5) Dreadful pain is the feature of the sounding of the fifth trumpet. The terrible horde of demons that torment men by inflicting such pain upon mankind. "And in those days men shall seek death and shall not find it, and shall desire to die and death shall flee from them" (9:6). The Lord suffered terrible pain from the hands of men upon the cross, Peter in his first epistle speaks of the suffering of Christ

many times. The righteous retribution of God will catch up with the world of Christ rejectors.

6) The sixth trumpet brings forth death, the 200 million horsemen from across the river Euphrates administer death on an impressive scale. The third part of men are killed by the fire and by smoke and by brimstone which issued out of their mouths (9:18). One must solemnly remember that the Lord passed through death, and to Him death was really death, God's just judgment upon sin.

7) The seventh angel sounding the trumpet brings to a conclusion the purposes of God for Israel. The enemies are all judged, this subject is later taken up in Revelation 19-20, and the Lord shall reign upon the earth, Israel shall enter into their inheritance. The prophets and the saints of a bygone day shall at last inherit all things (11:18). This is the grand outcome of the cross of Christ, without this the wondrous counsels of God would be frustrated, but Christ has died and secured all things.

Also note there is an earthquake with the sounding of the 7th trumpet, and when the Lord died upon the cross there was an earthquake according to Matt. 27:51-4.

THE MESSAGE OF THE TRUMPETS

No doubt these trumpets are prophetic, and shall be fulfilled in deserving judgments upon the world in a day to come. However, at the same time there is a message for the praying people of God. First, their prayers are heard in heaven as indicated by the incense altar. Here is another point they should observe, the Lord is working according to a plan, this will come to fruition in the last days. The nations must be dealt with, and in a way that shall bring home to them their guilt in the crucifixion of the Son of Man. As noted, these trumpet judgments are in a series that have attachments to Calvary. The great sin of the world in the rejection of Christ shall surely find them out.

THE ANGEL WITH THE LITTLE BOOK

Here is the third great consolation concerning the problem of the silence of God to the cries of His people. The angel and the little book.

Now again, the problem arises as to the identity of the angel, is he Christ ? This more or less has been dealt with at the beginning of this chapter, but a little more must be said of the angel here.

Because his face shone as the sun does not necessarily make him the Lord, the face of Moses shone, the righteous shall shine as the sun in the kingdom of their Father in Matt. 13:43. Again, this angel swears by Him that liveth for ever and ever, and acknowledges the creative power of God. Christ being God could only swear by Himself as Heb. 6:13, there is none greater. The angel here is swearing by one greater than himself, so this therefore could not be the Christ.

The same point arises as with the angel of chapter 8, that is, he is an angel of the SAME KIND, this is as "another horse" in 6:4, and used 5 times in chapter 14 of a series of angels, each introduced by "another angel".

THE MESSAGE OF THE ANGEL

The subject must be kept in mind that these chapters contain a message to hearten believers who in trouble are praying and there seems to be no answer from God. This is the third great consolation that emerges, consider the message that is contained in this vision.

The whole description is symbolic, each detail has a deep meaning to Israel and to all that will suffer in the coming Tribulation.

1) The angel clothed with a cloud would suggest the cloud that dwelt upon the Tabernacle and that went before Israel in the wilderness journey. The faithfulness of God is here, He will not forsake His beloved people.
2) The legs as pillars of fire carries the same suggestion, the cloud by day but the pillar of fire by night. This would convey that by day or by night the Lord is with His people although at times He seems to be silent to their crying.
3) The face like the sun would speak of the coming kingdom, this is sure, nothing can frustrate the purpose of God that His people should reign with Christ.
4) The rainbow again would indicate the faithfulness of God, this is the way the rainbow is used in Gen. 9:13 to Noah. God is a faithful creator, and will be faithful to every covenant including that made with Israel.

5) The angel placing one foot on the sea and the other on the land denotes that the reign of our Lord shall be from shore to shore, from the river to the ends of the earth.

6) Seven thunders utter their voices and John was about to write these things. However, he was told not to do so. The implication of this is really simple, when believers suffer and they seek God in the matter seemingly in vain, there is much that they cannot understand, the ways of God are mysterious, not till the Judgment Seat of Christ shall be revealed the "reason why".

7) The little book seems to be prophecy as in verse 11. Of course this is the grand subject, God is fulfilling His eternal counsels and in the course of these the lot of many believers is to suffer. So with John the eating of the book would speak of experience, the tasting of the things of God experientially. The book was sweet in the mouth, how interesting to consider prophecy, it evaluates the mind and heart of the inquirer. The swallowing of the book was another thing, bitterness is the real portion of those who live when the prophecies are being fulfilled, and that seems to be the message here in the little book. Prophecy cannot fail, all must be fulfilled, but prophecy entails much suffering to those faithful to God and His Word at the time.

8) The most encouraging thing of all is the words which the angel spoke in verses 6-7, "That there should be delay no longer". Then the time of waiting shall come to an end, the silence was for half an hour in heaven, and came to an end. Eventually God moves when His time is ripe, prophecy shall be fulfilled and the prayers of the saints shall all be answered. This is presented more fully in the next chapter.

"The mystery of God shall be finished as He hath declared to His servants the prophets". The mystery here would seem to be that of which Paul spoke in Romans 11:25 the blindness in part that has happened unto Israel. God is working with all nations but especially with the nation of Israel, they have promises, covenants etc. and to all these God will remain faithful, hence the rainbow. It is interesting to note that Rom. 11:25 goes on to speak of the "fullness of the Gentiles coming in", and that has already been seen in Revelation 7. There the Gentiles are brought into blessing and in this chapter the Lord then takes up the mystery of the blindness to Israel until the time of restitution. Presently this mystery is in operation, Israel remains in unbelief, the Gentiles are coming into salvation through the gospel.

THE TWO WITNESSES OF CHAPTER 11

The contents of chapter 10 is for Israel, whereas that of chapter 11 is for the world, it is never left without a witness.

Who are these witnesses? Some identify them as being the 144000 that are mentioned in chapter 7 and 14. This is most unlikely, as they are similar in character and works to two individuals in the O.T. that is Moses and Elijah, so these must again be individuals. Bedsides, the 144000 are preserved through the tribulation whereas these are slain, and resurrected and are caught up to heaven (11:11-12). While they have the characteristics of Moses and Elijah that does not mean that they are that Moses and Elijah, perhaps one of them is the promised one who would come in the spirit and power of Elijah.

When do they prophesy ? Again there is a great difference of opinion as to whether the first half of the seventh week of Dan. 9 or the second is in mind. It is most likely the second, the tribulation period, and the world is not left without a witness in the greatest time of deception. They are killed by the Beast, and it seems to be in the duration of his diabolical season of terror, the Great Tribulation.

How do these fit into the pattern of this section on the silence of God ? This also along with the altar, trumpets and the angel with the little book is a source of encouragement to the suffering and praying believers in the time of trouble.

1) They ministered in a time of extreme weakness. Just as Moses when it may be said the people stood with their back to the wall, yet the evil Pharaoh and his followers perished. Also in the days of Elijah the terrible rebellion and departure of Israel was in full swing, Elijah stood up for God and was gloriously vindicated. In both cases the enemy was overcome. Israel in the last days shall face a greater than Pharaoh, and in the nation itself a greater departure than in the days of Ahab, yet the Lord shall as in the past sort all things out. He is able to bring order and stability out of confusion.

2) In spite of the enemy, there must be a witness, that is the meaning of the word "martyr" one who is a witness even unto death. While it is

true that God will judge the world, yet the mercy of the Lord is seen in giving space for repentance as with the trumpet judgments in 9:20-21. These two servants are the greatest of men, endued with power from God to witness right in the enemies' camp concerning grace and impending judgment.

3) There is as usual an Old Testament background. "These are the two olive trees and the two lampstands standing before the God of all the earth" (11:4). Joshua and Zerubbabel are called these in Zech. 4, and the idea is that they are nurtured from above for the great task committed into their hands. So with these witnesses, power is available either to witness or to suffer. "I will give power unto my two witnesses" (verse 3). "These have power to shut the heaven that it rain not" (verse 6).

4) Again, how encouraging to read, "When they shall have finished their testimony" (verse 7). The suffering ones shall not be killed before their time, the question of life and death is in the hands of God and not men. All can be faithful unto death as the church of Smyrna was exhorted by the Lord.

5) The four kinds of miracles referred to in verses 5-6 are interesting. The fire to consume and the shutting of the heaven that it rain not are reminiscent of Elijah. He was faced with religious opposition in Jezebel who worshipped Baal, and to a lesser extent the political opposition of Ahab. The turning of the waters to blood and the earth smitten with all plagues are a throwback to Moses. He faced chiefly political opposition in Pharaoh, and to a lesser degree from the religious magicians in Egypt.

The fire was to consume the falsehood and mockery as seen with Elijah in 2 Kings 1. The lack of rain was a sign of the displeasure of God with His broken laws. Apostate Israel is in mind here as in the days of Elijah.

The water changed to blood and the plagues are upon the earth, which is the seat of that which is political, and would suggest the kingdom of the beast. In the Tribulation both political and religious powers are against the believers, but they shall be overcomers.

6) The city Jerusalem here is called Sodom and Egypt. It is called the "Holy City" in Matt. 4:5 because the Lord was there, and again in Matt. 27:53 because the resurrected saints went into it. On the contrary, here it is called Sodom which speaks of corruption and Egypt

which would suggest violence, both were present in the earth leading up to the flood in Gen. 6:11-12. The same will characterize the reign of the beast in the last days.

7) The three woes are enlightening, these speak of the most ferocious of the judgments of God. The first seems to be the release of many demons in 9:1-12. The ministry of the two witnesses seems to be the second woe according to 11:14, and the third woe will be the coming of the Son of Man in judgment as hinted at in v 17-18. The ministry therefore of the witnesses is very severe to the world. At least, the praying saints are delivered from these.

8) Finally, the witnesses are so like their Lord. They as He ministered with miracles, these of judgment whereas the Lord's works were with grace. Like Him, they will be killed and resurrected, and like Him they shall be caught up to heaven. The world was guilty in the time of the rejection of the Lord, and will be just as guilty in the final days of this old world. Mankind has not changed, all is just the same.

THE FINAL PASSAGE, 11:15-18

Here at last the prayers of the saints are answered. The Lord begins His wonderful reign, and how beautifully the material is written here.

(1) The announcement of the coming reign v 15
(2) The extent of His reign, all the kingdoms of this world
(3) His right to reign because of who He is, the Almighty etc.
(4) The power to take the kingdom and to reign 17
(5) The result of His beginning to reign. This is twofold

To the nations a curse, there is anger instead of humility and repentance, they destroyed the earth and they in turn shall be destroyed.

To Israel comes the blessing. That Israel is intended is evident by the reference to the servants, the prophets, they entered into death, and here experience resurrection. This seems to be the resurrection of the Old Testament saints, they are not included in the rapture of the church. There the dead in Christ are raised, this is Ephesian truth, "In Christ", Old Testament saints are in the Lord but not in Christ, the body.

They that fear His name both small and great would be the living saints who shall have endured the Great Tribulation, similar companies appear in Rev. 20:4-5.

IN CONCLUSION

The prayers of the saints are answered, but the encouragement is contained in this section 7-11 to be patient and to wait God's time.

(1) The altar teaches that their prayer are before God, all is heard.
(2) The Lord however has a work of judgment to complete as seen in the trumpets.
(3) The angel and the book teaches that the counsels of the Lord stand, and all shall eventually be fulfilled, God cannot be hindered.
(4) The witnesses to the world are a testimony and a reminder to the world that God hates sin.
(5) The Lord shall soon come and judge the enemy, and Israel shall enter into the promised inheritance.

Verse 18 ends this section, verse 19 belongs to the next.

CHAPTER TWENTY-SIX

A Practical View of ch. 7-11

A s with the last section, so with this, an ethical examination of it is bound to reap relevant blessing.

There is much food for thought in a practical application to these chapters, for instance, the exercise of prayer as in ch. 8. The danger of deception can be seen in the trumpets, and over against this would be the TRUTH in the "book in the hand of the angel" of ch. 10. The grand subject of witness appears in ch. 11 and the wonderful incentive of reward that concludes the section.

The structure of the four chapters in pairs must again be brought forward.

A. An angel, prayer and the trumpet judgments cover 8-9.

B. An angel, the Book and the witness judgments cover 10-11.

The first part ends with idolatry in (9:20) and the last part ends with those who fear the Name of the Lord (11:18). This section indeed lends itself to practical application.

THE GREAT SUBJECT OF PRAYER

1) Silence does not mean that God has not heard or that He does not consider, the period of silence was ended in half an hour. To

burdened praying people on earth time may be long, delay may seem to go on forever, but to heaven the time really is short. One thousand years is as one day with the Lord in 2 Peter 5:8. When people are suffering pain and affliction, a short time seems to be very long indeed. The happy thought at the beginning of this passage, is that the time of silence is bound to come to an end, God manifests Himself in His own time.

2) Note also that the prayers of the saints here are seen as collective. The praying people may not necessary gather together, but the praying of many individuals even apart, for the same thing is seen as one. It brings to mind the words of the Lord concerning prayer "If two of you shall agree on earth as touching anything that they shall ask, it shall be done for them of my Father which is in heaven" (Matt. 18:19). They may not gather to pray, but wherever they are, they pray for the same thing, united prayer is very successful. The prayers of the saints here are heard.

3) The need was so great that there was no such a thing as a "non praying saint" upon the earth. Verse 3 speaks of the prayers of ALL the saints, the burden at the time was so great that prayer was the only source of strength and hope.

4) The much incense that was added cannot be the prayers of the believers, these are mentioned apart. The incense can only be the intercession of Christ Himself, and would likely also include the intercession by the Spirt of God as in Rom. 8:26. Note that it is MUCH incense that was added in verse 3. How much the Lord engages for His people one cannot really envisage, His love and concern for suffering saints, and all saints can be seen in this short reference.

5) All ascends up before God in verse 4. We know from other references in Scripture that the Lord as High Priest sifts the prayers of His people and takes away the dross and then presents that which is of Himself to God. The golden plate on the mitre of the priest comes to mind in this, "It shall be upon Aaron's forehead that Aaron may bear the iniquity of the holy things which the children of Israel shall hallow in all their holy gifts ... that they may be accepted before the Lord" (Exod. 28:38).

6) The angel added the incense but he did not offer it, (Revised Version) as seen earlier in these writings, the angel is not the Lord, rather the Lord is seen in the "Incense Altar", one of the holy vessels in the

Tabernacle that speaks of Christ Himself as our Great High Priest. As that altar was a cubit square it would speak of the universal interest and intercession of the Lord for His people, hence we read here of All the saints.

This passage would encourage to pray as similarly the Lord's exhortation in Luke 18:1 that men ought always to pray and not to faint.

THE TRUMPET JUDGMENTS

These are judgments indeed and must be taken as literal, after all the plagues of Egypt were literal of which these passages are parallel. The trumpets are similar to the bowl judgments which are called the "last plagues of the wrath of God" and they are literal for they are called plagues. The fact that in the fifth trumpet judgment they were to hurt not any green thing or the tree teaches that the judgment upon the trees for the time being was finished, and that the judgment then was upon the bodies of people.

But why such details in these judgments ? Another question, why the plagues of Egypt ? The answer to the second question becomes the answer to the first. It is distinctly told that the plagues on Egypt were a judgment upon the gods of Egypt. "Against all the gods of Egypt I will execute judgment, I am the Lord" (Exod. 12:12). An example of this would be the darkening of the sun, because the people worshipped the sun as a god. The same axiom is seen with the trumpet judgments, "And the rest of the men who were not killed by these plagues yet repented not of the works of their hands that they should not worship devils and idols of gold, and silver, and brass and stone, and of wood, which neither can see, nor hear nor walk" (Rev. 9:20). Verse 21 is the result of the idolatry, murders, there will be no fear of the government of God. Sorceress would indicate the refusal to seek after God, fornication is the rejection of the moral laws of God, and theft is the rejection of the law of God concerning the rights of man. Man without God is first deceived into worshipping that which is not God, and the moral breakdown surely follows. Consider the trumpets in this light.

The first trumpet brought forth a judgment upon the trees. Now trees are used extensively in the making of idols as in Isa. 40:20, "He ... chooseth a tree that will not rot: he seeketh unto him a cunning workman to prepare a graven image". In perhaps a lesser way today there are many who put a greater value upon the countryside than on the living God Himself.

The second judgment is upon the sea and all the commerce that the sea and ships would speak of. We live in the greatest business times of all, many people are married to their career or business, in plain words, they have made idols of them allowing them to consume their life and shut out God. Such a warning to the people of God, He must have priority in our lives and all the rest is to be accepted as gifts that are to be received with thanksgiving and not idolized in the heart.

The rivers and waters are next affected. Water is essential to life, Egypt depended upon the river for its wellbeing, therefore it speaks of the necessities of life. However, again these things can so occupy the heart, either the lack thereof, or the hording for future use, and God is again left out. The Lord gave a warning about this in Matt. 6:25 stating that there should be no anxiety concerning what one should eat, drink and wear, rather there should be trust in God and laying up of treasure in heaven.

The fourth judgment is upon the sun, moon and stars. Men love darkness rather than light, the dark deeds of the flesh are idolized in this generation. But in another way, a lot of idolatry today is linked to the sun and stars, the sunshine is cheerful, but again, use it to the blessing of the body and not to excess.

The demons are let loose with the fifth trumpet. Note that the green grass is not to be hurt this time, God values creation but not to the extent that it should be worshipped. There is a terrible movement towards demonology in this day, and along with the demon comes idolatry as taught in 1 Cor. 8.

Note the perversion that is suggested by the sounding of the fifth trumpet, the setting aside of the truths of God by the perversion of those truths.

a) A descent and a resurrection is hinted at in 9:2 and is in direct contrast to our Lord in Eph. 4. He has descended into the lower parts of the earth and has ascended above all things, here it is a fall; no doubt because of pride and the pit, another counterfeit of Satan appears in this fifth judgment.

b) The darkness of verse 2 is in contrast to the light of revelation, and of Him who is the Light of the world. Light features in the holy city of chapter 21.

c) The locusts appear as horses, perversion again, to call evil good and good evil.

d) These creatures had faces as men but hair as a woman in verse 7-8. Again the perversion comes out, the setting aside of headship as clearly taught in the Scriptures of truth.

e) The teeth as lions would again be another perversion. This would be after the pattern of the beast in chapter 13:2 who has the mouth of a lion. These are parts of a lion, but the blessed Lord appears in the figure of a lion in all His fullness and majesty.

f) The sting is in the tail, the bitterness is at the end. The terrible deception to those who serve sin and the devil, Judas found this out to his awful cost and ended in hanging himself. The pleasures of this world and slavery to idolatry of any kind end with the bitterness of loss, and of banishment from God. The contrast is with the believers in the experience of chastening, at first bitterness and grief, but afterward it yieldeth the peaceable fruit of righteousness in Heb. 12:11.

g) This horde of demons have a leader, a king over them in verse 11, his name being Apollyon which means destroyer. Such a contrast to the Lord whose Name is Jesus because He shall save His people from their sins; sinners saved by grace love that blessed Name.

A LOOK AT THE 200,000,000 HORSEMEN

This is the sixth trumpet judgment, and six being the number of man in the Bible, presents the full glory of man. Such an army and such a description. This will be typical of the armies of the last days who shall engage in the battle of Armageddon etc..

Here the horsemen are described in symbolic language declaring the glory of man which of course leads to his own destruction.

Glory is to the fore, the sheer size of the army and the wonderful things said about them, consider as follows:-

Their breastplates are of fire, jacinth and brimstone, this presents violence on a great scale with the third part of mankind slain.

They have heads as lions, here again the part of a lion but incomplete as seen already, the lion like head would speak of pride and haughtiness as in Isa. 2.

Fire comes out of their mouths, smoke and brimstone, how different from the mouth of the Lord who spoke words of grace, and the mouths of the babes and sucklings who perfect praise to God (Matt.21:16). Contrast also the mouth of the believer in Rom. 15:6 glorifying God. The mouth that at one time was full of cursing and bitterness (Rom. 3:14) after confessing with the mouth the Lord Jesus as in Rom. 10:9 then begins to praise God.

Again the believer carries a message that saves and destroys not, the gospel heals and gives life.

Verses 20-21 are important, what is worshipped in the heart is surely manifested in the life, all comes out in practice.

Murders, taking away the life of man

Sorceries, the deceiving of man's mind

Fornication would be against man's body

Thefts is taking away man's possessions

THE ANGEL AND THE BOOK OF CH. 10

This is a mighty, a strong angel, yet he handles a little book, how often great men are called upon to handle little things, however those apparent little things are often great in the sight of God. On the other hand, how often the servants of God weak and insignificant in themselves, are called upon to handle the great things of God. Such is the case with the knowledge of God in the gospel in 2 Cor. 4:7 "We have this treasure in earthen vessels that the exceeding greatness of the power may be of God and not of us".

Perhaps four dispensations are hinted at in the fourfold description of the angel here. The rainbow is suggestive of Human Government as in the days of Noah when the bow was first seen. The cloud is Israel in the wilderness and at that time the Law was given. The face as the sun is in keeping with this time of grace when the glory is seen in the face of Jesus Christ as in 2 Cor. 3:18. The legs as pillars of fire could perhaps be applied to the setting up of the Millennium, when the Lord shall trample all His enemies beneath His feet. It is good to take notice of the dealings of God with mankind at different times.

The angel in Dan. 10 had eyes as fire, and feet like fine brass, howbeit he was just an angel as here. These wonderful created beings take their character from their Lord.

This description of the angel forms a great contrast with the demons of chapter 9. His face described "as the sun" is in contrast to the perversion of faces of men with women's hair. The clothing with the cloud which speaks of the glory of God, as opposed to the breastplates of IRON which generally betoken evil in Scripture.

THE LITTLE BOOK

The book was little, or small in the eyes of man, it was just like the Manna. The Manna was small upon the ground, denoting man's inadequate view of the great heavenly movement of the eternal Lord Jesus in coming into the earth.

The book was open, not sealed as in Dan. 12:4, the time will come when the remnant in the Tribulation will fully understand the prophetic writings as in Matt. 24:15 where the Lord said "Whoso readeth let him understand".

Again, the sealing of verse 4 of this passage could be towards the world, the natural man cannot understand the things of the Spirit. The thunders were heard publicly but the meaning was hidden from the world as with the voice from heaven in John 12, the Lord heard the voice while others heard thunder.

The book was given to John and he was given instruction to eat it. In his mouth it was sweet as honey but in his stomach it was bitter. How practical, the great joy of looking into the Prophetic Word, but when one is involved in the fulfilling of the prophecy then bitterness can be the experience. In fact, any part of the Word which a believer makes part of himself in the working out thereof shall bring forth bitterness from some direction. It is still the same, the godly in Christ Jesus shall always suffer persecution (2 Tim. 3:12).

The encouragement is there however in the command "Thou must prophesy again", to get the Word in, is necessary to use the opportunity to pass it on to others, such an exhortation is given to Timothy in 2 Tim. 2:2. Great lessons appear in all this. The open book is before all believers, great in our eyes, one must eat of it to the joy of the soul, the living out will be bitter but not without its joy in suffering for Christ, and it can all be passed on to others with power.

THE ANGEL AGAIN

Before leaving this chapter a few further remarks must be made in a practical way concerning the angel.

1) "He spake with a loud voice as when a lion roareth" (verse 3)
   The Lord Jesus is seen as the Lion of Judah in ch. 5 this angel takes his character from his Lord.
2) His absolute loyalty to the Lord comes out, he seeks the glory of Christ, and heralds with joy the kingdoms and dominion given unto Him.
3) The foot upon the sea and the other on the earth would indicate that the reign of the Lord will be from shore to shore, and to the ends of the earth. Angels shall ascend and descend upon the Son of Man (John 1:51).
4) He swears by Him that liveth for ever. His allegiance to the Eternal One. His oath is most instructive and can be seen in a threefold way. The fact that the Lord is eternal, and in power He is the source of all things created in heaven, earth, and under the earth, and His wisdom comes out in the statement, "There shall be delay no longer". All is planned, and nothing can frustrate the plan, the eternal counsel shall surely stand.
5) The mystery of God, as seen earlier relates to Israel, the blindness now of that nation will continue until the fullness of the Gentiles comes in.

In summing up, the rainbow would depict the faithfulness of God, and the cloud the eternal glory of God. The sun would indicate the righteous reign of the Lord Jesus and the legs as pillars of fire would set forth His power, the power of a man is in his legs as written in Ps. 147:10.

This chapter to Israel and to all that read, makes clear that God will reign supreme, and anyone who is on the Lord's side is on the winning side.

THE TWO WITNESSES OF CHAPTER 11

Practical points arise in this chapter.

1. Service and its principles seen in the witnesses 1-7
2. Opposition and its outcome 8-10
3. Vindication and its glory 11-18

First consider the lessons in service that lies on the surface of this chapter. Many are so taken up with seeking to interpret who and when these two men minister that the practical side is overlooked. One can surely take character from two of the greatest servants that shall appear in the last days. These serve in the most difficult time of all, faced with the greatest powers of opposition that ever servants of God encountered. Their service was also of a "condemning nature" in order that when the Lord eventually judges, all would be left without excuse. Consider a few salient lessons from their ministry.

THE MINISTRY OF THE WITNESSES

1) They were able to work with each other. It is good when servants of the Lord can work with other fellowservants. This is evident with the return from exile of Israel, Nehemiah worked with an Ezra and so on, sometimes not together but they complemented each others work. Paul mentions so many of his companions who were fellow-labourers, and fellow- prisoners in many of his epistles. In this light consider Col. 4 and Rom. 16, the latter has often been described as a list of Paul's mighty men. True, a servant of God is sometimes a loner as Elijah, Philip and Apollos, but this is not the normal in Christian service.

2) These were men of power, and that power did not come from themselves. They have power to shut the heavens that it rain not, and to smite the earth with plagues (Verse 6). They had power with heaven and earth. It is made clear that this power comes from God and not themselves in verse 3. Moses and Elijah both had this character that they thought little of themselves, Moses was the meekest man in all the earth, and Elijah was so afraid of Jezebel that he wanted the Lord to take him home.
Again, the power was ever present, neither temporary nor occasional, they were able to smite the earth with plagues as often as they would in verse 6.

3) They were clothed in sackcloth, they were sober and serious in their ministry. Sackcloth of course was the sign of mourning, and they therefore had a burden in the message they preached and in the miracles of judgment they performed. They no doubt had a compassion for the people who were unrepentant and perishing. Servants of this calibre would be desirable in these days, servants who really believe what they preach, and do so with great compassion; men with a burden as the prophets of old.

4) The service was rendered in fellowship with God and the Spirit. The olive trees in verse 4 would imply this. The background to this is the passage in Zech. 4, the golden lampstand and the supply of oil by way of golden pipes from the olive trees. No doubt, among other things this speaks of the supply of the Spirit to Joshua and Zerubbabel for the task before them. The same principle applies here; men of the Spirit indeed.

5) These are protected by God until their ministry is finished. No matter how strong the enemy, God is all prevailing, His purpose will be accomplished in the servant He has raised up.

6) There is a contrast today with the minister of the New Covenant, he avenges not himself as these witnesses do. Consider the submissive words of the apostle in 1 Cor. 4. "Even unto this present hour we both hunger and thirst and are naked and are buffeted, and have no certain dwelling place. And labour working with our hands, being reviled we bless, being persecuted we suffer it. Being defamed we entreat: we are made as the filth of the world and are offscouring of all things unto this day". The witnesses in the last days can judge those who hurt them, the minister of the gospel today endures all things. The reason for this difference is the times, today God is dealing in grace, but with the witnesses the time of judgment will have commenced.

7) They had power over waters, to stop rain and to turn water to blood. These miracles are reminiscent of Elijah and Moses, in both cases the miracles of judgment were signs as well as an effort to bring about repentance. These as all servants, work toward a transformation in those who hear.

8) The witnesses finish their course. Paul had this before him in 2 Tim. 4, and also in the sermon he preached in the synagogue at Antioch. He spoke of John the Baptist fulfilling his course, and David like-

wise with the words "he served his own generation". However of king Saul he remarks, "God removed him" as if to say this disobedient man did not finish his course (Acts 13).

9) One final point, these servants are vindicated, after being killed they rise again before all their enemies. They are caught up to heaven, as already remarked, just like their Lord before them. Paul speaks in this way of the vindication of the servant when the Corinthians had so bitterly criticised him. "Judge nothing before the time until the Lord come, who both will bring to light the hidden things of darkness and make manifest the counsels of the heart, then shall every man have praise from God" (1 Cor. 4:5).

No doubt any servant of God in any dispensation could well study with profit the ministry of the two witnesses of this great chapter.

A FEW FINAL COMMENTS AT THE END

Here is the bringing in of the answer to the praying people as already elucidated, but a few encouraging features must be briefly considered in closing this chapter.

All will be headed up in Christ (Verse 15) the Lord shall enter into His inheritance and the purpose of God to commit all into His hand will come to pass. In this way the righteous rule of verse 17 will come forward.

The thought of this provokes worship from the elders and the living creatures in verse 16. Truly, the meditation of the glorious station that belongs to our Lord, and the place He will righteously receive produces worship in the heart of the devoted believer.

The time of reward shall surely come as in verse 18. A few remarks about this reward would be reassuring.

First, the well gifted in the prophets and the lesser in the saints will both have rewards before God. Again, the word "saints" is the result of conversion, whereas the "prophet" is the outcome of the call of God to service.

Second, those that fear the Name of the Lord will not be forgotten. Perhaps they had not much in the way of service to offer, but they feared and revered the Name of the Lord. This is worthy of great reward in the sight of God.

Finally, the small and great are mentioned. There will be no respect of persons with God, faithfulness counts perhaps more than the degree of the calling and gift. Note that the small comes first here, so like our God to encourage the weak.   The small and great occur often in Scripture,and are worthy of serious study.

Verse 19 really belongs to the next section, chapters 12-14.

CHAPTER TWENTY-SEVEN

The Manchild and the Dragon

The key to the understanding of the Revelation is in the seven distinct sections, and the chapters now approached form the centre of these. Each of the sections deal with a problem encountered by a persecuted people, and each commences in some way with a reference to the Tabernacle in the wilderness. This same formula is followed in this section, but a difference arises that makes it stand out from the others. The first three parts up to chapter 12 run in a parallel order to the three parts after ch. 14 which make chapters 12-14 the middle part, and distinct as having no other parallels in the book. This point alone apart from the significant material makes this section prominent, and no doubt the most important of the seven.

However this distinction does not make this section a parenthesis, rather it is part of the unfolding plan of the book, and is essential to complete the message the book contains.

The last verse of ch. 11 really belongs to this section, (11:19) and as usual with a new part, commences with a Tabernacle reference, namely, the ark of the covenant. What does this signify, and what is the whole section about ? As with the other sections so here, a definite theme runs through the three chapters. Note the following subjects:-

1) A great space of time is covered. The fall of Satan and many angels are seen in the dragon casting stars to earth with its tail, this goes

back to the beginning of time. The final reign of the Son of Man brings the material forward to the Millennium preceded by many judgments. With this in mind, whatever God would bring to the fore is something that has marked all time.

2) Many personages appear in the section
The woman clothed with the sun
The Manchild who is to rule the nations
The dragon with the heads and horns
The archangel Michael who is victorious
The beast coming up out of the sea
The beast coming up out of the earth
The 144000 again, standing on Mount Sion
The Son of Man on the white cloud
Besides the fallen angels of chapter 12:4 and the loyal angels of 12:7.
All these personages are mighty in power and authority.

3) However, the manchild appears at the beginning of chapter 12 and the Son of Man closes chapter 14. There is little doubt that both of these can be identified with Christ. He is the manchild produced by the woman, and He is the Son of Man at His return, Christ is all, and all the promises of God, in Him are yea and Amen.

4) It is important to see that there are two opposing sides. One side would be those who are for God, the woman, the manchild Michael, the good angels and the 144000, these are all on the Lord's side. The enemies comprise the Dragon, beast, false prophet and the fallen angels. This is the age long struggle of good and evil, light and darkness. Perhaps they could be arranged on opposite sides as follows:-

The woman	The beast
The Manchild	The false Prophet
Michael	The dragon
144000	Fallen angels

5) Can these personages be identified ? The symbolism helps the student of Scripture to do so.

a) The woman can only be Israel. The woman represents many people as in the case of the bride of chapter 19, and the scarlet woman of chapter 17. The woman then is all Israel.
She is clothed with the sun, the glory that belonged to Israel such as is seen in the blessing of Rom. 9:4. "Who are Israelites, to whom

pertaineth the adoption and the glory and the covenants and the giving of the law, and the service of God, and the promises. Whose are the fathers, and of whom concerning the flesh Christ came."

She has a crown upon her head. Israel is destined to reign over the nations of this world some day.

The twelve stars are in keeping with the twelve tribes of Israel, and the dream of Joseph in Gen. 37:9.

She brought forth the manchild who will rule the nations, as already declared in Rom. 9:4-5 Israel produced the Christ.

b) The man child as already stated must be Christ, He alone has the authority to rule the nations with a rod of iron. This has been received of the Father in 2:27, and the reward to the overcomer in that passage is to rule with Him in like manner. The Son of Man in 14:14 is the same person, here 12:5 is destiny, there in 14:14 is fulfilment.

c) The dragon is identified for us in 12:9 and in a fourfold way.

As the devil, he is the accuser of the brethren.

As Satan, he is the adversary against all God's workings.

In the serpent he is seen religiously, the same serpent that beguiled Eve in Eden.

As the dragon, he is seen politically with the heads and crowns.

As such he is behind the political evil that is perpetrated on earth.

d) Michael is the archangel, the chief of the angels. There is only one archangel, thus the very highest of the angels is brought into the conflict.

e) The beast out of the sea is the lie in contrast to the truth of God. It is he that shall eventually sit in the temple and declare that he is God (2 Thess. 2:4). Violence personifies him, he shall be a world leader of the last days, who shall begin successfully in the eyes of man, but shall then begin to destroy. He will be the cause of millions of deaths.

f) The beast out of the earth is also called the false prophet. He therefore will impersonate Christ, and is the one of whom the Lord spoke "One shall come in his own name, and him you shall receive" (John 5:43). This would be the antichrist.

g) The 144000 seem to be the same as in ch. 7 who were sealed of God to be preserved through the Tribulation. Perhaps they shall bear the news of salvation to Jews and Gentiles, and the message of the coming King.

h) The stars of 12:4 can only be angels that fell with the fall of Satan, no other suggestion is feasible.

WHAT IS THIS ALL ABOUT ?

With many of these great personages crowns are mentioned which would suggest kings and kingdoms besides the mention of rule, thrones and so forth. Consider these references:-

1. A crown of twelve stars in 12:1
2. Seven crowns on the dragon's heads 12:3
3. The man child to rule nations 12:5
4. The man child caught up to the throne of God 12:5
5. The kingdom of our God in 12:10
6. The ten horns with ten crowns 13:1
7. The dragon gave him his throne 13:2
8. The Lamb on Mt. Zion, always to do with the king 14:1
9. The Son of Man, a golden crown on His head 14:14

The three chapters evidently have a common subject, that of kings and kingdoms. This has made history in the past, the kings emperors, dictators and national leaders of every sort. This fact will also close earth's history, the kings and kingdoms of the last days. Daniel received a vision of all this in the "metallic image", each metal corresponding to a nation that would seek to destroy Israel. God puts a title upon the whole operation, "The times of the Gentiles". These three chapters have to do with the final phase of the "times of the Gentiles".

However, the chief point is that many great nations in the past and those that shall feature in the final stages are "antichrist", it was always a general pastime to persecute the people of God. Many dear saints found this difficult to understand, and would no doubt ask the question "why has God made the persecuting nations so strong and mighty" ? Why is power on the side of the enemy ? This very problem is dealt with in this central section. The people of God are weak in the eyes of the world, and the powers arrayed against them are so powerful. The strength is with the enemy, as was the case with Egypt, Babylon, Rome and Germany to name a few. .

The consolation to suffering as such is in these chapters, the order is so neat as the material unfolds. God's permission is seen towards the nations, but the inner plan can been seen in His handling of those nations, hence the "ark of the covenant" which is a type of the throne of God.

Chapter 12 is a look behind the enemy lines, the dragon who is Satan in political form is the source of the rising of nations against the Christ and His people (Psalm 2:1-2).

Chapter 13 brings forth the final kingdom that the manoeuvring of Satan will advance, the empire of the beast with ten horns and ten crowns. Alongside him, the religious side is seen in the lamb-like beast, the false prophet. How those nations come to power and the ensuing persecution is the burden of ch. 13.

Nevertheless, all is for but a short time, forty two months.

Chapter 14 brings in the bright side. The mighty nations who trouble the people of God are doomed. The Son of Man shall come, this is the title in which He inherits the earth, and in which He is assigned full control over all nations. On His head is a crown of gold, a victor's crown, glorious as the gold indicates. Judgment and perfect rule are the outcome. These chapters demand a closer look.

BEHIND THE ENEMY LINES IN CHAPTER 12

If anyone desires to study the ways and activities of the powers of darkness, then this chapter must be considered in order to be forewarned.

1) Satan is very active throughout the chapter.
   He is seen casting stars down to earth v 4
   Also seeking to devour the manchild v 4
   He is called the deceiver of the whole world v 9
    Closer still, he is engaged as the accuser v 10
   He makes war in heaven in v 17
   The persecution of the woman depicting Israel comes from him in v 13.
   The flood comes out of his mouth to drown the believers v 15
   Now in all this he appears as the dragon with seven heads and seven crowns which indicates that all this activity savours of the political

scene. Chiefly his opposition is against Christ and the woman Israel, and her seed, believers in v 17.

2) Other titles emerge in verse 9 as God exposes him to all that read. His titles are fourfold here, which would indicate the wide world platform for his activities, in fact it is so stated in the words "which deceiveth the whole world" (verse 9).

He is called the devil and Satan. Devil means "the accuser" and as such he accuses the brethren, note the title "brethren" not the saints which is their relationship to heaven, to such there is no condemnation (Rom. 8:1). Nor of believers in their relation to their faith, but the brethren, suggesting that the interrelation of Christians to each other that gives him the best ground for accusation. The brother in Christ must manifest love to his brother in the faith so as not to allow the devil to get an advantage.

As Satan, which means "the adversary" his opposition is more arrayed against the work of God, the service believers render unto God seeking to promote God's things upon the earth. As the devil he is chiefly against the life and testimony of the believer, and as Satan he attacks the work the believer is seeking to do unto his Lord.

3) He is also called "the old serpent". this would be his religious activity in contrast to the political work as seen in the dragon. It was as the serpent that he beguiled Eve which led to the severing of both Adam and Eve from the communion with God.

He is called the OLD serpent, suggesting he was like this from days of yore, even from the beginning of time. This religious activity Paul refers to in 2 Cor. 11:3 "But I fear lest by any means, as the serpent beguiled Eve through his subtlety, so your minds should be corrupted from the simplicity that is in Christ".

4) However, a closer look at this chapter manifests the weakness of the enemy. In all his works there is much action, which in turn brings much sorrow upon humanity, but his failure runs throughout the entire chapter. Follow the passage again in this light.

a) He failed to cast down all the stars, the greater part continued in their course. No doubt this refers to the fall of angels in the past, but all did not fall: in this book of Revelation many references are made to angels, and sometimes to millions of angels who are all loyal to God.

b) He failed in his intention to devour the man child, He was caught up to the throne of God. This can only be Christ, "she was delivered of a son" (R.V.), true, Christ was the son of Israel being the son of Abraham, He was also the eternal Son of God. Some writers interpret this man child to be the church, this would be contrary to the meaning of the figures presented here, Israel, the woman did not produce the church, and again, the church appears as the bride of Christ, not as a man child or a son. Also it must be taken into consideration that Satan is seen as the dragon waiting to devour the man child because He is destined to rule. To the church he would have appeared as the old serpent as in 2 Cor. 11:3, and not as the political dragon. However, the dragon fails, the man child will one day rule the nations with inflexible judgment, the rod of iron.

c) He deceives the whole world, but he cannot deceive the elect, they shall prevail and will refuse the lie, they shall be willing even to die for the truth. The great number of saved people in chapter 7 were not deceived, or the 144000 which are only the firstfruits of the great harvest of souls (14:4).

d) Satan as the devil accuses the brethren, but who can lay any charge to God's elect ? Christ has died, His blood has brought about reconciliation, and peace is made. Romans 8 is the great passage to do with this assurance, none can accuse, the perfect work of our Lord Jesus for the sinner who believes, closes the mouth of all accusers.

e) The war in heaven also ends with failure and defeat. The dragon is cast out of heaven knowing he has but a short time (verse 12). The bitterness of final defeat is known to Satan and to the demons that follow him, they cry "Art thou come hither to torment us before the time" (Matt. 8:29). Paul was aware of the defeat of darkness in Rom. 16:20, "The God of peace shall bruise Satan under your feet shortly".

f) The persecution of the woman in verse 13 also fails in its mission. The woman being Israel in the last terrible days escapes, the two wings of a great eagle which carry her into the wilderness are figurative of the all preserving power of God. While it is true that many of Israel shall be slain, yet the attempt to wholly wipe out that nation fails, the woman is preserved. All this is a throwback to Exodus, Pharaoh tried to wipe out the nation of Israel, they escaped into the wilderness, and God speaks of carrying them on eagles' wings in Ex. 19:4. History will repeat itself.

g) Even the flood issuing from the mouth of the dragon fails in its intention, the earth, meaning other nations, helped the woman. The flood of God succeeds in its purpose in Gen. 6:8 but the flood of the dragon utterly fails.

h) Finally, the war against the seed of the woman is also lost in verse 17, they still exercise obedience to the commandments of God, faith in the Lord Jesus, and continue in testimony unto Him. The seed could perhaps be the spiritual children of the woman Israel, namely, those of the Gentiles who believe the testimony and who will become followers of Christ and the kingdom. The persecuted Jews are figured in the woman, and the seed could identify Gentile believers.

The tremendous passage of time as already noted at the beginning of this chapter, needs further explanation. The opening verses go back to the fall of Satan and many angels with him. The verses also cover the call of Israel and its destiny to rule one day as seen in the woman. The time then swings forward to the birth and ascension of Christ, and on to the end times, the great subject of prophecy from 6-17. The devil from the beginning of time unto the end appears as the enemy of God, and His people. So this instructive chapter covers much time, and also exposes Satan in weakness and eventual defeat.

CHAPTER 13

This chapter is often taken up by itself, yet the full meaning cannot be grasped without the contents of chapter 12, and that of 14. Few would start to read a book in the middle, the information that goes before is necessary to the understanding of the whole. So with this, and each section of the Revelation. Chapter 12 is concerned with the operations of Satan, and through the chapter as the dragon, he is in opposition to God's future kingdom. Israel and the man child are both destined to rule, so Satan would seek to oppose and delay them. Chapter 13 is what Satan has in mind, and deals with the presentation of his kingdom to the world. This kingdom and its king is depicted as a violent beast, and the religious leader who comes in his own name is likewise seen as a beast. In short, ch. 12 he seeks to put down God's kingdom, and in ch. 13 he sets up his own kingdom.

A few remarks on the chapter will make this clear.

THE FIRST BEAST 1-9

Most prophetic students will have noticed the similarities that occur between this beast and the writings of Daniel, especially ch. 7. Four beasts are described in that chapter depicting four different nations. Perhaps that chapter has a double interpretation, looking back to the days of Empires that existed up until Christ came, and in another way prophesying of other nations that shall arise together in the last days. However, the important feature here is that the symbols describing the first beast are borrowed from the description of all four in Dan. 7. There is no need to go into detail in this, a comparison can easily be made by those interested, but what is the message of all this ? Simply progression, the features of each successive nation are carried forward to a climax in this beast out of the sea.

Several times in the wording the verb "to give" appears.

The dragon gave him his power and throne 2
This is repeated in verse 4
There was given unto him a mouth speaking great things 5
Power was given unto him to continue forty and two months 5
It was given unto him to make war with the saints 7
Power was given him over all kindreds, tongues and nations 7

Six times this last occurs which significantly is the number of man in the Bible.

Now who gives this man his power ? Many suggest it is God in His sovereign way giving all these to a man. However, all the references to giving are surely to be interpreted in the light of the first occurrence, "the dragon gave him his power and throne and great authority" . The devil himself in the guise of the dragon is the giver and so throughout the passage. This is similar to Job 1-2, God gives Satan a freedom to do as he will, but within certain limits. So here, the dragon of ch. 12 by God's permission produces the beastly man of ch. 13. Verse 1 is translated by other versions as "He stood upon the sand of the sea", meaning not John but the dragon, thus supervising the rise of these evil personages.

A few more remarks are necessary to the understanding of this great movement:-

1) The power which was offered to the Lord in His temptation by Satan and refused in Matt.4 is offered to this man and he is willing to accept the position.

2) The head wounded to death is not the beast himself but a feature of the whole movement. Those heads are interpreted as being 7 kings or kingdoms which means that somewhere along the line one kingdom suffered a death wound and was raised up again, more about this in chapter 17.

3) Just a few brief remarks as to the character and course of this king.

a)Out of the sea means that this king shall arise out of the Gentile nations. Howbeit, the seas also stand for wickedness as in Isa.57:20

b) Seven heads are an aggregation of features from the past empires headed up in one man

c)The ten horns with crowns are ten great nations amalgamated into one great confederacy

d) The dragon gets glory and homage from many through the beast

e) He is victorious in warfare bringing fear upon the nations

f) He is an orator, a mouth is given him, the organ of speech

g) His ministry is that of blasphemy against God's Name and his tabernacle and them that dwell in heaven (verse 6)

h) He makes war with the saints, that is, tribulation saints

i) He shall continue the reign of terror for 42 months The blasphemy against the Name could well be the mockery of the revelation of Christ, and the blasphemy against the tabernacle and those who dwell in heaven, could be a mockery of the raptured church. The young lads in 2 Kings 2 mocked Elisha in asking him to go up and to disappear as did Elijah.

4) Note the power given to him to continue 42 months. As already suggested, this power comes from the dragon, and seemingly he thinks that 42 months will be enough to accomplish his purposes in wiping out Israel. After all, the Lord Jesus in His three and a half years ministry did all the Father's will, and accomplished what God had purposed. So the dragon or Satan copies the man child, as God was in Christ, so shall he be behind his prodigy who shall reign with terror for three and a half years.

5) The elect are preserved from the deception in verse 8, the Lamb is brought in as the true purpose of God from the foundation of the world. The appeal goes forth to those who have ears. This phrase is

repeated to each of the churches in 2-3 but with the addition of "What the Spirit saith unto the churches", this is absent here, the church will be no longer on earth when these kings shall appear.

THE BEAST OUT OF THE EARTH 13:9-17

This second beast is what one would term, "The Antichrist", meaning one who is predominantly against Christ, who will impersonate Him, the counterfeit Christ. Just a few points are given to describe him, but enough to identify him. He comes up out of the earth, the earth which God has blessed, the earth that is to be subjected to the Son of Man. When the earth comes into blessing, the land of Israel shall have chief place. Israel produced the true Lamb, and most likely this counterfeit lamb will also be a Jew. The counterfeit must need arise out of the land of Israel would be the reasoning of Satan. He also has two horns like a lamb, this identifies him as the antichrist, he is like a lamb but not "The Lamb". The horn in Scripture speaks of power and authority, the Lord had a twofold authority in His ministry, His Words and His Works. Note the reference in Matt.7:28-9 to His words and Matt. 9:8 to His works.

The false christ is featured in both these ways in this chapter, verse 14 refers to what he says "an image should be made unto the first beast". Then in the same verse his works are mentioned as well, "the miracles which he has power to do" . The result of his ministry is great deception and great fear. He uses several ploys to bring the masses under the sway of the first beast.

1. By deception, he is as his master, a deceiver in verse 14, how different the Lord, who was the Way and the Truth, and of His Father, God.
2. By idolatry, the image will no doubt be attractive, and incidently, idolatry rests in the heart of every man. The Lord would only ascribe worship to God in Matt. 4:10.
3. By fear. The threat of death, and that an horrible one forces the people to worship the image lest they be killed.
4. By boycott. One can neither buy nor sell without the mark of the beast. The outcome of this would be that both businesses and individuals who had not the mark would be boycotted, helpless to trade in any way.

5. By works. This akin to the deception, the Lord used His works to testify to those who did not believe His words, that His claims were genuine. The works of this false one shall be used in that direction. It is worthy of note here, that in the ministry of the true Christ the people ascribed the works from God to the devil (Matt 12). In the ministry of the false christ they will ascribe the works of the devil to God.

As to the mark, this can either be on the forehead or the hand in verse 16. Those who will be ardent fanatical followers of the beast will be more public, and have the mark in the forehead, really wearing the colours they would say.

The others subjected by fear etc. choose to have the mark upon the right hand only.

THE NUMBER OF THE BEAST V 18

Much has been written on this, and much fantasy. Note the words "Here is wisdom, let him that hath understanding count the number of the beast". This is similar to Matt. 24:15. "When ye therefore shall see (that is tribulation saints) the abomination of desolation spoken of by Daniel the prophet stand in the holy place, let him that readeth understand". This simply means that when these prophetic events are there in reality, the understanding of these Scriptures shall be clear. The coming generation of tribulation saints will understand the number of the beast, and not until then shall this verse be fully understood. However, six is the number of man, and three is the number of revelation, on the third day the dry land appeared. It is also the number of resurrection as this revealed that the Lord was all He claimed to be. The three sixes is the full revelation of man in all his glory and depravity at the same time. Men like these are reserved for the last days.

Finally, note the counterfeiting of the Name of God in verse 6 and the number of the name of the beast in verse 18.

CHAPTER TWENTY-EIGHT

The Coming of the Son of Man in ch. 14

Chapter 14 is the Divine side of the great three chapter section to do with kingdoms and kings. Ch. 13 has considered the coming kingdom of the beast, the earthly glory and the darkness it represents, ch. 12 is the source of that kingdom, the dragon working from times past towards this end. All will be short lived, the greatest empire this world will ever see shall last for only 42 months. The Lord Jesus shall prevail, and this is the content of our present chapter.

THE LORD JESUS IN THE RIGHT PLACE, VERSE 1

This opening verse is in direct contrast with 13:1-8. There is a definite play upon words.

1) The Lord Jesus has the right title, The Lamb, this is in contrast to the dragon in 13:1. "He stood on the sand of the seashore" is the better rendering of the verse, meaning that not John, but the dragon stood on the sand. Here is the Lamb who can fill the throne of God, in contrast to the dragon, that fearful being.
2) Again He was standing on Mount Zion, the rightful place. He is the one who is destined to reign, Mount Zion is always linked with David and the kingdom of God.

3) Again, Zion is a rock, the solid rock in contrast to the sand of 13:1. The Lord spoke a parable about this in Matt 7. The house built upon the sand cannot endure when the storms of judgment come, but the house built upon the rock will stand. The kingdom set up by the Lord shall endure not for a mere 42 months, but for a thousand years and into eternity.

THE 144000 ON MOUNT ZION VERSE 1-5

These were with Him, the Lord has faithful followers who will enter into blessing with Him.

The number is the same as in chapter 7, that is, 144000. There is no warrant whatsoever for making these to be a different company as some suggest. The thing to really notice is the number, the same as those who were sealed in chapter 7, not one of them will be lost. The dragon could cast some stars to earth but these cannot be moved, they continue faithfully throughout the terrible times.

They have the name of the Lord and of the Father upon their foreheads. In consideration of the followers of the beast the choice was to have the number either on the forehead or the hand, those most fanatical would choose the forehead. All of these on Mount Zion have the name upon their foreheads, no mention is made of the hand. All are forward and bold for the Lord. Again they have a double name, that of the Lord and the Father, the double portion belongs to them.

These are called the "firstfruits" in verse 4. This means that a harvest will follow, and this harvest is seen in verse 15.

This vast number of 144000 is only the beginning, millions more shall follow, the Lord will be successful in having faithful followers in those dark times. All followers of the Lamb will reign with Him, hence they are on Mount Zion, whereas the followers of the beast shall suffer eternal pain in verses 9-11.

The voice like many waters is another contrast. The dragon opened his mouth to send forth water as a flood in 12:15 but here are many waters, representing power, and how much more powerful here than ch. 12:15

They were purchased from among men (verse 3 Revised Version) this is of course in contrast to the "not being able to buy or sell" without the mark of the beast in ch. 13. God comes in and purchases this great number of souls from the earth, and the kingdom of darkness is powerless to stop Him.

These have not been defiled, the "lie" shall have no hold upon them, the image did not attract them, they have the power to keep themselves chaste. The "women" here would be suggestive of the scarlet woman of ch. 17 who subtly attracts many nations, but she is powerless to attract the 144000.

These follow the Lamb wherever He goeth. They do this without force, or threat, nor are they deceived in any way. The love for the Lamb, their faith in His claims and the coming kingdom will attract them voluntarily to Him.

Perhaps the greatest contrast would be in the "new song" of verse 3. The hidden mystery of the number of the beast in 13:18 can be learnt upon earth by those who have understanding. The song in heaven sung by the 144000 can be learnt only by revelation from God, and in heaven, not on the earth. Here is understanding that earth cannot know. Songs in the Bible speak of "experience" among other things, here in experience, and the joy of the heavenly benefits.

In all this it is evident the Spirit of God is contrasting the Kingdom of our Lord, with the earthly kingdom of the dragon and the beast. The superiority of this over the old is the great message in the whole section, and is bound to be a comfort to suffering believers.

THE FIRST THREE ANGELS. 6-13

The second part of this chapter follows the same pattern, all is in contrast to that which has gone before in chapters 12-13.

This time the material is in a series of angels, three of them are mentioned, and after the vision of the Son of man, another three angels complete the series. Consider the first three angels.

The first angel has the everlasting gospel. A gospel that cannot be silenced, this in contrast to the "lie" of the beast which will last for forty two months only. The everlasting gospel exceeds time, and is "a message about creation" it would seem from the wording of verse 7, "worship Him that made heaven and earth and the sea and the fountains of waters". This is a message similar to Psalm 19:1 "The heavens declare the glory of God".

This gospel is for all nations, and to bring to the worship of the true God, rather than the worship of the beast and the image in chapter 13 and in verse 9 of our chapter. With the beast and false prophet there are lies and deception, here is the truth, and the creation to prove it.

The second angel has a message of doom (verse 8). "Babylon is fallen is fallen", the fact that the fall is repeated, makes it clear there can be no mistake, the kingdom of the beast is doomed from the start. This is in contrast to the everlasting gospel proclaimed by the first angel.

The third angel comes with a warning, in verses 9-11, the followers of the beast will be overwhelmed by the wrath of God.

In chapter 13 the people fear the wrath of the beast, and take his name in the forehead or hand, but this is to reject God, and the great judgment will be meted out to such. An apt title for these verses would be "It is better to fear God than man". The contrast can be seen with the 144000 in verse 1.

Perhaps the political scene is taken up with the second angel, Babylon, the religious world with the third angel in the worshipping of the beast and image. All will fail, God has no place in the wisdom of this world.

There follows a beautiful passage on the faithful who shall not be deceived by the lie in verses 12-13.

1) The patience of the saints, they will wait patiently for the coming of the true King, and will endure all suffering that they are called upon to experience.

2) They keep the commandments of God and the faith of Jesus. They obey the commands of the true Lamb and not the commands of the false lamb which are seen at the end of chapter 13.

3) They may be called upon to die, but such a sacrifice is really a blessing, "Blessed are the dead which die in the Lord from henceforth". This is blessing indeed, not only to die and to be with the Lord but to have a foremost place among that lustrous company. The "from henceforth" raises a difficulty, perhaps this means from the rise or the reign of the beast of ch. 13. This would mean that the greater the times of persecution the greater the honour to die for the Name of the Lord. On the other hand, it may be read as in the margins of some Bibles, "from henceforth says the Spirit", (verse 13) this would mean that on entering death they would enter into rest and blessing. The first idea is preferable.

4) The blessing is so precious to heaven that the Spirit cannot be silent and comes in with His comment, "they shall rest from their labours and their works do follow them". This is important, indicating that in spite of terrible tribulation and adversities, these believers put in much labour for their Lord, then enter into rest. Their works would speak of their righteous works, the Christian ethics they maintained in the midst of such difficulties.

Verses 9-13 of this chapter show the two destinies for eternity, those who follow the beast are to be tormented for ever, and those who follow the Lamb will enter in to the eternal blessedness and the reward for their works will follow them.

THE SON OF MAN ON THE WHITE CLOUD 14

This is the last reference to the Son of Man in the Bible. Often it has been pointed out that the first reference in the N.T. is found in Matt. 8:20 "the Son of Man hath not where to lay His head". The rejected Son of Man who had no resting place for His head, will eventually appear with the crown of gold upon His head. However, there is another contrast between the two passages that may not be noticed. Both passages have to do with discipleship, followers of Christ, in the Matt. passage the would be disciples were not willing to endure any hardship, but this reference to the Son of Man is linked here with those who follow Him even to death in the previous verse.

This is the third descriptive passage in Revelation that presents the Lord Jesus in symbolic language. As in the others, the head and the hand of the Lord are the fore. The golden crown upon His head is the glory and position that belongs to Him, whereas the hand speaks of what He is about to do. Who He is, and what He does, this double combination is often found in Scriptures. The crown is a "victor's" crown, and is in contrast to the crowns upon the heads of the dragon and the horns of the beast in the previous chapter. Those crowns are "Diadems" but this is victory. The beast will have glory according to this world, but the Lord will have the victory, and the glory besides when He comes crowned with many diadems (Rev. 19:12). The white cloud however would speak of glory as in the tabernacle of old.

The voice of the angel to Him "to reap" is not a command, rather agreement with His actions, the amen of heaven to His righteous judgments.

The harvest would be in a good sense, the completion of the firstfruits of verse 4. No doubt this is the saved of Israel, and likely of Gentiles as well. The earth was reaped in verse 16, this would be the gathering of the saved of earth similar to the wheat from the tares as in the parable in Matt. 13. The judgment of unsaved Gentiles follow in the next verses.

THE VINTAGE OF THE EARTH 17-20

Two more angels complete the series to six, and these last two have to do with the vintage of the earth. One comes out from the temple and the other from the altar. The angel of verse 15 which spoke of the harvest was also out from the temple, out from the temple would be the source of the judgment, the presence of God. The separation of the true from the false in Israel and the vintage judgment to Gentiles issue from the presence of the "Righteous Judge". The angel out from the altar would speak of the prayers of the suffering saints being answered. This would refer back to 6:9:10, those under the altar who pray, "how long O Lord ... dost thou not judge and avenge our blood on them who dwell upon the earth". These prayers are now answered, hence the angel from the altar. He is the angel of fire, fire from off the altar brings forth judgment in 8:5 as in this case. On the other hand, fire from the altar in Isa. 6 brought forth fitness to do the service of God. Here it is the judgment, and the prayers of the martyrs answered.

The judgment is mighty, the blood-bath of verses 19-20 can only be Armageddon as in chapter 19, where the beast, false prophet and all the followers shall come to a swift end.

"The vine of the earth" is important. Israel was God's vine in Isa. 5, but they failed to bring forth fruit. The Lord Jesus is the true vine in John 15:1-3, and believers are the branches, the heavenly people. Here is the false vine, the movement professing to be of God as the false prophet, and the beast setting himself up as God, but all will be destroyed. This vine is cast into the wrath of God, the Lord Jesus ascended into the glory of God. Verse 20 with verse 10 of the chapter shows that this vintage judgment is upon the kingdom of the beast.

The section is complete, here is God's answer to the work of the dragon down through the ages, and the later uprising of his kingdom. it shall last only 42 months, but the rightful king shall come forward, He has moral quality for He is the Son of Man, He has power for He sits upon the cloud of glory. He can judge, the sharp sickle is in His hand; and He will judge, the wrath of God shall be manifest. It is good to be on the winning side, the side of the Lord Jesus, God's Man, God's righteous King.

CHAPTER TWENTY-NINE

Practical Thoughts from Kingdoms ch. 12-14

This remarkable section of God's Word that sets forth the working of Satan, and the overall triumphant workings of our God through His beloved Son, is bound to yield a bountiful harvest of practical teaching. In this light consider the enemy as in Rev. 12:-

1) His names and titles are fourfold, suggesting the universal aspect of his activities. He is the "old serpent" that is, religiously from the beginning of time, the same that beguiled Eve in the garden of Eden. He is still the deceiver and the source of all falsehood as in the present time. It is well to remember the warning of Paul "As the serpent beguiled Eve" (2 Cor. 11:3).

In the political scene he appears as the "dragon", fierce and fiery. Much of the hatred towards God and the persecuting of God's people on a national scale has its source in the dragon. Still there is more to come, yea in a greater way than ever and finally heading up in the Great Tribulation. The deception of the serpent and the political evil of the dragon is ever present in this old sin torn earth.

He is also called the Devil and Satan, one is his role as the accuser and the other as the adversary. As noted already in these writings, the devil accuses especially the failure of the personal life of the believer, and as Satan he opposes any service the believer seeks to do unto God. Again one must be reminded that he accuses the brethren, the family name of the Christian, his accusations are chiefly concerning the sad relationships of believers as brethren. The Judgment Seat of Christ in a special way will deal with this evil, "why dost thou judge thy brother" (Rom. 14:10-13).

2) In the previous chapter of this book the varied activities of the devil were pointed out. The solemn thought is that he never changes, he is the same today.

He is still out to crash to earth the star-like Christians who would seek to shine as luminaries, one must be on guard constantly.

Also, he is seeking to devour anything of Christ that is produced by God in the life of the Christian.

He accuses the believer and hinders his work by night and day, when men slept the enemy sowed the tares in the field (Matt. 13).

He is at war with the believer now as he will be with the archangel Michael then.

He is still the persecutor of the godly using the ways and powers of the ungodly to do so.

He would seek to send a flood of deception or trouble to destroy the believer once for all, and rid the earth of that testimony as in the case of Job. However, God does not always permit this, or sometimes the devil is restricted, again as in the case of Job.

By these, and many other ways his awful activity is noted in Rev. 12.

THE ANSWER IN THE WHOLE ARMOUR OF GOD

What is the answer to all this ? It can only be "the whole armour of God" as in Ephesians 6.

1. The loins girt with the girdle of truth is the answer to the deception of Satan, error is exposed by the truth (Isa. 8:20).

2. The breastplate of righteousness surely leaves no room for accusation, the accuser is silenced when righteousness prevails. The devil could not accuse the person of Christ as perfect righteousness was always there.

3. The best remedy against his persecution is to have the feet shod with the preparation of the gospel of peace. "How beautiful are the feet of

258 ALPHA AND OMEGA

them who preach the gospel" (Rom. 10:15). The preachers of old found this out as often God came in and saved the ringleaders of the persecution, such was the case with Saul of Tarsus.

4. When trouble comes as a flood, it is a time of testing which indeed would overwhelm, if it were not for faith. The shield of faith is the antidote to sorrow and trouble. Faith steadfast upon God will understand that He will not cause His child a needless tear.

5. The helmet of salvation looks up to where Christ is on the throne of God, this preserves the mind and life and the designs of the dragon to destroy utterly fails. "Set your mind on things above, not on things of the earth, for ye are dead and your life is hid with Christ in God" (Col. 3:2-3). God is working in our lives in view of His eternal purpose, and the helmet of salvation keeps that great design in mind, and preserves from the devouring enemy.

6. Satan is engaged in open conflict with every believer, and the sword of the Spirit which is the word of God is the defensive weapon against his devices. The Lord Jesus used that sword so skilfully during the temptation in the wilderness.

Therefore, the believer clad in all the armour of God is strong against all the subtle and powerful attacks of the devil as seen in Rev. 12.

EXHORTATION IN CH. 13

As for chapter 13 the raising of the beasts on the political and religious scene, and the effect upon the world has been dealt with in the previous chapter. Just a few remarks are necessary to see the practical implication in this passage which surfaces in the exhortation given to the saints in verses 9-10.

"If any man have an ear let him hear". This is to the individual who has hearkened to the Word, such shall have understanding to interpret the events both political and religious that take place upon the earth. In other words "to be able to discern the times" as our Lord taught. He ascribed to the Pharisees the ability to read the signs concerning the weather, but they were not able to interpret the wonderful visitation of grace from heaven in the person of Christ. "How is it that you do not discern this time"? (Luke 12:56) The hearing ear shall understand by the current events the movement of evil powers on the one hand, and the heavenly on the other.

Verse 10 is difficult, one way of reading is as the R.V. "If any man is for captivity into captivity he goeth". This simply means that believers of that time will bow to the will of God even to captivity. Such will say in the face of all adversity, "the will of the Lord be done". The A.V. seems to be more correct and gives a sound reason for the faith and patience of the saints in knowing the sowing and reaping principle in the governmental dealings of God with the nations. He that captures shall be captured himself, and he that kills with the sword shall also be himself killed with the sword. The fact that believers know this great principle, strengthens their faith, and with patience they await the vengeance of God. It is a comfort to know that evil cannot endure.

Before leaving ch. 13 another practical point emerges from verse 18. "here is wisdom, let him that understandeth count the number of the beast". This is a blessing to have understanding, such will not be deceived by the old serpent, and will perceive the ultimate outcome. Wisdom would be knowing how to act, to be wise like the wise virgins and not to be as the foolish ones. The understanding would preserve from all deception. The number 666 is the number of a man, any man, so if one could examine self in the light of Scripture one would soon discern the old man, and see the principle working in others, especially the beast of the last days.

Therefore in both these passages in ch. 13 the idea of spiritual understanding will preserve. To know the principle of sowing and reaping and to receive consolation therefore, and to discern the number of the beast and to be forewarned, all this is God given understanding.

CH. 14 AND THE 144000

It is not the service of the 144000 that is presented in this passage, rather their loyalty to Christ and sanctification of life. Also the preserving hand of God upon them.

They are with the Lamb, their faith will give place to sight. The Father's Name is in their forehead, and would indicate complete dedication to Him, this relationship will be enjoyed on earth during dark days, and comes into fullness in their position with the Lamb on Mount Sion.

Intelligence again comes forward in the new song, here is the wisdom of experience and the addition of the song of the Lamb. They come out of the same school as Moses, delivered from a greater tyrant and tribulation than that which was experienced by Moses and Israel. Yet they have a beginning to their spiritual experience, they were redeemed or purchased from among men. This could either be their experience of salvation, or that of being taken up by God for service in being separated as in the case of Acts 13 when Barnabas and Saul were separated unto the work to which God had called them. Probably both things are in view.

The total consecration to Christ is their main asset in verse 4. These are virgins, speaking of their spiritual purity. Most if not all of the false doctrines past and present allow the flesh to operate similar to the heathen temples of old that made fornication a feature in their religion. These are morally clean and doctrinally pure. Then the positive side is seen in their following the Lamb whithersoever He goeth. It is the Lord they follow, He leads and they follow, the will of God controls all their movements.

Then in their mouths was found no guile, or as the Revised Version puts it, "No Lie" meaning that they were totally separated from the lie which of course sums up all the deception associated with the coming beast movement, in this they were without blemish.

Such an example all this is to Christians today, these will be surrounded by mighty opposing forces and yet abide faithful to the Lord, morally and doctrinally clean.

THE ANGELS IN THE CHAPTER

The six angels also present a great lesson, especially the way each occupies his own place in service.

Of the first three, one has a message, a gospel and delivers it faithfully. The second has a declaration to proclaim, even the fall of Babylon, and at the same time bringing the charges of its crimes against it. The third heralds a warning concerning the consequences of worshipping the image and receiving the mark of the beast.

Verse 14 presents the Son of Man and this is followed by another series of three angels. One announces that the harvest of the earth is ripe, and speaks of the Lord's right to reap the harvest. The second angel in this series has nothing to say but something to do. He with his sickle gathers the clusters of the vine of the earth, this is judgment. This angel will be in agreement with the angels in the parable of the tares who gather the tares for burning (Matt. 13). Likely the time is the same, except that the parable of the tares is distinctly Israel, this in Rev. 14 is wider and includes Gentiles.

Finally, the last angel also has something to say, the vintage is ripe, and the time of judgment has come.

Yes, each angel in his place and each complementing each other in the work they are called to do. Surely Christians today could learn from this.

THE SON OF MAN ON THE CLOUD

Finally, the Son of Man is found in the midst of the angels, three on each side of the passage in verse 14. Here is total vindication, the righteous ways of our God are seen in the humble Man now exalted. He enters into His rights over the earth here as the Son of Man. Also as the Son of Man He judges accordingly and has a crown of glory and victory upon His head. It is so with all that follow Christ, such as the 144000, the time of vindication will come. All this seems to be the practical import of this great chapter of the Revelation.

CHAPTER THIRTY

The Blood of the Martyrs in ch. 15-18

C hapters 15-18 form the 5th section of "The Revelation" and as in the previous sections, it deals with a problem encountered by persecuted believers.

This section begins with a song in 15:3 and ends with "rejoice over her thou heaven" in 18:20. It also begins with harpers of heaven starting their song, and closes with the harpers of earth silenced forever in 18:22. Yet the theme is terrible, the martyrdom of believers. However, the victory and the joy are on the side of those same believers.

The section has four clear cut divisions in keeping with the four chapters of which the section is comprised.

1. The preparation of the seven angels with their bowls of wrath. The heavenly singers, and the temple in heaven. (ch. 15)
2. Each of the angels pouring out his bowls upon the earth (ch. 16)
3. The description and doom of the scarlet woman in 17
4. The city Babylon and its final doom. (ch. 18)

CHAPTERS OF GREAT THINGS

One who reads these chapters carefully cannot but be struck by the repetition of the word "Great". Truly this word occurs often in the book of Rev. but is most paramount in these four chapters. Here is the display of the wisdom and power of mankind in the presentation of Great Things.

In 16:19 one reads of the "great city" and this is repeated in various forms throughout the four chapters.

Then the city is identified as "Great Babylon" in the same verse (Verse 19).

This is followed by the introduction of the "great whore" in ch. 17:1, this is the first time she is mentioned in the book.

Ch. 17:5 speaks of "Mystery Babylon the Great"

This symbolic women is admired with great admiration or wonder in 17:6.

The great city reigning, is explained in 17:16.

Again 18:10 speaks of the great city, as well as 18:18-19.

The great city must be Babylon, either literally or symbolically and the great woman is most definitely symbolic. These two make up the "great things" of the world that is coming to a final end in these chapters.

THE LORD HAS GREAT THINGS ALSO

A great sign can be read of in 15:1 and of great and mighty works in 15:3 under the judgment of God poured out in the seven bowls. "Great heat" occurs in 16:9 and a "great voice" in 16:17, and a "great earthquake" in 16:18. The series of bowl judgments come under the heading of the "Great Day of God Almighty". Chapter 16:21 speaks of "great hail", every stone about the weight of a talent, and this plague is further described as "exceeding great".

Chapter 18:1 presents an angel as having "great power" and another mighty angel as taking a stone as a"great millstone" in 18:21. The power of these great things are so overwhelming that "great Babylon" finally falls in 18:2.

In all this it is easy to see the great forces, that of good and evil, of light and darkness, come into severe conflict in the last days, and to see that righteousness and truth shall prevail.

WHAT IS THE THEME OF ALL THIS?

While references concerning the blood of the martyrs are scattered throughout the book of Rev. yet this section seems to gather together the majority of these references. Consider such as in 15:2, the victors over the beast and over the image, are standing in glory before the throne of God on the crystal sea. No doubt these have suffered violent death because of their allegiance to the coming King, the Lord Jesus, and who refused the defilement of idolatry in the image. These are overcomers, who will overcome the dragon by the blood of the Lamb, and by the word of their testimony, and who love not their lives unto death (12:11). These are the "Blessed dead from henceforth" spoken of in 14:13. Now they are before the throne and a song of victory is upon their lips.

A most interesting reference is found in 16:6. The angel of the waters declare "They have shed the blood of saints and prophets and thou hast given them blood to drink for they are worthy". This confirms the basic reason for the seven last plagues, and the warning to all that afflict the people of God because of their testimony, retribution is sure to follow.

Again in reference to the "great whore" the same condemnation issues from God. "She was drunken with the blood of the saints and with the blood of the martyrs of Jesus" (17:6).

The very closing verse of the section confirms this, "In her were found the blood of prophets and of saints and of all that were slain upon the earth" (18:24).

All this is in keeping with the words of the Lord in Matt. 23:35, "that upon you may come all the righteous blood shed upon the earth from righteous Abel until the blood of Zacharias son of Barachias whom ye slew between the temple and the altar".

It is quite evident that the theme of chapters 15-18 is to do with the persecution of God's people unto death right from the beginning of time and unto the climax of this vicious action in the last days. The great things are man's power in putting the saints to death, and God's great things are the judgments upon the heads of the perpetrators of such evil. Hence we read of the "wrath of God" in 15:1 and 15:7. Also, "just and true are thy ways" (15:3), that is, in judgment. Again, " true and righteous are thy judgments" in 16:7. The whole thing is summed up very pointedly in 18:20 "God has avenged you on her", that is, upon the scarlet woman.

HOW WILL GOD PERFORM THIS JUDGMENT ?

One of the most interesting facts about the Rev. is the Old Testament background that is seen in most if not all of the seven sections. It has been noted in these pages that the whole book is saturated in Old Testament imagery. When dealing with section 8-11 the seven trumpets had a definite background in the fall of Jericho. In like manner this section on the blood of the martyrs has an Old Testament background from the early part of Exodus. Follow this through:-

1) A ruthless king, Pharaoh sought to abolish the nation of Israel, many children were drowned in the river. Here in Rev. 15-18 are Great Babylon and the kingdom of the beast with the same designs against Israel and saved Gentiles.

2) The magicians opposed Moses very much, of whom Paul warned "Now as Jannes and Jambres withstood Moses so do these also resist the truth" (2 Tim. 3:8). Paul was speaking of the last days. Jannes and Jambres and all such like as in Paul's day with those of the last days are all part of the scarlet woman of our passage.

3) The people of Israel called upon God in Ex. 2-3, so do these in Rev. 8-11 and the answer comes in our chapters under consideration, namely 15-18.

4) Egypt was plagued with plagues very similar to these mentioned in chapter 16.

5) Egypt was destroyed, Babylon is fallen as the counterpart, meaning not only the city but the empire.

6) The song of Moses in Ex. 15 is again sung in Rev. 15 and added to this is the song of the Lamb. These are the first and last songs in the Bible.

What God has done in the past He can do again, and will indeed do so as in this section.

A CONTRAST WITH EXODUS

Miriam sang the song of Moses accompanied with a timbrel which is a woman's instrument. Jephthah came to Mizpeh unto his house and behold his daughter came out to meet him with timbrels and with dances. (Judges 11:34). "The singers went before and the players on instruments followed after, among them were the damsels playing with timbrels" (Psalm 68:25). Here in Rev. 15 it is not women but men, and they are playing harps and not timbrels, all this speaks of maturity. David played the harp, it seemed to be a man's instrument in Bible times. This voices the fullness of understanding that shall be expressed in heaven.

Another contrast is the addition of the song of the Lamb to the song of Moses, the fullness of revelation has come in. Moses was a man of the types, these saints, like the church today, rejoice in the fulfilment, not the shadows but the body.

Another great contrast is in the dividing of the waters. In Ex. 14 the Red Sea was divided to let Israel escape, but here the waters of the Euphrates are dried up to let the enemies of the beast come forth. And so he proceeds to his destruction with the coming of the Lord in chapter 19. In both instances the enemies of the people of God are utterly destroyed.

Now to look at the four chapters in a little more detail.

THE SEVEN ANGELS OF CH. 15

This section compares with the others in opening with a reference to the Tabernacle of old. The sea of glass here answers to the laver of the court of the Tabernacle. The reason for this particular reference will be considered in its place, but first the seven angels must be examined.

While many sevens run throughout the Rev. the most outstanding ones are the seven churches, seals, trumpets and the seven bowls of judgment in these chapters. The first two series, the churches and the seals are handled by the Lord, but the trumpets are sounded by angels and the bowls are also poured out by angels.

The churches, the Lord's testimony upon the earth and the seals which are events throughout time, are both in the hand of the Lord as most well know. The trumpets and bowls are definitely judgments of the last days and angels have much to do with that as in Matt. 13 etc.. These bowls are called the last plagues of the wrath of God and accordingly are in the hands of angels. Note a few interesting facts:-

1) These angels comprise a "sign". (Verse 1). This is the third sign in the Book of Revelation. The first was the woman clothed with the sun in 12. The dragon also in 12 formed the second, and these angels with bowls of wrath make up the third. Often triple signs are found in Scripture and with the same formula, the final one is always judgment. The first of these triple signs occurs in Ex. 4 with Moses at the burning bush and the others can easily be traced in the Bible.

2) These angels have the last plagues of the wrath of God. The wrath of God is generally accounted upon the earth, (1 Thess. 2:16). The trumpets etc. having gone before, these bowls would complete that earthly wrath leading right up to the coming of the Lord in ch. 19.

3) The angels are mentioned in verse one and then again in verses 6-8 and into the next chapter, therefore verses 2-5 form a parenthesis.

4) The angels proceed out of the temple, indicating the presence of God, the source of the judgments which are according to righteousness. In verse 8 the temple is filled with smoke, symbol of the presence of God similar to the glory abiding upon the tabernacle in Ex. 40. In both cases no one can go in, the presence of God is there, if Moses was not able to go into the Tabernacle then no one else could do so. In the Tabernacle and the temple of Solomon the Lord was there in blessing, but here in judgment.

5) The angels are clothed in pure white linen which would signify true and righteous judgment against an offending people who give glory to another instead of God (Rev. 9:20).

6) They are also arrayed with golden girdles around the breasts. Under law the ceremonies had to give way to the law of need as in the case of David eating the showbread. Also in the Lord touching the leper in Mark 1, the same ceremonial law had to give way to the law of love. But in these angels the time will then have come when love will have to give way to holiness, and the glory of God will demand judgment. Longsuffering as in the days of Noah will then come to a complete end.

7) One of the living creatures gives each angel a bowl full of the wrath of God. The living creature is life, God is life and the deadness of the unrepentant people must be dealt with. The fact that the bowls are full indicates that iniquity will then come to the full and judgment will have to be meted out.

THE SEA OF GLASS

In the previous lines it has been pointed out that verses 2-5 of ch. 15 form a parenthesis. This even more emphatically highlights the key to the whole section.

This sea of glass answers to the "laver" of the Tabernacle and was for cleansing. The fact that fire is mingled also indicates cleansing, for fire burns away all the dross.

Aaron and the priests who washed both hands and feet at the laver had in a sense gone through the water, but the people in our passage are upon the sea, these have not been defiled with the beast, his image or his mark. They had gained the victory in contrast to those in 16:2 "there fell a noisome and grievous sore upon the men which had the mark of the beast, and them which worshipped his image". These in 15:2 were overcomers. Peter well illustrated this, he walked upon the sea in Matt. 14, then began to sink when he took his eyes off the Lord. He cried out and the Lord was immediately beside him and he then walked upon the sea with the Lord back to the ship. These upon the sea of glass are victorious overcomers.

How did they overcome? By loving not their lives even unto death. These are before the throne, as the sea of glass was before the throne in 4:6. These have been martyred and thus they introduce the subject of martyrdom that runs right through these 4 chapters.

No doubt they were the cream of saints, and those left behind in such troubled times may well question the ways of God. "Why has God allowed such to be taken away from us"? However, the time has come for this to be avenged, hence the last plagues; God in longsuffering allows the slaying of believers down through the ages, but the time of retribution will come at last.

These martyrs sing the song of Moses. Israel crossed the Red Sea and Pharaoh was doomed. These stand upon the sea of glass and the beast is doomed. In both cases the song of Moses is the experience of deliverance and the laying low of the tyrant.

The song of the Lamb is added as it is through the Lamb the victory is eventually gained. All glory and praise is unto the Lamb. The King of Nations is no doubt the Lord in verses 3-4 and the setting up of His Millennial kingdom when righteousness shall reign.

In verse 3 the qualities of the Lord to reign are set forth, and in verse 4 the power of the Lord to establish the kingdom is presented, and He shall be the centre. In all things He must have the pre-eminence.

THE SEVEN BOWLS OF WRATH

These are poured forth upon the source of the persecution that was drenched with the blood of the martyrs, and the reason is given in 16:6. "They have shed the blood of saints and prophets and thou hast given them blood to drink for they are worthy".

1) The first angel pours his bowl upon the earth and the second upon the sea. How fitting as the two beasts of ch. 13 arise out of the sea and the earth, and these are the source of the martyrdom. The earth comes first here as the second beast who comes out of the earth represents religious persecution. The result of the first plague is noisome sores upon the bodies of the people who follow the beast. The 6th plague upon Egypt in Exod. 9:11 was similar to this, and it hit the religious section of the nation. The magicians who opposed Moses could not stand in the court of Pharaoh.

2) The sea is affected by the second angel, and becomes as the blood of a dead man, this is, it was congealed. All in the sea died, the water being too thick to maintain marine life. The political beast of ch. 13 comes out of the sea, he was of the dragon, the mark of death is there. Also the nations depend upon their economy and commerce and this is swallowed up in the plague.

An instructive contrast to the plagues of Egypt appears here. The judgment plagues upon Egypt increased in severity, first to cause irritation like the frogs, lice and flies. Then property was affected in the murrain upon livestock. The hail was upon livestock and also upon the bodies of people, many died who were foolish enough to disobey the word of Moses to stay indoors. Finally, the life of every household was touched in the last plague, the death of the first born. Here in these plagues of wrath the bodies of people are affected from the very first and death comes from the second. These plagues are more severe than those on Egypt.

3) The third angel poured his bowl upon the waters and they became blood. This was the first plague upon Egypt but it comes third here because of its message in verse 6. Guilt is brought home to the heart, note also that none of these lead to repentance in v 9.

4) The fourth angel affects the sun, men were scorched with fire and great heat. Although no comment is made by heaven or angels this is no doubt similar to bowl three. Down through the ages a great many choice saints were scorched and burnt to death while tied to a stake. Here again is retribution from the righteous God. They blasphemed the name of God and repented not, they are as steadfast in their unbelief as the martyrs were in their faith. The reference in 7:16 of the persecuted people fleeing into the wilderness to suffer from the heat of the sun has also a bearing in this, again retribution is foremost.

5) The fifth angel with his bowl affects the kingdom of the beast and brought forth darkness. This is more severe that the ninth plague of darkness upon Egypt, there the darkness was felt, very sinister, but here it is felt by pain, they gnawed their tongues for pain. Still no repentance is forth coming because this plague betokens the condition of the beast followers, they were in darkness and of darkness.

6) The sixth angel pours his bowl upon the Euphrates and it is dried up. As noted earlier, this is similar to the dividing of the sea for Israel to pass through. It was a deliverance to Israel but death to Pharaoh and his host. Likewise this drying up of the Euphrates will prove to be the destruction of the beast and his kingdom.

   A parenthesis comes in between the 6th and 7th bowl, and the narrative hastens on to Armageddon. Here in verse 13 is the trinity of evil, the dragon is the false Spirit unseen, the beast is the counterfeit God, and the false prophet is no doubt the false Christ. The deception in the symbolism of frogs out of the mouth of this false trinity is the doctrine and miracles of demons luring the nations unto the destruction of Armageddon.

   The people of God are addressed in this parenthesis as in 18:4, there to separate, here to keep themselves. They are exhorted to watch, watch the development but to keep aloof from it all. Also to watch for the coming of the true King, He that is faithful and true.

7) The seventh angel seems to bring forth a sort of summary, many features are brought forward that would speak of Armageddon, the fall of Babylon and the actual coming of the Lord. The islands and mountains falling away is the language of chapter 6 which indicate the convulsions that accompany the return of the Lord as the Son of Man. This bowl is poured into the air, from whence the Lord shall eventually appear, and Babylon especially is mentioned as being the course of the persecuting element from the beginning to its final doom. Here especially appear the great things. A great voice, a great earthquake and great hail upon the great city and so on.

The earthquake is the last of four that occur in the Revelation and speaks of the instability of anything built upon this sinful earth. Well has one of old said, "They build too low that build beneath the skies". Like the jailor in Acts 16, his indifference was shaken by the earthquake, and he then sought the things eternal.

The Lord's displeasure is seen in the great hail, each stone about the weight of a talent. This is similar to Joshua 10:11 where the Lord cast down great stones from heaven upon the opposing kings. The result was that more were slain with the stones than with the sword of Joshua.

The sad thing that emerges out of it all is the unrepentant attitude of the people in verse 21. It would seem that there was room for repentance right up to the final moment of the Lord's return. They repented not in verse 9, they blasphemed God and repented not in verse 11. Finally they blasphemed God in verse 21. The world of men is never ready for the judgments of God, although warned, and given evident signs of its reality.

CHAPTER THIRTY-ONE

The Woman and the City ch. 17-18

These two chapters continue with the section to do with the blood of the martyrs, and contain the direction of the final plagues of ch. 16, a certain city referred to as Babylon.

These two chapters have proved to be most difficult over the years and most commentators freely admit this fact. Difficulties always arise as to the identity of the scarlet woman in ch. 17, and is she different from the city of ch. 18 ? Is one chapter the religious system and the other the political concept ? The chapters are indeed fraught with difficulties.

It seems most likely that both chapters consider the same thing as there is an interchange of ideas between the two. Consider some of these:-

1) The woman is called a city in 17:18, and the city is referred to in the feminine gender in 18:3. HER fornication, HER delicacies, and come out of HER my people in 18:4 and so on. In fact from verses 3-6 of ch. 18 the city is referred to as HER no less than eleven times.

2) The clothing is the same. In 17:4 she is arrayed in purple and scarlet and decked with gold and precious stones and pearls. This is over against 18:16, "Alas that great city that was clothed in fine linen and purple and scarlet and decked with gold and precious stones and pearls".

3) The woman has a golden cup in 17:4, and 18:6 refers to the cup which she has filled to the double.

4) The kings of the earth have committed fornication with the woman in 17:2 and of the city it is said "the kings of the earth have committed fornication with her" (18:3).

5) In both chapters the blood of the martyrs is to the fore. "The woman was drunk with the blood of the martyrs of Jesus" in 17. "And in her was found the blood of prophets and of saints" in 18:24.

6) Both are traced back to Babylon. "Mystery Babylon the great"in 17:5, and then in 18:2 "Babylon the great is fallen".

7) The order of the chapters is significant. The woman appears in 17 and the city in 18 then in 19:1-2 the rejoicing in heaven over her destruction is noted. This goes back to 17, but why is the city of ch. 18 missed ? Likely the great whore includes the city; for the city is not referred to again in the Revelation.

Many other comparisons can be made but this may suffice to show the obvious relations of the woman to the city as if they both were one and the same. A few suggestions can be made in this observation.

The first is that the woman is as God sees the system, and the city as man sees the same thing. This idea often occurs in Scripture such as Dan. 2 with Dan. 7. The first is man's view of the empires and their glories depicted as precious metals. However God sees the same nations as monstrous beasts in ch.7.

No doubt there is greater development in Dan. 2 and 7, and the vision may go forward to the line up of nations concurrently in the last great conflict.

Again, chapter 17 could be looked upon as the source of the persecuting system, and the city its final expression, the climax of that same system. In the woman is seen the character, course and circumstances that bring about her final doom, and in 18 that doom is enlarged upon.

That both stand for a religious system is evident. The woman is idolatrous in opposition to the true testimony of Jesus and puts to death those faithful to Him. This woman like the woman of chapter 12 is the symbol of many people as in 17:15. The religious element appears also in the city. She traded in the souls of men in 18:13, and the holy apostles and prophets rejoice over her in heaven for God has avenged them in 18:20.

As suggested earlier, religious opposition to the truth has always been present from the days of Cain who slew Abel right on to the end times culminating in the events of these two chapters.

Now a few remarks on each chapter is necessary to put each in the setting of this section, that is the four chapter martyr section.

THE SCARLET WOMAN OF CH. 17

The reason she is brought in at this juncture of the book is because she represents a religious system and as such is the source of the shedding of all the blood of those who were faithful in their testimony to God during all time.

Her judgment is announced right at the beginning in 17:1. The time will have come when the cry of ch. 16:17 shall go forth "It is done", that is, the revenge of God upon the perpetrators of the death of the martyrs.

It is a wilderness scene, this is as God sees her. Man sees the glorious city in 18. Perhaps the wilderness here is the counterfeit of Satan because Israel were led through the wilderness at the beginning. The wilderness no doubt also betokens desolation, nothing in her for God in spite of much religious boasting.

She commits fornication and not adultery. This proves she was never joined to the Lord, profession was there but without the reality.

She rides the beast in verse 3. The woman is seeking to lead as in the case of Eve with Adam. Ahab also bent to the rule of Jezebel and Herod was manipulated by Herodias. In these instances the Divine principle of headship is set aside.

She is deceived. She thinks to ride the beast, no doubt sees in him great potential and will seek to use him in her system. However, the beast carries the woman in verse 7, he in fact is using her world wide influence to get himself to the top. When he gets there he destroys her as in verses 16-17. The whole system seen as a woman has no doubt in mind the story of the foolish woman in Prov. 9:13-18. In her deception she thinks that slaying the saints and prophets is doing God service as in John 16:2.

A FEW POINTERS

Her description appears in verse 4 and betokens riches and affluence. It takes a lot of money to keep Christendom going and all this is far from the simplicity of the early churches in the Acts. Large cathedrals, fantastic buildings costing millions of pounds have been set up claiming to be to the glory of God. This is far indeed from the sentiment of Paul "as poor yet making many rich" (2 Cor. 6:10).

Great Babylon of verse 5 shows the source of the system. It springs from Babylon of Gen. 10 and 11 which seems to be the beginning of idolatry and the perversion from truth to error in such a subtle way that to the deceived, the error is the truth. Again Christendom revels in great names, many a sect goes back to its founder, people love to be under a great name.

The mystery of verse 5 would be alongside the mystery of iniquity of 2 Thess. 2:7, which is identified there as a great religious movement of the last days.

The terrific influence is noted here and causes wonder even in the apostle John in verse 6.

She is called the great whore in verse 1

She influences the kings of the earth in verse 2

She is the cause of the abominations of the earth, verse 5

She sitteth on many waters which are people nations and tongues in verse 15

She reigns over the kings of the earth in verse 18

She is the mother of harlots, she has many children, many offshoots of religious persuasions.

It all started with Nimrod who was a hunter and not a shepherd, hence the character throughout time of hunting and putting to death the witnesses from God which is the theme of this part of the Revelation.

Her doom is before God, she will be deceived by the beast, and in the will and programme of God the beast shall bring about her downfall in verses 16-17. This will be as follows:-

The woman who has world wide influence shall come to the notice of the ambitious king, the beast. If all the religions of the world today were amalgamated into one great movement and one man gets to the top to direct all as he pleased, that would be advantageous indeed. This is exactly what is to happen, and the woman features the climax of "the council of churches" movement as seen in our day. The beast has authority but not complete in the ten kingdom confederacy. He uses the woman, the religious movement, and carries her to achieve his ends. When he gets to the top, he then destroys the woman, the religious system so that nothing shall oppose his great programmes. His idea is to set himself up as God so that he alone is worshipped as in 2 Thess. 2:1-6. The woman thinks she is serving God but is deceived by Satan the dragon, and finally removed to make way for Satan's masterpieces, the beast and false prophet of chapter 13, and also at the close of this chapter.

A FEW WORDS ON THE BEAST

The events concerning the rise of the beast in these verses goes before those of chapter 13. Here the horns have received no kingdom as yet, but in 13 they are crowned, that is, kingdoms belong to them then.

These 10 verses cover much ground and are an important development of the last days. Consider the order.

1) The source is seen in verse 8. It is the powers of darkness that brings forth the beast king with such an ambitious programme. The Lord Jesus came forth from heaven, even the glory to do the Father's will, and to make possible the Kingdom of God as seen in the church. Here the blueprint is of God, but copied by the dragon, the beast comes from the abyss to do the will of the dragon.

2) The seven heads are seven mountains or kingdoms. This looks back to the development from the past. Empires a plenty have been in the historical past but only those who are in the development to the last days are included here. As many teach, and it appears to be so, the five that are fallen, this is, in the past, were Egypt, Assyria, Babylon, Persia and Greece. All these persecuted Israel or had some great part to play in their history, some making great attempts to wipe out the said nation. These are in the past. The head described as "Now is" would answer to Rome then in power at the time John wrote this book. This would be head number 6. The seventh is still to come and would be the ten kingdom confederacy. This would break down economically or in some other way, (the head with the deadly wound and healed (13:3); but when taken over by the beast, the ambitious king, all will prosper - this would be the eighth. The beast stands for both king and empire, the person who rules forms the empire. The programme can easily be traced.

The woman, the religious influence, has been in power since the beginning in Gen. 10, yea, even from the days of Cain. In the last days this influence increases in power and authority and dominion.

Alongside this is a political rising, the ten nation confederacy experiencing ups and downs.

A king arise out of this confederacy seen as a beast in Rev. 13. He is the little horn of Dan. 7 who is very ambitious to get to the top by conquering and seeking to conquer as in Rev. 6:1-6.

He sees the world wide influence of the harlot and joins the movement. The system personified by the woman seeks to use him and so rides the beast as if to direct. But it is really the beast who is carrying the woman, using her for political advantage.

Eventually the little horn, the beast becomes the supreme leader of the ten kingdoms and makes a seven year covenant with Israel to protect them from the kings of the north and south. Coming up to the middle of this covenant, that is three and a half years, the beast has no more use for the religious influence, the harlot and with sudden and tremendous force destroys her, using the ten kings to burn her with fire.

The reason for this is his ambition to set himself up as God, (2 Thess. 2) and the woman would need to be removed. This is one of the trigger points that issue in the Great Tribulation. She would oppose him as her allegiance is to the one God, howbeit deceived in seeking God by religion and not by Christ.

This chapter then records the destruction of the religious woman who has been responsible for the blood of the faithful men and women throughout the course of the ages. The time of vengeance will have come and the Lord shall use the power of the beast to destroy her, and so to recompense the blood of the martyrs.

THE CITY OF CHAPTER 18

In the previous pages the similarities between the woman and the city have been noted. On the strength of this, both seem to be the same thing. If such be the case, then the judgment of the city in 18 is the same as that of the woman in the previous chapter, and taking place about the middle of the seven year period. The fact that the city is not mentioned any more throughout the Revelation would suggest that this is so. The woman is burnt with fire (17:16), the city is also burnt with fire, "she shall utterly be burnt with fire" (18:8). "They shall see the smoke of her burnings" (18:9) and again repeated in verse 18. Note it is HER burnings.

The contents of the chapter point in this direction that both are the same judgment.

1) The announcement of the fall of Babylon by an angel in verses 1-3. It is an angel that also announces the judgment of the harlot in 17:1. The earth is lightened with glory as if to say "the darkness has been removed".

2) The crimes that call forth the judgment in 3-6, the spiritual fornication with the kings of the earth, and her riches and influence. Two calls come in here, the call for the faithful to separate from her, and the call from heaven to judge her. This proves that the chapter has nothing to do with the kingdom of the beast, to be part of that is to receive the mark and to worship the image. This is a system in ch. 18 and not a kingdom.

3) The suddenness of the judgment is seen in verses 7-8, she least expected it, she was complacent, then in one day the judgment fell.

4) The mourning of the kings of the earth is seen in 9-11.

5) Verses 12-14 note the past merchandise of the city, and all are religious trappings, the list ends with the souls of men. These could be the people caught up in the system and who become fanatical slaves to what the woman and city represent. All is to the losing of their souls.

6) Again the mourners are seen in 15-19. These could be like the silversmiths of Acts 19 who suffered loss of trade because of the gospel. These suffer loss by the destruction of the religious system.

7) The call from heaven to the apostles and prophets to rejoice over the judgment, "God hath avenged you on her" (Verse 20).

8) The action of the angel casting the millstone into the sea with the announcement that the violent judgment is sure and final, this can only be of the religious system (Verse 21).

9) The pleasure is all over in 22-23. The entertainment, skilful industry, and the social life with its attendant evils will be closed forever.

10) The final verse 24 is the reason for the judgment, and a fitting close to the section which has for its subject, "The Blood of the Martyrs".

A summary of these four chapters is given in chapter 19:2. "For true and righteous are His judgments, for He hath judged the great whore which did corrupt the earth with her fornication, and hath avenged the blood of His servants at her hand". This includes all of chapters 15-18.

CHAPTER THIRTY-TWO

Chapters 15-18 Viewed Practically

This section dealing with the treacherous deeds of those who slay the martyrs of Jesus, and their just revenge, also yields a great harvest of practical suggestions. Chapter 15 is easily divided into two parts, verses 1-4 are blessing verses 5-8 are judgment.

Here very distinctly two classes of people are presented, the saved and their blessing, and the lost with their terrible doom.

Right at the beginning of this section is a sign, one of three in the Revelation and this forms a series as elsewhere found in Scripture. Triple signs as noted previously are first found in Exodus 3-4, Moses at the burning bush, these were concerning Israel in bondage and their deliverance, with the judgment of their enemies. Here again the last series of triple signs also concern Israel and their deliverance from the enemy and the judgment that follows.

The three signs in Revelation are the woman, Israel in ch.12, the dragon also in ch. 12 and the seven angels of wrath in this chapter.

These correspond with the three signs at the burning bush. One was relating to a serpent, and the sign in ch. 12 is the dragon. Another concerned Israel in the flesh, and this corresponds with the woman in ch. 12. The last one is always judgment, the turning of the water into blood which became the first of the 10 plagues upon Egypt, corresponding with the bowls of wrath here, one of these turns water to blood in ch. 16.

The enemy, God's people, and the judgment are the subjects in both sets of signs. This has a practical import, here is the patience of the saints, the Lord soon comes in to defend and deliver His own, judging the enemy in the process.

Consider the overcomers in verse 15:2 they are upon a sea of glass, this is seen empty in chapter 4 now full, yes, a place is prepared for the people of God. A sea of glass in which it is impossible for people to sink, not so with Peter in Matt. 14 who when walking upon the water began to sink. Many failures are met with down here but there will be none up there.

This sea of glass answers to the laver, there will be no need of washings up there, nothing to hide, crystal speaks of purity in the Bible, these are made pure by the blood of the Lamb.

They overcome four dreadful things. The beast, they feared not man as exhorted in Matt. 10. The image, which speaks of idolatry and covetousness, their possessions were in a better place. The mark of the beast, which is identification with the apostate world. This is in contrast to those of ch. 14 who have the mark of the Father upon their foreheads. The last thing they overcome is "the number", this is man in the flesh. These were overcomers in all these.

The harps of God are found three times in Rev. and always accompany a song, hence praise. So with the 24 elders in 5:8, there it is praise unto the Lamb. In 14:2 the harps are used in a personal song of praise based upon the experience of the 144000 they alone can sing that song. Here the martyrs in 15:2 are with the harps of God, all that they are and have, God is the source. It is interesting to note that harpers are again mentioned in the close of ch. 18 there in the hands of the ungodly and silenced because of judgment. Together then, there are four references to harps and harpers, three to do with the godly and one with the ungodly, as usual in the Scriptures the four is divided into a three and a one.

Another interesting fact is that there are no wind instruments used by saints in heaven, the trumpet is used by the Lord in chapter one and four, and by angels in 8-11. The trumpet is for battle and gatherings of the earth. Heaven is for praise; hence the harp.

The song of Moses is the first and last song in the Bible. Moses is here described as the servant of God, not the leader. This takes up from the first chapter of Joshua, Moses my servant is dead, but his work goes on right into the last days in the song. There is an addition to the song here, that of the Lamb. The song of Moses is the judgment over the enemy as in Ex. 15 here is added the exaltation of the Lamb, the Messiah entering into His rightful place. Moses knew little of this.

The song presents the Lord in a threefold way, His title as King of nations depicting His sovereignty, His works, they are great, and His ways are righteous and true. All this is to do with God revealing Himself in a governmental way to this world. He showed His ways unto Moses and His works unto the children of Israel (Ps. 103:7). Israel knew God's works in deliverance etc.. But Moses knew God's ways, the principles by which He acts and moves. This was a very mature knowledge of God, many see His works in their own conversions and lives but how many understand His ways ? These martyrs are very mature, the song includes experience of the works and ways of Jehovah.

Millennial features appear in 15:4. the Name Jehovah in contrast to the beast. This will be the centre of gathering and worship in the coming kingdom age.

Note a few lovely points on "the gathering centre". The gathering is to the Name, JEHOVAH. Holy is the character of the one to whom they gather. The attraction to the Name comes from all nations. Worship is the purpose of the gathering. These ought to be the features of churches today, in a real way the Lord shall enjoy this homage in the Millennium.

The second part of chapter 15 portrays the judgment, the seven angels are the main object of the vision, but before these are seen, as ever the saints are secure as in verses 1-4.

The seven angels are described in a twofold way, clothed in pure and white linen, and having their breasts girded with golden girdles. The garments obviously speak of purity, what God requires, and the gold of Divine righteousness, this is what impurity meets with. Here is the righteousness of the judgment upon the beast and his kingdom which lack cleanness. The unclean must be judged from His presence. The symbol of brass as judgment is usual in a scene like this, but here the nature of God is offended by the corruption of Babylon, hence the righteous Divine judgment as seen in the gold.

The ark is mentioned in this section. This is the covenant with Israel, now fulfilled in Christ. These are delivered under the covenant of the blood of Christ, the new covenant. The temple is called the tabernacle of the testimony in heaven and the angels issue forth from this. All else in testimony came from the same source, the law from heaven, God came down, the gospel as a light from heaven as in the case of Saul of Tarsus, the Spirit came down etc.. If the message is not received, then the judgment comes from the same source.

CHAPTER 16 THE ANGELS

As noted in past pages of this book this section contains the great things of both man and God. The great things of man really interest the believer but little, however every believer should admire and enter into the good of the great things of God. These angels of chapter 16 do that, and have part in the same.

Angels are of special interest to the church as seen in 1 Cor.:-

a) Paul speaks of the apostles being a spectacle to the world to angels and men, angels watched the apostles and saw the Christ likeness there (1 Cor. 4).
b) In 1 Cor. 11 the angels are watching the behaviour of the believers especially the head covering of the female.
c) In 1 Cor. 13 one reads of the tongues of angels, yet these are not as important as the edifying ministry in the church.
d) Eph. 3:10 indicates that the church is an object lesson to angels, there they see the wonderful grace of God.
e) Added to this is the fact that the church shall govern angels in the Millennium in 1 Cor. 6. In all this surely it is meant that we can learn from angels.

Angels are the chief part of this great vision in Rev. 15-18, their service is seen in chapter 16 and the aftermath of their work is detailed in chapter 17-18.

In the going forth of these angels many lessons can be learnt by even the simplest believer. Consider a few of these:-

Where they start from is important, the temple in heaven (15:6). All service should have this in view, all must start from God and His clear direction.

"Go your ways" (16:1) here is clear indication of the path the Lord would have them take. Such was the Lord in the days of His flesh, "in all thy ways" is what the devil omitted in the temptation. The Lord

Jesus followed only the path that His Father had set before Him. Paul speaks of "my ways in Christ which I teach in every church" in 1 Cor. 4:17.

Each angel has his own sphere of service, one to the earth, another to the sea, another to the rivers. One affects the sun, another the beast, another the river Euphrates and the last one affects the air. They are not all doing the same thing except pouring out their bowls, but all work the same judgment as from the Lord.

In this light the effect is different. Angel one affects the flesh of men, and angel two, the sea, symbol of commerce and shipping. Another affects the waters that none can drink, symbol perhaps of the pleasures of men. The sun is then affected, the light of men. The beast, the kingdom of men is affected, and the destiny of man in the frogs. Finally the headquarters of men in the city. These angels have a ministry that bites and is felt; would the ministry of saints were the same, except for good and not for judgment.

A contrast to these effects and spheres can be well applied to believers today.

We war against the flesh in 2 Cor. 10

We ought to trade with our God given talents

The river of life for men is our proclamation, John 4

Christ must be presented as the Light of the world

We must advance the kingdom of our Lord Jesus as in Acts. 8

Our destiny is the glory

The city upon which we set our mind is the new Jerusalem, and not the cities of this earth.

Before leaving this great chapter note the searching sections that emerge. The retribution in 5-6, they shed the blood of martyrs and are given blood to drink. Here is the sowing and reaping principle, and it is ever true even to the people of God.

The readiness of verse 15 is important. Readiness as in Sardis, and careful not to be found naked as in Laodicea. The exhortation to these churches is embodied in this appeal.

CHAPTER 17 THE WORLD RELIGION

Verse 3 of this chapter speaks of "being in the Spirit" and this occurs four times in the book in an interesting connection.

The first occurrence is in chapter one, John in Patmos and the second in chapter 4 where John is caught up to heaven. Here are earth and heaven, and one can expect to be "in the Spirit" in heaven, but the same can be true when on earth.

The next two occurrences of the phrase are found in verse 4 of our chapter then in ch. 21:10. Again a great contrast is evident, one speaks of the false bride and the other of the true bride of Christ. Such a contrast, the wilderness and the mountain, corruption and purity, destruction and glory.

The description of the woman in this chapter is in keeping with what the world looks for in religion, and it is ever so.

1) Influence as in verse 1 and 15, to influence much people and many great religious movements strive for numbers above all else.
2) Clothing and ritual figure much with most religions these days. This of course stems from the high priestly garments which finished with the law by the bringing in of Christ.
3) Gold, jewels and adornment with precious things. Riches are much to the fore in world religions. True, it takes money to keep any church or movement going, expenses must be paid, but this is aggrandisement, the adornment of rich buildings etc.. Many religious groups today boast of their riches.
4) The cup would speak of unity, and today a movement is in progress to bring together all the churches of various persuasions into one great whole.
5) Babylon is long standing, and speaks of the tradition handed down. Again this is a great part of many religions, the great traditional heritage from the glorious past.
6) The political affinity is again sought by many religions. The mingling of religion and state is seen often in the O.T. Pharaoh and the magicians are a case in point, so with Balak the king and Balaam the prophet. This will be the situation in the last days, the woman here is religious and the beast is political and one rides the other.

CONTRAST THE NEW TESTAMENT BELIEVER TO THIS

The two or three in Matt. 18:20 affect the Lord, a church does not depend on numbers, rather spirituality.

Clothing of the sisters is dealt with in 1 Tim. 2 and a sister can present a godly attitude in the way she dresses. It must be modest and as becoming saints.

Spiritual riches are to be desired rather than material riches. The rich man of the parable in Luke 12 was not rich towards God.

Riches are all right and useful if carried well, but nothing can make up for the spiritual riches, Paul speaks of being poor yet making many rich.

Unity of the Spirit is the teaching of Eph. 4. The lack of unity in the church at Corinth was the cause of all their problems.

Rather than tradition handed down, the true believer ought to have the ear for the commands of our Lord Jesus, he is Lord of all.

Complete separation from the political world and the religious world is the call to the believer in 2 Cor. 6. Our citizenship is in heaven, a pilgrim character is what the believer ought to be in the sight of God. As for the religious world, the call comes in ch. 18:4 to come out of her my people.

WHAT REALLY IS FOUND THERE

Empty profession is there. The word "harlot" used to describe this system proves that the followers are not genuine, they were never joined to the Lord as in Eph. 5:30.

Uncleanness and spiritual fornication are there, and very often the natural lusts of the flesh are unbridled as well.

How terrible, the names of blasphemy characterize this woman. That is, the system takes upon itself names that belong only to God, to apply these to humans is blasphemy.

The woman stands for the rejection of all Bible loving believers.

There is no place for the truth where error prevails.

The abominations speak of idolatry, this can not be only towards lifeless objects but to living persons as well. Even believers can fall into this error.

The Lord Jesus who came in grace is also rejected. All truth is embodied in Him, and to disagree with His Person and work is error indeed, He is the test of all doctrine and practice.

CONTRAST THE TRUE BELIEVER

A believer is joined to the Lord in 1 Cor. 6:17
A believer is sanctified in the Spirit in 1 Pet. 1:2
They give the Lord Jesus the rightful place in their lives.
Their love in measure goes out to all the people of God, as in
1 Cor. 13
Such keep themselves from idols as 1 John 5:21
They love the Lord Jesus and life is conducted with Him in view.
To grow up in Him in Eph. 4:15
To walk in Him Col. 2:6
Eventually to be conformed to Him Rom. 8:29
Now seeking to put on Him as a garment in Rom. 13:14
And while waiting for Him, serving Him 1 Thess. 1:10

THE PRESENTATION OF CHRIST IN ALL THIS

In such a chapter that warns of present evil that shall steadily increase, there appear lovely pictures of the Lord Jesus.

1) He is seen as JESUS in verse 6. The Meek One but in whom salvation is found in contrast to the profession that is the character of the woman system.
2) The LAMB is seen in verse 14. In this character He is exalted above all and made Lord of lords and King of kings.
3) The KING appears also in verse 14, all will be subjected to Him after His righteous and powerful judgment deals with all His enemies.

The faithful followers also appear with Him in verse 14.
They are "Called", this is grace.
"Chosen", this is sovereignty.
"Faithful", this manifests the wise choice, they shall not
fail Him.

THE CITY IN CHAPTER 18

A few words will suffice here in a practical way. In the exposition the suggestion has been made that the woman and the city are but two views of the same thing. So all that has been said about the woman is true of the city. However, a few important things come to the fore in this great chapter.

This is what the world seeks after and shall see in this fullness in the last days.

1) All nations are affected by the grandeur of this city
2) Pleasures wine and uncleanness are the order of the day
3) Commerce and riches are typical of the desires and pursuits of the occupants
4) Self glorification is the character of its people.
5) A long list of pleasures appear in verses 22-3, such are the world's pursuits
6) The source of all is the devil in v 23

A word of warning comes from the pen of N. T. writers.
Love not the world (1 John 2:15)
Conform not to the world (Rom. 12:2)
Beware of friendship with the world (James 4:4)
Avoid the wisdom of this world (1 Cor. 1:20)
Keep no company with the fornicators of this world (2 Cor 5:10)
Care not for the things of the world in 1 Cor. 7:34. and so forth.
Exhortations to be separate from the world abound in the Bible.
This is the world that is depicted in this city of Rev. 18.

HEAVEN IS AFFECTED BY THIS CITY

Their sins reach unto heaven, the righteous there cry for just judgment while the mercy of God waits (Verse 5).

Heaven is called upon to rejoice over her judgment in verse 20.

This goes forward into chapter 19 where three of the four halleluiahs concern the woman who is the city.

This world with its pleasures and pending judgment is no place for the people of God, "come out of her my people that ye be not partakers of her sins, and that ye receive not of her plagues" (Verse 4).

CHAPTER THIRTY-THREE

The Seven Judgments of ch. 19-20

These two chapters compose the sixth section of the Revelation which is the shortest so far.

The suggestion put forth in these writings is that each section of the Revelation deals with a problem that would arise in the minds of the persecuted people of God at any given time. This of course leads up into a climax in the last days.

While this section is short, but two chapters, yet the question that arises is a very important one. When the beloved and persecuted people of God consider the confusion, the departure from God and the open defiance against God and all righteousness. It is then the question will be asked, "Can God really judge the world, can God sort all these enemies out"? Yes, He can and will, and the Spirit inspires John to gather together in this section seven great judgments that shall lead to the defeat of all the enemies of God and of His people.

THE SEVEN JUDGMENTS

1) The woman of 17-18 comes first. God is not deceived, all the hypocrisy and false pretences are seen by God. She has already been dealt with in chapters 17-18 but is brought forward again to be included in this series of judgments.

2) The beast is also summarily dealt with in 19:19-20. He will be the personification of political violence as is the woman of religious deception. One is Satan as an angel of light and the other as the roaring lion. The beast will be cast alive into the lake of fire.

3) The false prophet is likewise dealt with, he will be the arch deceiver of Israel, but he shall deceive no more. The lake of fire shall be his doom as well (19:19-20).

4) The armies of the nations of the earth with all their leaders shall be drawn to the plain of Megiddo and shall also come to a swift end. They will choose to fight against Him who is upon the white horse and shall be consumed by His word, the sword that issues from His mouth.

5) Satan also comes into his long awaited judgment. Here is the seed of the woman finally crushing the head of the serpent.

6) The passage goes on finally to the end of the Millennium and the nations (those not engaged in Armageddon) will be consumed with fire out of heaven. It is at this point that the earth shall pass away.

7) The last to be judged will be those who have died without Christ right from the beginning of time. This comes last as if to suggest the reluctance of God to mete out judgment, but His righteous character proclaims so it must be.

Yes, God is able to judge all who are in opposition to Him, and He will do so at the appointed time.

Another enemy is destroyed in these chapters but is not mentioned in this section. It is not until 21:4 that it is announced "There shall be no more death". The last enemy to be destroyed is death (1 Cor. 15:26).

THE TABERNACLE REFERENCE

As previously noted a Tabernacle reference comes early in each section and is an indication of the theme of that section. The first section on the churches begins with the Lampstand, the theme is testimony, and the Lampstand in the Tabernacle is a similar symbol of this.

The Tabernacle reference can clearly be seen early in this section, and that is the fine linen clean and white of 19:8. This of course looks back to the court of the Tabernacle which was made of fine twined linen in Ex. 27. But why this, what can this mean ? The fine linen that composed the Tabernacle was the display of God's righteousness to the world without. Also the place of safety is indicated as being inside the court, a figure of salvation. Both ideas appear in these chapters. Here is a wonderful display of the righteousness of God manifested in the judgment of the universe. Here also is the goodness of God in providing salvation as in the Bride of Christ, the church, and the out working of righteousness in the lives of those who compose the church. The linen is the righteous acts of the saints. This is the display in glory of God recompensing the faithfulness of His saints, and all according to their works. Behold the goodness and severity of God as in Rom. 11:22.

Israel also come into their promised salvation in ch. 20.

COMPARISON WITH SECTION TWO

Early in this book attention was drawn to the seven clear divisions of the Revelation, each forming a distinct section, and the fact that together they were written in a series of inverted parallels. This section comprising 19-20 is therefore over against the second part that recorded the opening of the seven seals in chapters 4-7

The main themes of the seal section are repeated here in section six. Howbeit, there is great advancement, all is carried to a permanent conclusion. These are most profitable to consider.

1) The counterfeit king who emerged in the first seal (Chapt. 6) is here destroyed by the King of kings. He that is faithful and true.

2) The second seal produced wars, but here in chapter 19 is the final war, the war to end all wars, Armageddon.

3) The famines are the burden of the third seal, but here is abundance and plenty. The birds even can eat to their full.

4) The fourth seal called forward the pale horse and its rider whose name was death, and hell followed. Here death and hell are cast into the lake of fire, this is the second death.

5) The fifth seal depicted a scene in heaven, the martyred souls crying for just vengeance. Here that vengeance is manifested and the same servants are enthroned.

6) Every mountain and island is moved out of its place in seal six. Here in this section the heaven and the earth pass away and there is found no place for them.

7) Silence in heaven was the outcome of the seventh seal. These chapters make it clear that the heavens shall no longer be silent, the longsuffering of God has come to an end. The terrible bursting forth of judgment is recorded here. Yet with all that, God delights in mercy. Chapter seven comes in with salvation in that seal section, the innumerable company of the saved in heaven. Here is the Bride, the church presented and Israel at last receiving their promised place as reigning in the kingdom of their Messiah.

It is interesting to see the three ways the church is presented in the Revelation.

In chapters 21-3 it is seen in the symbol of lampstands, that is, in testimony to this dark world.

In 4-16 the church appears as "elders" in heaven before the throne of God. This is the position after the rapture and before the revelation of the Son of Man.

Finally the church appears as the bride and this will be the future manifestation of the church during and after the coming of the Lord in kingdom power. Note, these ideas do not overlap, when the elders come into the book there is no more mention of the lampstands. When the bride comes into view there is no more mention of the elders. These seem to be the three views of the church as seen in three different times.

The lampstand is testimony now. The elder is intelligence in the glory, and the bride is the display of glory on into eternity.

1. THE JUDGMENT OF THE WOMAN

This remarkable chapter opens with four Halleluiahs, and these would compare with the four great outbursts of praise in chapter 4-5. Halleluiah means Praise the Lord, and occurs often in the Psalms. The last five Psalms could well be called "Halleluiah Psalms" because each begins and closes with Halleluiah, Praise the Lord. Mostly the use of Halleluiah in the Psalms is in the context of judgment, and this is the case in Rev. 19. Three of the Halleluiahs here have to do with the judgment of the women of 17 and the fourth has to do with the Bride of the Lamb. Here are the two brides in contrast, the false and the true. One is the counterfeit, mother of harlots committing spiritual fornication as in 17. The other is the true Bride and the purity is seen in the clean and white linen garments. The contrast in the two women cannot fail to be noticed.

One is a harlot the other is a virgin (2 Cor. 11:3).

The first woman is for the beast, the second for the Lamb.

Babylon is connected with the first and the New Jerusalem with the second in chapter 21.

The harlot woman is for time only, the bride eternal.

Corruption is the feature of the first, purity the second.

Judgment was the principle thought of 17:1 and the woman there has a part in events leading up to the Great Tribulation. Here the judgment only is noticed in 19:1-3, the reason for this is that these two chapters present the ability of God to judge all opposition in His own time. She shed the blood of the martyrs, now the avenger of blood has caught up with her.

The judgment as far as earth is concerned will be swift, "in one hour is thy judgment come" (18:10). However, the judgment goes beyond time into eternity in 19:3, "her smoke rose up for ever and ever".

The fourfold praise to God of verse 1 is to the effect that God can judge the world, yet His hand in salvation is manifest. The words of praise in verse one sums up all. The salvation and glory would well apply to the bride of the Lamb, and the honour and power would be seen in the doom of the harlot. This power in fact carries right through the section in the just judgment of all the enemies of God.

2. THE BEAST IN 19:20

The conqueror of chapter 6:1-2 is conquered. The beast appears in 13:1 with ten diadems upon his horns, but here the Lord Jesus wears many diadems. He has the victory and the greater glory. It is wonderful that salvation came to Saul of Tarsus by the appearing of our Lord to him on the Damascus Road, but here the Lord destroys by His appearing, even the brightness of His coming (2 Thess. 2:8).

The events that lead up to this scene seem to be as follows:-

The Tribulation in the closing stages is augmented by the bowls of wrath which are the last plagues of the wrath of God. Somewhere about this time the beast and his armies compass Jerusalem and destroy it. (Zech. 14:1-2). Then the kings of the earth cross the Euphrates and array themselves for battle in the north of Megiddo. Tidings of this comes to the ears of the beast according to Dan. 11. The beast with his armies and accomplices proceed to Megiddo to engage in battle. Before the battle commences the Lord returns in glory according to verses 11-18 of our chapter. The forces of the East and the beast seemingly join forces to fight against Him that sits upon the white horse. Then the terrible slaughter of Armageddon takes place. The beast is taken and cast alive into the lake of fire.

3. THE FALSE PROPHET 19-20

The false prophet is never mentioned apart from the beast, so he must perish alongside the beast. This would teach us to watch our company, we may also be apportioned a share of their discipline if not careful. The great deceiver is now exposed. the Lord is the Faithful and True One. The false prophet is no doubt the false christ, the performer of miracles having their source in the dragon. This is the one that had that compelling influence to set up the image and cause all great and small to receive the mark of the beast. It is all only for a little while, like the one he followed, he too has his part in the lake of fire.

4. THE ARMIES V 19-21

The nations of earth today boast of their strength, yet the mighty armies of the mightiest nations with all their technical warfare are dispensed with in one verse of our Bible.

The northern powers have already been destroyed at this stage according to Ezek. 38-9. Also the kings of the south as in Dan. 11. The remaining armies of the east and the western armies of the beast are summarily dealt with in this verse. This is the battle of Armageddon, and this is not the first reference to it in the Rev..

Chapter 14 speaks of the blood bath, the blood extending for 200 miles and up to the bridles of the horses, metaphorically speaking, the people shall wade in blood.

Chapter 16 reads that the Euphrates will be dried up to make the passage for the kings of the east. The three unclean spirits there issuing from the trinity of evil deceive and compel all to come to the place of slaughter. The design of the dragon in this is not difficult to observe. It is to bring death swiftly to many people, to end their opportunities and to place them beyond the grace of the gospel. There could be an even deeper and more sinister design in the gathering of the nations. That is to seek to overcome God's Man, the true Christ. He knows he can but fail (Chapter 12), he has but a short time. Nevertheless he will try to overcome. It shall be as the temptation in the wilderness, Satan himself and his designs shall be defeated.

Chapter 9 is also linked to this battle and gives an idea of the tremendous amount of people that will be involved. The horsemen forming one side only amount to 200 million. No wonder the slaughter becomes such a blood bath.

5. SATAN, THE DRAGON 20:1-3

Here the might on the side of God comes out beautifully. Satan is strong, yea the strong man of the parable. An angel described as a strong angel however has greater power and lays hold of the dragon and renders him helpless.

The Lord spoke three parables that included the workings of Satan, and in all three he miserably fails. In the parable of the sower the devil takes away the good seed from the wayside, but he cannot touch the good ground. God continues to receive fruit from the gospel and the harvest is sure.

In the parable of the tares and the wheat, the tares sown by the devil shall eventually be gathered and consigned to the furnace of fire with their master soon to follow. The wheat prospers.

In the parable of the strong man already alluded to, Satan the strong man is overcome and bound by the stronger man, even Christ in His manhood.

The course of Satan is always downward. He was cast out from the presence of God in Ezek. 14. He will be cast out of heaven as in Rev. 12. He will be consigned to the bottomless pit in our chapter and eventually into the eternal lake of fire. All his followers shall be brought down with him.

Young men can overcome him in 1 John 2, even weak saints can resist him and he will flee.

Note the threefold expression of his captivity. The key to the bottomless pit, the great chain and the binding, (20:1). The chain and key are not literal of course, these would speak of great authority and power that cannot be surmounted.

His four titles are here again as in chapter 12, there active, but here rendered inactive in all four ways.

He will be bound for 1000 years yet he emerges just the same. He cannot be reformed or altered. The final revolt brings him into eternal pain and not into 1000 years of captivity.

6. THE NATIONS 20:8-9

There will be a great judgment of the nations in two stages. That of Matt. 25 at the return of the Lord when He sits upon the throne of His glory and the nations are brought before Him. This judgment precedes the Millennium and the saved are known as the sheep, and go into the Kingdom. However, they are human, and not in a glorified state as in resurrection. Hence children will be born, all will be confronted with the Word of God and Christ. Many will reject, and sin and death will still be present in spite of Millennial conditions. This is clearly seen in such passages as Zech. 14 where in some places the rain will be withheld because of the refusal to worship Christ. After 1000 years men will have increased tremendously upon the earth and Satan will be loosed for a little season, but little effort will bring about the revolt spoken of in this chapter. People can never be changed without the Lord. This is one of the many reasons for the Millennium, to prove to man his awful sinful depravity, that cannot be improved even in Millennial conditions.

Fallen man shall still be the same even without the devil who will be bound during the repopulation of the earth.

Again the nations great and mighty are dispensed with in one verse as previously the armies before them, "fire came down from God out of heaven and devoured them" (20:9).

The extensiveness of the revolt is seen in the threefold description here. The four quarters of the earth, as the sand of the sea, and they went up upon the breadth of the earth.

7. THE WICKED DEAD CHAPTER 20

Chapter 20:11-15 are perhaps the most solemn verses in the whole Bible. Here is the resurrection of the unjust, all those who have died without Christ. Although they will be raised with a form of resurrected body they are always called the "dead", in fact dead and death are mentioned 7 times in the passage. Dead in trespasses and sins (Eph. 2:1) they were spiritually dead in their lifetime and did not receive life in Christ through the gospel. Hence they carried their spiritual death into physical death and the grave, and from hence into the lake of fire, the second death.

These are judged according to their works. Perhaps three books at least will be opened at the judgment. The Scriptures no doubt, as the Lord said, "the words that I have spoken, the same shall judge him in the last day" (John 12:48). The book of life will be opened, alas no name there. The book or the records of the works of man as here. The book of works may be symbolic of the infinite knowledge of God concerning every person. Psalm 139 would bring this out, "There is not a word in my tongue but lo O Lord thou knowest it altogether" (Verse 4), and then the passage goes on to explain that nothing and no one can be hidden from God.

The second death is final and eternal. The first death will reign for approximately 7000 years, but the second death will reign for ever and ever.

These two chapters manifest that God can judge the world and that He in righteousness shall do so in His own time and way.

CHAPTER THIRTY-FOUR

The Practical Application of Rev. 19-20

In the previous chapter the theme of Revelation 19-20 has been traced. All the material is tied together to give the assurance that God can and will judge all that is in opposition to His rule and the Revelation of Christ. These two chapters can also lend themselves to a devotional and practical approach in a wonderful presentation of Christ at His appearing and the subsequent happy lot of those who believe in Him.

Chapter 19 can easily be divided into 2 sections

1. The false and true bride verses 1-10
2. The true and false king   verses 11-21

Consider first the coming of the rightful king, the true Christ.

Six wonderful verses (11-16) present Him in a twelvefold description. This is the last of four great symbolic pictures of Christ in the Revelation. The first appears in chapter 1, containing a tenfold display of the Glorious Man in the midst of the lampstands. Here is a twelvefold account relative to Israel and the nations. Much has been written about this marvellous passage, yet the depth is bound to be beyond the most experienced and spiritual of minds. However a few short considerations shall be necessary.

THE VISION OF THE LORD ON THE WHITE HORSE

1) The whole description is in the language of war. The white horse was usually the carriage of a victorious general in Roman times. His vesture dipped in blood would indicate the magnitude of the slaughter of Armageddon. The armies of heaven accompanying Him would be to oppose the armies of earth. The sharp sword would be symbolic of the terrible destruction when He but speaks the word, He will destroy all enemies by the breath of His mouth. The Lord makes war in verse 11, the winepress of the wrath of God is mentioned in verse 15. This is a "Holy War", even Armageddon.

2) Many devoted saints cannot fail to observe the stark contrast with the first coming of Christ.

There He rode on an ass but here upon a white horse.

In the past, the eyes of the blessed Lord shed tears and there are three references to this in the gospels, but here His eyes are as a flame of fire.

He was crowned with thorns upon the cross, here He is crowned with many diadems.

His humble name Jesus was written upon His cross, in this passage His name is called the Word of God, Faithful and True, King of Kings and Lord of Lords.

His garments were divided in the Gospels, here his vesture is dipped in blood.

On the cross He was alone, even forsaken of God, now all the armies of heaven accompany Him.

Gracious words proceeded from His mouth in the days of His ministry, in this passage the words of death and destruction issue from His mouth.

One could go on, every detail in this passage has a throwback to the days of the flesh of our Lord Jesus.

3) In this wondrous passage a great significance is placed upon the Names by which the Victor on the white horse is called. There are four in all.

(1) In verse 11 He is called "Faithful and True". This would be His character as revealed in the past. He was the faithful and true servant

and witness always, and this would correspond with the Gospel of Mark, being that of the "Servant".

(2) He has a Name written that no man knows but He Himself in verse 12, corresponding with the spiritual mysteries as depicted in the Gospel of John.

(3) His Name is called "The Word of God" in verse 13. This would be along the line of the Gospel of Luke. Great emphasis there is placed upon the clear messages the Lord preached. The parables of Luke are masterpieces of the wisdom and knowledge of God.

(4) The final Name written, "King of kings and Lord of Lords" appears in verse 16. This of course is parallel to the Kingly gospel of Matthew. There He was King of the Jews, here He is King of kings.

Consider further, "Faithful and True" is moral. For Israel and all nations He is faithful, His promises are dependable. He has the right quality to assess all and reward or discipline accordingly. Nothing can be hidden from His eyes which are as a flame of fire.

The Name no man knows, this would express Divinity.

a) The stone with a new name written which no man knows is given to the "overcomer in Rev. 2:17.

b) A new song is sung in Ch. 14 that no man can learn.

c) Here the Lord has a Name that only Himself knows.

All these "new things" speak of personal experience The Lord had experiences in His incarnation and subsequent ministry that was only known to God, a whole burnt offering.

The reference to the Word of God in verse 13 is God in human form, Humanity in order to communicate in revelation. This is John's word to present the incarnation of a Divine Person as in John chapter one. As a Man He could relate to humans although He was God, and as such He declared the Father. All this is summed up in Heb. 1:1, God has spoken unto us in (the person of His) Son. We know that the Son of God is come and hath given us an understanding ... this is the true God and eternal life (1 John 5:19). Old Bible preachers used to say, "nothing can be revealed after the Son", the N T. writers that followed interpreted Him. This Name "The Word of God" is for the church.

The King of kings in v 16 would be Royalty. The titles are reversed in 17:14. Here the King of kings comes first because the subject is "sovereignty", the bringing in of the peaceful reign of Christ. Lord of lords comes first in Rev. 17 because there the subject is authority, not the system symbolized by the scarlet woman, but that of the Lord Jesus, He shall have all authority.

The Lord Jesus is anointed above His fellows in Heb. 1:9 and this is certainly the case in these names. In summing up, the Faithful and True is for Israel and the nations. The Unknown name is for God. The Word of God is for the church, and the King of kings and Lord of lords is for the world and the kingdom.

4) The first and last of these names especially would be towards Israel while the war-like description is towards the enemies, the Beast and False Prophet and nations. However, at the coming of the Lord all these Names shall have Israel in mind. Israel rejected the Person of the Faithful and True One. His ministry was the Word of God, which was also rejected. His claim and the proof of Kingship alike were rejected, and his mysterious Person the Son of God could not be comprehended by Israel. These titles are for the nation Israel in that coming day. Israel shall receive Him is all His fullness.

To His enemies the white horse, the sword, the vesture and the armies manifest His glorious victory and their sure defeat.

Such a passage, the One who humbled Himself will be publicly exalted, this in turn produces worship in the hearts of His believing followers.

THE TESTIMONY OF JESUS 19:10

John fell at the feet of the interpreting angel to worship him. He saw the might and power of angels in the visions, power over fire, power over waters and many other things. One must realize the power of even one angel, 2 Kings 19:35 would demonstrate this, one angel slew 185000 warring men of Assyria. The angel before John is one of those that poured out the bowls of the wrath of God in ch. 16. He then took John to see the woman and the city in ch. 17-18, and was able to interpret the vision of the woman and the beast in ch. 17. He seems also to be the one who reveals the Bride in Ch. 19 and gives the command to write in 19:9. Such overwhelming power and understanding, John is overcome and falls down to worship this very angel. The angel will have none of this, and says "see thou do it not". This mighty angel is only an angel, a servant of God whose power comes from God just like John himself, and this is true of the humblest servant of the Lord as well as the so called "great". Angels serve in the sphere of earthly and heavenly things, so also the prophets, Apostles and the servant of the Lord in our day.

The angel draws attention to Christ. If such an knowledgable and powerful angel is not to be worshipped, much less human servants of God. Yet the tendency in religious circles is to "hero worship" the preachers and servants of God, especially they who are the special instruments of the power of God and channels of the knowledge of God. The angel draws attention to Christ in a beautiful twofold way. "The testimony of Jesus is the spirit of prophecy".

Consider the testimony of Jesus. The Bible with all its various doctrines and means of presentation is not for the curious mind to unravel as one would solve puzzles. Rather the whole revelation together presents a PERSON, and that person is Jesus, His human name by which He came into the world. The eternal Son became a man and this is the witness of the Word of God. Right from the beginning God spoke of the seed of the woman and the seed of Abraham in Genesis, the first book of the Bible. All this anticipated the coming of the Perfect Man. Even the wood in the tabernacle displayed the same ideal Manhood. So with the offerings and the great prophecies concerning the "Servant of Jehovah". All the different lines meet in the glorious Son of Man. All testify unto Him, this is the testimony of Jesus.

How often in meetings prophecy is treated the wrong way. Some have the reputation of being "prophetic scholars" and unwittingly draw attention to themselves instead of to the Person of the Son of Man. Fantastic statements concerning the future (often misleading) draw large crowds. The point is being missed, all prophetic teaching should circle around the the Lord Jesus, He must have His rightful place. He is the spirit of prophecy.

The prophecies concerning Israel shall eventually be fulfilled when Christ is recognized as their Messiah. Prophecies concerning the world shall be fulfilled when the resurrected Man rules the World (Acts 17:31). The prophecies that embrace the church will come to fulfilment when the Bridegroom comes and glorifies His Bride. Jesus is all and fills the picture as verses 11-21 go on to record.

THE OUTCOME OF THE GOSPEL

Ch. 20 of the Rev. is wonderful in its scope and predictions, and the source of excellent material from which to preach the gospel. How often the Spirit of God has put fear into souls through the preaching of this passage. Practical reflections also can be harvested from a consideration of this section of the Scriptures.

Here the outcome of the gospel is seen. Judgment and joy, banished and blessed, the gospel divides humanity and affects eternal destinies. The message itself comes out in many subjects, Jesus, the Word of God, the first resurrection, that of the just followed by the resurrection of the unjust. Also the book of life and the lake of fire. Such amazing subjects for any evangelist to get his teeth into, and subjects that are favourite with the Spirit of God in the salvation of lost souls.

CONSIDER THE ENEMY, SATAN.

Satan the adversary to God and to His people is traced often in Scripture. God would warn and safeguard as to the enemy of souls. The Lord in the gospels spoke three parables that made reference to the ways of the devil and Satan.

That of the strong man in Matt. 12   Satan's strength.

The parable of the sower in Matt. 13 Satan's stealth.

The wheat and the tares in Matt. 13 Satan's subtlety.

However, it is the Revelation that fully exposes him as in ch. 12 for instance, and it is in this chapter 20 that declares his final doom.

He is fully exposed in verse 2, even his titles and ways which have already been considered in Rev. 12

He is strong, but has less power than the strong angel who binds him in verse 1. Note the threefold assertion of him being rendered helpless. The key, the chain and the bottomless pit. All these are symbolic of God's power to disclose the lesser power of the enemy.

After being bound for 1000 years he is released again and has a fruitful field to work upon, even the depraved and fallen heart of man which has remained unchanged even in perfect Millennial conditions.

Satan alone is released, no other soul or demon will have this experience. As the Millennium was the final test for fallen man, so this releasing is the final test of Satan. In both cases there is failure, the people and the devil will be destroyed together in verses 9 and 10 respectively.

The final method of Satan is as the first in Gen. 3 that is the use of deception, "He will come out to deceive the nations" (verse 8). This charge is also pointed to Satan in verse 10 "the devil who deceived them".

His final downfall is also seen, he is cast into the lake of fire, this is final, no release from this is possible even for ever. Alas, all who follow him shall meet the same fate in the following verses.

All this information is most solemn, the intention of the Spirit is to produce fear of God and not of puny man.

THE UNBELIEVERS 11-14

Throughout the Revelation Christless sinners are referred to as "those who dwell upon the earth", apparently one word "earthdwellers". In this chapter all that they have is taken away from them. The earth passes away in verse 11, all they trusted in will be gone forever. Something even more alarming follows, they are raised from the dead. Even though they will experience a resurrection and appear in a resurrected body to be judged, yet they are constantly called "the dead". They never took the gift of life in Christ and continue to be dead in trespasses and sins (Eph. 2:1). Into eternity they are known as the dead. The word death and dead occur seven times in verses 12-13. God's perfect and righteous judgment.

The Judge is Christ Himself, the Giver of life, His words are spirit and life if received (John 6:63), the same words shall judge in the last day if refused (John 12:48). The judgment throne of the Lord Jesus is described as "A Great White Throne".

A throne because of the majesty of Him that sits upon it. He is King of kings.

It is White because of the purity and righteousness with which judgment shall be meted out.

It is called Great because of its universal effect and the eternal doom that will issue from its judgment. Millions shall stand before Him to be righteously judged, every mouth will be stopped and all banished from the holy presence of the Judge.

The Books are opened, (verse 12) there must be at least three kinds of books. The book of works, God's infinite record and knowledge of every deed committed by every person. Then the Book of Life, this implies that provisional grace was offered and refused. Finally, The Word of God, the Bible which is the witness to God at all times.

At the resurrection of believers it will be said, "death is swallowed up in victory" (1 Cor. 15:48). Here it could be said "life is swallowed up of doom", this is the second death.

THE BLESSINGS OF BELIEVERS

However, a more cheerful note emerges from this searching chapter, that of the eternal blessings of those who believe the gospel. Believers endure reproach now as in 1 Cor. 4:8-13. They suffer for righteousness sake and for Christ's sake. Reproach is only for time, here the rest and blessing is entered into.

There is a reminder of the past in the language used here.

1. Their walk and message was the "Word of God" in verse 4.

2. Zeal was manifested in their witness to Jesus, verse 4.

3. In faithfulness, they were not deceived by the worship of the beast, although refusal was very costly, verse 4.

4. They were steadfast in their faith, even unto death, willing to lose the life down here rather than to gain it.

Their reward will be Authority as seen in the thrones, this will be during the Millennium and into eternity. They had traded with their pounds and talents in life and enter into the prepared glory. This is the completion of the first resurrection. Christ was the firstfruits, afterward those who belonged to Him at His coming, even the rapture of the church, then the end or rearguard, Israel as recorded here.

One must acknowledge that generally the information here concerns the Tribulation, however all the blessings recorded will be true also of the believers in this time of grace. Both times are in view. Verse 5 is the saints that will come out of the Great Tribulation, and verse 6 includes all saints. The worship as priests would embrace the holy priesthood of which Peter speaks in 1 Pet. 2, and the reigning as kings would be the royal priesthood also of 1 Pet. 2. Such is the blessing of the redeemed, God is faithful, nothing shall fail of His promises and purposes for the believer in Christ.

CHAPTER THIRTY-FIVE

The Eternal State of Rev. 21:1-8

The final section of the Revelation is now before us, and it makes a fitting end to the Revelation and in fact to the whole Bible, a message of glory and assurance. Here is the contrast with how the Bible begins in the early chapters of Genesis, here is the end of the old creation and the bringing in of the new. In Gen. 3 death enters and now "no more death" (21:4) and such like contrasts have been ably brought out in most commentaries on the Revelation.

The greatest however is the creation itself as recorded in Gen. 1

In the beginning God created the heaven and the earth.

Here John saw a new heaven and a new earth, this coupled with verse 5 "behold I make all things new".

The waters gathered together were called seas in Gen. 1:10 but here there is no more sea.

The first two days of Gen. 1, brought forward the principle of "separation", separation of light from darkness and the waters separated above from the waters beneath. Here the godly in verses 1-7 are eternally separated from the ungodly in verse 8.

The third day of Gen. 1 brought forth the land and vegetation. Over against this is the tree of life bringing forth twelve manner of fruits in Rev. 22:2

In day four the sun and moon were set for light and rule. Here the rule is from the throne of God in 21:5.

The fifth and sixth day brought forth life and headed up in the man, and the garden of Eden was his domain. Note verse 7. "He that overcometh shall inherit all things, and I will be his God and he shall be my son".

The Lord came in the evening to walk in the garden, no doubt to commune with the man, and here the tabernacle of God is with man in verse 3.

A difficulty stands in the way of interpreting this section of Revelation. The first is, "where does the section end"? In one way it would seem that the section ends with 22:5. Rightly, this is the end of the visions, and verse 6 to the end appears to be a kind of epilogue or postscript. However, if the section is parallel with chapters 1-3 then the material from 22:6-17 must be included. Therefore it seems that the section runs from 21:1 to 22:17 and the remaining verses 18-21 form a conclusion similar to the introduction of chapter 1:1-7

The parallel between ch. 1:8 to 3:21 to this section in 21:-22:17 has already been set out in the "Outline of the Rev." in the first chapter of this book. A reminder of this would be profitable here.

COMPARISON OF A. 1-3 and A. 21-22.

1. I John a prisoner 1:8	I John saw 21:2
2. New Jerusalem 3:12	New Jerusalem 21:2
3. Alpha, Omega 1:8	Alpha, and Omega 21:6
4. Him that overcometh 2:7	He that overcometh 21:7
5. In the Spirit 1:10	Carried in the Spirit 21:10
6. Go no more out 3:12	Unclean not enter in 21:27
7. Lamb's book of life 3:5	Lamb's book of life 20:27
8. Tree of life 2:7	Tree of life 22:2
9. New name upon him 3:12	Name on foreheads 22:4
10. Shortly come to pass 1:1	Shortly be done 22:6
11. Angel 1:1	Angel 22:6
12. Words of this prophecy 1:3	Prophecy of this book 22:7
13. Behold He cometh 1:7	Behold I come quickly 22:7
14. John fell at feet 1:17	John fell down 22:8
15. The churches 2-3	The churches 22:16
16. Spirit saith, Hear 2:7	Spirit says come 22:17

The second difficulty is concerning the subject matter. Verses 21:1-8 are definitely the unfolding of the eternal state of both saved and unsaved. Does the material then from verse 9 continue the eternal state, or does all revert back to the Millennium? It would seem that this is the case and proofs to that effect will be considered in these pages.

THE SUBJECT MATTER OF THE SECTION

The subject matter of the chapters issue in 4 main themes.

1. The eternal state in 21:1-8
2. Millennial conditions 21:9-22:5
3. The New Jerusalem in both these states.
4. The final words of the angel, of the Lord, and of John, finally the Spirit and bride speak. (22:6-22:17)

The best way to understanding is to deal with these subjects in that order.

THE ETERNAL STATE 1-8

If the suggested division is correct, then only these verses speak of the eternal state in the Revelation. Seven as touching the saved and one verse (8) concerning the unsaved. Add to this the one verse in 2 Pet. 3:13 and the total is eight in the N.T. To this could be added Isa. 65:17 and 66:22, the total is ten in all. Why so little information about the endless condition of the saved? Because things will be so glorious and wonderful that they defy description in human language. It would seem as if God were to say "Wait and see". Verse 5 confirms this, John is no doubt marvelling at the glory of the vision, perhaps wondering is it real, surely it is too good to be true. God comes in with the assuring words "write for these words are true and faithful". Of course the wonderful features of the New Jerusalem will continue into the eternal state, but with greater weight.

A PURGING FIRST IN VERSE 1

This is the order with God, purging must come first. This of course is seen in the previous chapter where all the enemies are dealt with, namely, the Harlot, Beast, False Prophet, Satan, Armies, the wicked dead and death itself. The heaven and the earth also pass away. Whether this is the actual substance passing into nothing, or else the character and form undergoing a change is a long debated point by many Bible scholars. The first is not impossible, as the Lord formed the first earth out of nothing, He is able to reverse this, there is nothing impossible with God. How easy it would be for God to create again a new heaven and earth. Really there is nothing here to suggest that the present earth undergoes a change to that which is called "new". There is no necessity for the living God to recycle things. In no way can an old thing become new. The new covenant is not the old covenant made anew, rather the passing away of the old, and the new is established (Heb. 8:13). In the same way the old creation is passing away (Heb. 1) and will totally pass away under the judgment narrated in the previous chapter, and the new will take its place. "The first heaven and first earth passed away" is a clear statement of chapter 22:1.

This scene of verse 1 is not without its practical import. While Ephesians speaks of the heavenlies, Colossians speaks of the earth. Through the gospel we first die to this old world as in Romans 6, and based upon this is the exhortation, "love not the world" in 1 John 2:15. We then understand that we are crucified unto the world in Gal. 6:14. Here the whole scene is to pass away.

The fact of no more sea is important also. It has claimed the lives of millions of people. It is a symbol of the nations in wickedness without God. The sea also would indicate "separation" as in Acts 21:5-6. Paul prayed, kneeling upon the shore, then departed by ship and the beloved Christians went to their own homes. There will be no separation in the eternal state.

THE PLACE IN VERSE 2

The place of the eternal is called a new heaven and a new earth. Now new means new in contrast to that which is old, but also carries the thought of being "ever new" . This will never wax old and will never loose its freshness and fullness or be depleted of its energy.

God's ways are marvellous, and in the first creation with it waters, fruitfulness etc. all was provided for the man, then finally the Lord made the man, and placed him in the prepared environment. The reverse to this operates in the new creation, the people are prepared first and when all the people are gathered, then finally the new heaven and the new earth will be created. It could be expressed simply as "in the first creation God first prepared a place for a people, in the new creation God first prepares a people for a place". 2 Cor. 5:17 teaches this, "If any man be in Christ he is a new creation". Perhaps the words of our Lord "I go to prepare a place for you" has this in mind among other things.

Again, all will be everlasting in keeping with the everlasting covenant of Heb. 13:20. The covenant has not only present blessing in mind but advances on to the eternal state of things.

Another feature of the new creation is the absence of the sea. Remarks have already been made concerning this.

Another feature is the New Jerusalem, and four pieces of information are given about it in verse 2.

1) It is called "the holy city", in keeping with the character of its maker. Everything about the new creation is bound to be holy.
2) It is named "New Jerusalem" , in keeping with the character and context of new things. Things never to wax old, ever to retain their freshness.
3) The source is from God himself "coming down out of heaven from God" (verse 2). This is what God is working up to, first an earthly Jerusalem then a heavenly and spiritual according to the principle of 1 Cor. 15:46, the natural before the spiritual. It would seem that the city is more important than the new heaven or earth, there is a more detailed description. The heaven and earth likely are created to display the holy city.
4) Prepared as a bride adorned for her husband. This preparation has been going on for a long time.

John the Baptist prepared a people for the Lord.

Now, the Spirit is preparing the church by gifts in Eph. 4.

The adornment is the linen of 19:8, the righteous acts of the saints, which are in preparation now in the lives of His people.

The husband is Christ, and would speak of care sustenance and affection. When the Lord is called the "Bridegroom" the thought is of the glory that belongs to Him.

Note "John" is omitted in R V.. What is an earthly name in the presence of such heavenly splendour. Like Moses at the bush who cried "who am I", and Paul speaking of the resurrection calls all human effort but dung or waste in Phil. 3.

THE GREAT DECLARATION OF VERSE 3

A great or loud voice is needed to declare great truths, and this voice is from the authority of the throne. God's ultimate purpose is to dwell with men.

This is first seen in the visits of God to the garden of Eden.

The Tabernacle in the wilderness expresses the same. God came as near to the people as possible, but the veil was ever in between, a testimony to the inadequacy of the sacrifices.

The Lord in incarnation came amongst men, but as a Man of Sorrows, the eternal glory of that august Person was veiled in human sinless flesh. Howbeit, it was manifested at times such as in the transfiguration.

The coming of the Spirit to dwell among the believers and in them personally is a great advancement in this desire of the living God.

Here is the completion of all the work of God, the successful work and sacrifice of Christ makes it possible for this desire of God to be fulfilled. The day will surely come when "The Tabernacle of God will be among men, and He shall dwell among them". Perfect relationship is expressed in "they shall be His people and God Himself shall be with them, and be their God". All this in a perfect environment, no sin, darkness or death.

THE PERFECT CONDITIONS

If the Tabernacle is seen in verse 3 then the work of the altar comes forward in verse 4. The sacrifice of Christ has reversed all the sorrows and terrible conditions of man brought in by the fall of the first Adam in Gen. 3. Tears like those of David, Jeremiah, Paul and millions of other saints, tears because of the havoc that sin has wrought, like those shed by the Lord at the grave of Lazarus, shall be no more.

There will be no more death, the last enemy shall be destroyed, because the sinless One entered into death and conquered it once for all.

There will be no more sorrow and crying, all such can be traced back to the fall. The Lord became a Man of Sorrows and acquainted with grief. All this is ended by the victory of the cross.

Pain, dreadful pain, the lot of fallen man, the agony of the ageing process and passing away of the body shall be no more. The Lord endured pain in His sacrifice, physical, mental and spiritual pain that the most devout believer can never fathom. All these marks of the fall will all be in the past. The life of God is the possession of the believer. The passing away of these former things is because they belong to the old creation.

THE GREAT ASSURANCE V 5

This is the new creation coming to the fore, "He that sat upon the throne", there could be no greater authority or power. The certainty of the utterance is most encouraging, "Behold I make all things new". John may well have thought that all he saw was too good to be true, especially the things of verse 4. However, God anticipates this, and the Lord said unto John, "Write for these words are true and faithful". The writing is to impart assurance to all who believe. The word "faithful" is of course the faithfulness of God to such mighty promises, as indeed all the promises of God. The "true" would refer to what God had in mind in Christ in contrast to all the shadows of the past.

Further words from God to John follow in verse 6. "It is done", meaning that all has come to pass, faith believed God's word, and waited for this blessed state. At last all is accomplished.

"I am Alpha and Omega, the beginning and the end". Two ideas are embodied in these words, the beginning and the end has to do with creation. In the beginning God created the heaven and the earth as in Gen. 1:1. Not only is He the beginning of the creation but also its end, the purpose of its creation shall come to fruition. The "Alpha and Omega" are the first and last letters in the Greek alphabet. This is related to the revelation of Christ "The Word" as in John 1, the mind and purpose of God revealed in the Lord Jesus. Perhaps the Alpha would be seen in the past Scriptures, especially in John, and the Omega is seen in this book of Revelation.

The passage then goes on to Tabernacle ideas again in the "water of life", this is the fulfilment of the laver. Those who approached the Tabernacle were thirsting after God, seeking and longing for His presence. Such in the tabernacle order had first to wash at the laver, a testimony to their lack of fitness for the presence of God. Here the water of life is given as in John 4. Fitness for God's presence is there because of the possession of the very life of God. "Freely" would speak of the grace of God, all is without human merit.

THE NOTE OF VICTORY IN VERSE 7

The overcomer appears again in verse 7, this is one of the parallels with the first part, the church section of the Revelation. The thirst and longing for God was such that all obstacles were overcome. All this came by the Spirit of God and not human strength, the Lord dwells in the believer.

"Inherit all things" is a summary of all the eternal blessings of verses 1-6. The language of the remainder of the verse is strange, and yet so promising. It is put in a mysterious way "I will be his God and he shall be My son", one would have thought that Father and son would be the right relationship. The reason for this is the full thought of sonship, which is always with a view to the glory. Heb. 2 speaks of bringing many sons to glory, and Rom. 8 of the manifestation of the sons of God at the revelation of Christ. Here is the full thought, sons in the future eternal state.

Another reassuring point here is the individual standing. It is not they shall be my sons, but he shall be MY SON. this means that individually each believer is known and appointed by God to enter into full sonship. Known of God as in 1 Cor. 8:3.

This is the passage on the "eternal state", and quite a lot of the material is presented in threes.

Three things are called new, the heavens, the earth and the city.

The city is called three things, the holy city, the New Jerusalem and the bride.

Believers referred to in relationship to God v 3. Changed conditions in v 4, and overcomers in v 7.

Believers have three great promises. Life in fullness v 7, the inheritance of all things, and the wonderful full relationship of sons. Actually quite a number of triads appear in the passage.

The thirst is apart from works, but the fountain of waters is the result of the cross work of our Lord Jesus.

Four words would sum up the material of this rich passage.

The Purging, the Place, the Purpose, and the People.

THE ETERNAL STATE OF THE UNBELIEVER

Verse 8, one verse only covers the sad eternal loss of those who died without salvation in Christ. They were judged according to their works and found guilty in 20:12. These are lost not because of Adam's sin but their own.

There are 8 classes of sin recorded in the verse and these fall into three categories.

1) The fearful and unbelieving would be to do with the message of the gospel from God. The fear of man rather than God on the one hand, and the refusal of the gospel on the other. The fearful would imply that they heard the message, understood it and considered it, but were afraid of the cost of discipleship.
2) The abominable, murderers and fornicators, these are a manifestation of uncleanness, hatred and lust, the lack of control of one's passions.
3) The last three, sorcery, idolatry and lying would be the error in contrast to the truth of God in the first category. A person usually imbibes evil teaching when the truth is rejected. The seducing spirits in 1 Tim. 4:1 took away from the truth of God, and the doctrine of demons is substituted in its place.

The liars are not merely those who tell lies, but the deception of "the lie" as in 2 Thess. 2:11. In Matt. 24:5, 11, the Lord gives warning about Satanic deception. Paul in Rom. 1:25 writes about changing the truth of God into a lie. Those who make a lie, or deception are mentioned in the final verse of this chapter.

All is most solemn, and gospel preachers should continually have this judgment passage before them.

CHAPTER THIRTY-SIX

The Millennium and the City

I t would seem that from ch. 21:9 the angel takes John back to former Millennial scenes. Proof of this can be seen in some of the subjects that appear.

The Lamb is not mentioned in verses 1-7 that treat of the Eternal State, but is mentioned seven times in the remaining section, v 9, 14, 22, 23, 27, 22:1 and 22:3. The Lamb speaks of mediatorial service which will be needed in the Millennium for the nations etc., but not in the perfection of the Eternal State.

The nations are mentioned in ch. 21:24-6, showing the division in mankind which will be absent in the Eternal State.

Sin is still present in ch. 21:27.

Healing is needed, this cannot be in the new earth when tears, death, sorrow, crying and pain will be in the past. (v 4).

The wife of the Lamb in verse 9 would imply that rejection and reproach is still remembered.

Again, the scene completely changes. An angel, who had to do with the pouring out of the judgment bowls, is the guide. This would suggest another phase, the Millennium coming in after the last judgments. Also the statement, "I will show thee the bride the Lamb's wife", why is this if John had already seen her in verse 2? Actually the sight of the city in verses 9-10 comes before that of verse 2.

Again, for the fourth and last time the expression,"In the Spirit" occurs, and in each case the location and the scene is dramatically changed.

When the two sections are compared side by side the difference is bound to be obvious.

Chapter 21:1-7	Chapter 21:9-22:5
No Lamb mentioned	The Lamb seven times
People as Sons	As bondslaves
Word "new" four times	New not mentioned at all
New Jerusalem	Jerusalem without the word "new"
Spring of water 21:6	River of water in 22:1
No measurements	Many measurements in 15-17
No wall or precious stones	The wall and stones prominent
Link with the Tabernacle v 3	Link with the temple v 22

God is the temple, the Lamb is the lamp etc., and there is the court of the Gentiles in verses 26-6.

THE NEW JERUSALEM, IS IT LITERAL?

The beautiful city appears in both states if one accepts the difference as already asserted. The question is bound to arise "is this city literal" ?

No doubt this is a literal city, the patriarchs looked for a city, especially Abraham (Heb. 11:10). Abraham was called out of a literal city and looked to God to provide another, but somewhat different, a city built by God and not man. Heb. 11:16 informs us that God has prepared such a city. The heaven and earth of verse 1 is literal so why should the city of verse 2 be different ? Paul's comparison of the earthly Jerusalem with the Jerusalem which is above in Gal. 4 is another indication of this.

The first city in the Bible appears in Gen. 4 built by Cain and called after his son Enoch. This New Jerusalem is the last city in the Bible, and the two make instructive contrasts.

1) The first city was built by Cain, a fallen man, this last is built by God (Heb. 11:10). In Rev. 21:2 the city comes out of heaven from God.
2) God is not mentioned at all in Gen. 4:17-24, the passage that deals with Cain's city. On the contrary, God is mentioned four times in

this "New Jerusalem" passage, besides, God is also referred to as the "Alpha and Omega, the beginning and the end".

3) Cain went out from the presence of God, but in this last city God dwells among men.

4) There are twelve names mentioned in the posterity of Cain in connection with the first city, all fallen men. However in the last city the names of the twelve apostles appear.

5) Lamech had two wives in the first city, this last is called a Bride, the one wife of the Lamb.

6) With Lamech and the first city appear hurt, wounding and slaying, all these things are passed away in the final city.

7) In Cain's city the people seemingly thirsted after entertainment, but in the new city they thirst after the water of life.

8) Possessions loomed large in the first city as in every city, but in the last city the overcomer inherits all things.

Many more like contrasts can be seen in these cities by close observation.

While the city is no doubt literal, yet it is described in symbolic language. The glory or brilliance was like unto a jasper stone (verse 11), this is not a literal jasper stone but the literal light is described as such. The same goes for the words "clear as crystal" in the same verse. Again in verse 21 the street of the city is pure gold as transparent glass, would indicate the purity of that habitation. The street would suggest movement and freedom to travel from place to place. Some have wondered at the "one street" surely this is not in keeping with such a vast city of such gigantic measurements. The idea is a central plaza, the Greek word is "Platia" and sometimes it is in the plural as in Luke 13:26 "Thou hast taught in our streets", meaning public places. The bodies of the two witnesses lay in the street, a public place in Rev. 11:8.

The foundations of the wall also are called precious stones and named after the twelve apostles. There must be some deep significance that the Spirit sees in the character of each apostle likened unto a certain stone. Most likely these stones symbolize the character and position of the apostles in the coming kingdom. The Lord encouraged the disciples with this promise in Matt. 19:28 "Ye also shall sit upon twelve thrones judging the twelve tribes of Israel". The apostles are precious to the Lord as is every saint. The apostles were in the foundation of the church in Eph. 4:11.

The city is also called a Bride, "I will show thee the Bride", then he showed me a city. (verses 9-10) Surely this speaks of the people that populate the city and not the city itself. The city often stands for the people as in Mark 1:33 "And all the city was gathered together at the door".

Just as the tabernacle was made of certain materials that expressed great coming truths, so this city expresses great factual truths in symbolic language. Again, as the tabernacle was peopled by priests, so this city is peopled with a company of saints composing the Bride of Christ.

The word "city" is used much in the passage and is depicted in various ways.

A holy city in v 2. Its character and purity is indicated
A great city in v 10 This is its universal authority
A foursquare city v 16 would be its perfection
A walled city in v 14 signifies its security
A measured city in v 15 is in keeping with Divine principles
A supernatural city v 23 is the presence of Divine Persons
A new city v 2 is God's final manifestation

CHAPTER THIRTY-SEVEN

The Glorious City, New Jerusalem

The description of the city is most orderly and instructive. If one can understand the symbolism used by God then light and appreciation is bound to be the outcome.

The description begins with glory and light in 12:11 and ends with the same note in 21:5, "they need no candle neither light of the sun for the Lord God giveth them light".

How like our God to close the section with the portion given to the saints of God, "they shall reign for ever and ever".

The detailed description is as follows.

1. The glory in 21:11
2. The framework, wall gates and foundations in 21:12-14
3. The measurements in 21:15-17
4. The most costly materials in 21:18-21
5. The presence of the Lord, its light and centre 21:22-3
6. Its influence upon the nations in 21:24-27
7. The wonderful conditions therein 22:1-2
8. The glory of its residents in 22:3-5

The brief examination of these is bound to yield much spiritual profit.

1. THE GLORY OF VERSE 11

How could it be anything only glorious. The full display of all God's purpose in grace, the Lord Jesus fully vindicated and God's chosen people at last fully perfected because of all the travail and pain that the Lord passed through. This thought is remembered by the constant references to the Lamb.

Again, God and the Lamb are in this city (verse 22) and the outshining of Divine glory is bound to be manifest by the presence of Divine Persons, a case in point is the holiest of all in the tabernacle of old. The Lamb, the Lord Jesus will have then entered fully into the predicted glory that follows His passion.

The church is there, eternally linked to Christ as the body is to the head, the fruit brought forth by His suffering and sacrificial death. The church is also destined to reign with Him in the most glorious kingdom this world has ever seen.

One stone is used to symbolise this glory. One stone speaking of the beautiful unity and harmony that will prevail there, this is a moral glory that exceeds all others. The stone would also denote permanency, the wonderful conditions will be everlasting as the throne of God. Of course, the preciousness of the whole scene is also denoted by the symbol of the jasper stone, how valuable to God is this complete company of His blood bought church. Clear as crystal is so fitting a description of this glory, all is righteousness without a spot or blemish to mar the purity of this city whose Builder and Architect is God. Here is life on righteous grounds. Here is the fullness of that precious faith through the righteousness of God as spoken by Peter in 2 Pet. 1:1. All is holy, the holy city of verse 2, the holy Jerusalem of verse 10. At last God has a place and a people in keeping with His own holy nature.

2. THE FRAMEWORK OF VERSES 12-14

This could be literal as every city has foundations etc., but the language conveys moral qualities also in the symbolic expressions.

First, the WALL, not walls, this is singular and is spoken of six times in these verses. Six is the number of man in the Bible, but not here the natural man manifesting the deep seated fall from his heart; rather the perfect man found dwelling there, man in Christ as he should be before his Creator and God.

The wall would speak of security, such were the uses of walls in ancient cities akin to Jericho. Not that God needs any wall to keep out intruders but the thought of safety is prominent. The idea of security and safety is expressed in another way in cities without walls in the Millennium (Zech. 2:4). A King shall reign in righteousness.

This security is held firmly now by faith in the words of our Lord, "I give unto them eternal life and they shall never perish", in John 10:28, and such like passages. Here however, all is fully entered into, the promises of God are discharged.

This wall is built of jasper in verse 18 and would suggest the holiness of God similar to the court of the tabernacle. Only those who are made righteous by the blood of the Lamb have the right to enter in chapter 22:14.

The "GATES" are next described. These number twelve and are situated three at each point of the compass. Several ideas are associated with gates in Scripture as follows:-

a) A gate was the place of judgment and discernment, the place where the judges assessed all things. Only those approved by God have place in this city.

b) The idea of "entry" is also depicted in the gates. The occupants have symbolically entered through these gates as in ch. 22:14 "Blessed are they that wash their robes, that they may have right to the tree of life, and may enter in through the gates of the city".

c) The fact that three gates face each direction proves that the gospel was for all, and equally so. The north shall not be greater than the south and so forth. God is no respecter of persons in His gospel.

d) The twelves gates also present "unity", the names of the twelve tribes of Israel are written thereon. The division under Rehoboam will be finally healed, this is also taught in Rev. 7 in the sealing of the tribes. Israel at last shall enter into their inheritance as promised by God.

e) Each gate is described as a pearl in verse 21. The Puritans believed that the parable of the "pearl of great price" was the Lord and not the church. They could well be right, for the parables of Matt. 13 are all beyond the church age and are to do with the "Kingdom of Heaven" and the church has no place in this. How could the Lord in poverty be termed a "merchantman" and in the parable the merchantman came upon the pearl of great price by accident. Surely this is not the language of the church which was chosen in Christ before the foundation of the world. Again he was seeking goodly pearls, and who are these ?. To keep in the context of Matt 13 the merchant man is the remnant in Israel seeking riches who comes upon the pearl of great price, even the Lord Jesus and sells all to obtain it, this leads on to the tribulation, the remnant will pay dearly for their allegiance to Christ. This being so, each gate here with the tribes of Israel upon them are seen in Christ and represent Him in the Kingdom. At last, Israel shall find the door of John 10:9.

The FOUNDATIONS are mentioned next. Just a few words in verse 14 but more detail is given in verses 19-20.

Foundations are meant to hold and secure the building, and in this way would speak of governmental authority. The names of the twelve apostles in these foundations carry this thought to conclusion. The Lord said that they would sit upon twelve thrones judging the twelve tribes of Israel (Matt. 19:28).

3. THE MEASUREMENT IN VERSES 15-17

A golden reed is the rule of measurement. Gold speaks of that which is Divine and heavenly, and is the measurement determined by God. The Lord God has His standards to measure all things.

This is similar to the shekel of the sanctuary often mentioned as in Ex. 30:13, 38:24, 25, 26, etc.. The thoughts and ways of God are so different from the people of this earth as in Isa. 55:8-9.

With the believer sadly his measurement is often according to the flesh. Paul has much to say about this measurement in 2 Cor. 10.

The angel measured the city and the gates thereof and the wall thereof. The Lord measures us at present, evaluating each word and deed with a view to reward. He is especially measuring the unity of the believer as suggested by the wall, the progress of the believer suggested in the gates, entering into new truths and experiences. Here is the reward, all who have position in this community have the right to that position by the measuring judgment of the Lord.

The number "twelve" is seen throughout these measurements. There are 12 gates, 12 tribes, 12 foundations 12 angels and 12 apostles likened unto 12 precious stones. Also the great figures are divisible by 12, the

144 and 1200 furlongs. Now the number twelve indicates SERVICE in our Bibles. Here is much to do with service, as the measurements are extensive so shall the service be so. Note in 22:3 "and His servants shall serve Him, and they shall see His face". Here indeed is intimate service and before the very face of God. Nearness, not as angels with veiled faces. The name in the forehead speaks of dedication, and with the curse removed etc., all service will be perfect and unhindered.

The city is "Foursquare" and this betokens the perfection that God had in mind seen in the foursquare altars in the tabernacle etc.. Certainly, the measurements of this city contain great volumes of truth to be investigated with much profit.

4. THE COSTLY MATERIALS 18-21

How precious the saints are to the Lord who bought them, and how beautifully they shall shine in their acquired glory in that great day. No wonder that the place and the people are depicted as precious stones and metals in this holy city.

1) Jasper in verse 11 and 18 is the stone that is identified with the city and the wall, no doubt the "holiness of God" is implied. This holiness is seen in verse 27 where nothing unclean or an abomination or that which savours of falsehood can enter therein.

2) Gold is mentioned three times in this descriptive passage.
   The city itself in verse 18 , the street was also of pure gold in verse 21, and the measuring rod in verse 15. Gold speaks of Divine glory and righteousness. The golden city suggests Christ is the centre of all things. The golden rod is His righteous assessment of all things, and the street of pure gold is the foundation of His redeemed people.
   This street or plaza has the idea of unity and only one objective. Matthew 7 speaks of the one gate and road that leads to life, here is the one plaza of arrival, the glory and unity of the blessed people that populate this glorious city.

3) The gold like pure glass is another reference to that holiness which is preeminent in all that hallowed dwelling.

4) The foundations of precious stones present the apostles entering into their promised inheritance and reward. No doubt each precious jewel is significant to the character of each apostle, but to try and interpret this would likely take one into the realm of conjecture.

5) The gates each as a pearl as already suggested is Christ, He is the means of the restoration and kingdom of Israel.

5. CHRIST AS ITS CENTRE 22-3

The passage clearly asserts that no temple is needed, the Lord God Almighty and the Lamb are its temple. This would signify three important points. First, the tabernacle and temple were types of the heavenly things to come, now that all has come to full manifestation the types are no longer needed. In the second place, the temple was always the centre, the gathering place of the people in their annual feasts to worship. The centre of this great community is the Lord God, the title linked with the first man in Gen. 2:5-7, and the Almighty is first mentioned with Abraham in Gen. 17:1. Here is the grand progression to the climax of what God had in mind. The Lamb in His mediatorial work is the grounds for it all. Not only have the people of God at last entered into the full display of the grace given unto them, but the Godhead also is satisfied. The third point is that God was hidden in the temple, freedom of approach was prohibited, but here all is out in the open and the people of God before Him without fear.

There was no need for the light of the sun or the moon to shine upon it, the glory of God lightens all, for God is light.

Its lamp is the Lamb (verse 23). Again the progression of doctrine, often in the Kings and Chronicles the reference to the lamp of David is mentioned. Here is the Lamb, but also the Lion of the tribe of Judah, the King of kings.

The saved walk in this light, walk suggest at ease, the tranquillity of the nations in the Millennium.

Attraction is suggested in the kings of the earth bringing their glory into it. This likely means that gifts etc. are offered similar to Solomon in his reign, he was recognized as glorious and superior by the nations bringing gifts to him..

The ever open gates of verse 25 indicates freedom from fear, and freedom of movement. The angels of God ascending and descending upon the Son of Man would teach freedom of movement as with the saints of God. The danger to the ancient cities came by night, the fact of no night in the New Jerusalem is indicative of perfect security.

6. THE CITY AND THE NATIONS 21:24-7

The nations are obviously those who came out of the great tribulation and were ushered into the Kingdom. Matt. 25:34 would bear this out, "Come ye blessed of my Father inherit the kingdom prepared for you from the foundation of the world". These are on the earth, but walk in the light of the city, and that light is God Himself and the Lamb according to the previous verse. These inhabitants of the earth are able to bring their glory and honour into the city. This could mean one of two things, either the people themselves are able to come into the city to worship etc. or their gifts and appraisal of the city is accepted. Likely the latter view is nearer the truth.

Verse 27 declares the holiness of the city, in that nothing that defiles etc. can enter into it. This entering seems to suggest residence, the right to dwell there, and not a visitation as may be suggested by the previous verse. Those who enter or dwell there have that right by being written in the Lamb's book of life. This apparently would exclude the nations, the residents of the city seem to be those who were saved during the time of grace upon the earth. Here is a clear distinction between the saints that comprise the church, the bride of the Lamb, and those who were saved either before or after the time of grace.

7. THE WONDERFUL CONDITIONS THEREIN. 22: 1-3

Here is an encouraging section, the perfect conditions in the New Jerusalem that will exist through the Millennium and into eternity. This passage presents the river, the throne, the street, the tree of life and the blessing. All speak of LIFE. The river is the river of life, the throne is that of God and the Lamb, the source of life. The street is for those who have received life, and the tree of life speaks for itself. The curse removed is to return to the condition before death entered into Eden, here is the blessing in contrast to the curse.

The river is interesting in that it is a culmination of thought from three other "river" passages.

1) The river in Gen. 2 that divided into four heads to water the earth. There the tree of life is also mentioned, and brings together these

thoughts of life which God had in mind, now all comes to fulfilment in this last chapter of the Bible. Here is the first and last river in the Scriptures, the number 4 in Gen. which stands for that which is universal, comes to the full thought of the nations in this section.

2) The river in Ezek. 47 has been much taken up by the ministering brethren over the years. Wonderful lessons can be derived from its different depths and so on. The full thought comes out in the Rev. passage. In Ezek. 47 the river is from the temple, but here the river flows from the throne. How often the Lord is presented as a Priest and a King, the Priest upon His throne as in Zech. 6. Here the temple denotes the Priest and the throne the King, the Lord entered into the full place that belongs to Him, and the blessing of life of which the river speaks is the glorious result.

3) The final O.T. passage is Zech. 14:7-8. This is a Millennial scene, and the river is upon the earth and is called living waters. This is divided into two, one part flows towards the eastern sea and the other towards the western sea. Here are literal waters with a spiritual meaning, life is manifested in Israel.

To sum up:-

The river of Gen. is a figure of that which is to come. The river from the temple in Ezek. is from the earthly Millennial temple, and that of Rev. 21 is from the throne in the city. The effect is felt upon the nations of earth as in the Zech. passage and more fully in Rev. 22.

The tree of life is on both sides of the street or plaza, likely the branches rise up and over to the further side. The tree bears a yield every month, and the leaves are for the healing of the nations. Here again it is evident that the city affects the earth. All this is symbolic to the effect that every need of man is fully met, days of peace and prosperity will be a feature of the Millennium.

8. THE GLORY OF THE RESIDENTS OF THE CITY 22:3-5

The occupants of the New Jerusalem are not only saved, but belong to the Lord in a special way being the Bride of Christ, those saved during the time of grace.

Life is the key factor in these verses. The book of life, the water of life and the tree of life in previous verses. The book of life would be the initial receiving of life, their names written there, and the water of life is the power and manifestation of that life, as one of the many implications of waters in the Bible is power (Rev. 1:15). The tree would speak of progress, growth, this also manifested on earth, and into the blessings of the city.

They served the Lord upon the earth, but that lovely occupation does not cease, His bondservants shall serve Him. He is the centre of their activity, all is unto Him. These are not bondservants by defeat, rather by love, the principle in the Hebrew servant in Ex. 21:5-6 is verily effective here, I love my Master.

They shall see His face (verse 4), bondslaves in many cases never see the face of their owner, but how different is this, the perfect intimacy between servant and Master.

His name upon their foreheads would signify perfect dedication to the Lord and to the service given. All this goes to forward the truth that the service is done willingly in a loving dedicated way, and the Lord appreciates this as they have access to Him. This is service indeed, and something to look forward to, service without the discouragement, hardships, and failures of the way now.

These servants walk in the light of the Lord, "no more night" would speak of the troubles and obscurity in the service of the past upon the earth. The Lord God is the title that is to do with covenants and relationship, and this is fully expressed here. Perhaps the illumination spoken of here is figurative of spiritual intelligence, a necessity in service for the Lord.

The closing point in this lovely description of the servants is the fact that "They shall reign for ever and ever". Note the order, salvation, the subject of life, service in these lovely aspects and final reward in manifestation.

CONDITIONS SEEN IN SEVEN NEGATIVES

One cannot fail to see the seven things that are absent in these conditions, even the seven negatives that have been pointed out by many writers in different forms. These present the conditions from the viewpoint of the things that are past making conditions perfect indeed. Note these negatives.

1. No temple 21:22	——————	Perfect worship
2. No sun 21:23	——————	Perfect illumination
3. No shut gates 21:25	——————	Perfect security
4. No unclean thing 21:27	——————	Perfect sanctification
5. No curse 22:3	——————	Perfect environment
6. No night 22:5	——————	Perfect energy, strength
7. No artificial light	——————	Perfect knowledge.

These things that will no longer exist will make the eternal abode a very happy place, and especially when all the positives are taken into consideration, all as perfect as God can make it. No wonder Abraham and the patriarchs looked for this city.

THE SEVEN MENTIONS OF THE LAMB

As already noticed the Lamb is mentioned seven times in the description of the New Jerusalem. A few words of reflection on this will bring this chapter to a reassuring end.

1. The first thought is RELATIONSHIP, the bride of the Lamb in 21:9. Romans chapter 8 appreciates relationship with Christ, here is the climax.
2. ADMINISTRATION is seen in the twelve apostles of the Lamb in 21:14. This is similar to the service already considered.
3. WORSHIP, the object of worship is the Lamb in 21:22. This is suggested in the Lamb being the temple, the place of worship.
4. KNOWLEDGE, the Lamb is the light of the city 22:24. Light is used of knowledge often in Scripture, and this seems to be the idea here.
5. LIFE, this is seen of course in the Lamb's book of life in 22:27. Salvation and life are recurring themes respecting the Lamb.
6. THE THRONE, this is the centre in 22:1. Where the Lamb is must be the centre, all is unto Him.
7. Finally, THE OBJECT OF SERVICE in 22:3, the Lamb shall be in them, this would intimate that the Lamb is the focal point of all service. His efficacious death will always attract faithful service to Him as the Lamb. "They shall see His face".

Chapter Thirty-Eight

The Encouragement in the Conclusion

The concluding verses of the Revelation form an interesting comparison with the opening verses of the book. This is bound to be as the whole book is written in chiasm form. The seven main sections as noted are over against each other in an inverted parallel form, the first being similar to the seventh, the second to the sixth and so forth. No marvel therefore if the "introduction" of 1:1-8 forms a parallel with the "conclusion" of 22:6-21.

Verse 6 of our chapter covers the same ground as ch. 1:1. The angel, the bondservants, (a bondservant here, namely John) and the imminent future of the events, even the burden of the book.

"Things which must shortly come to pass" becomes, "things which must shortly be done".

"Behold I come quickly" in verse 7, 12 and 20 is a throwback to "Behold He cometh with clouds" in 1:8.

The "Blessing" also comes in for repetition, "Blessed is he that readeth ... and keep those things which are written therein". The formula is almost word for word in 22:7 "Blessed is he that keepeth the sayings of the prophecy of this book".

Note also that John is named in both sections, 1:4 "John to the seven churches" and "I John" of of 22:8. In fact "I John occurs in 1:9. He is never mentioned by name in any other part of the book.

"The time is at hand" is shared by both sections 1:3 and 22:10.

The titles Alpha and Omega, the beginning and the end occur in 1:8 and is repeated in 22:13.

The theme of Testimony is seen in both places. The testimony of Jesus Christ (1:2) is over against "I Jesus have sent mine angel to Testify unto you" (22:16).

A reference to the Spirit begins and ends the book. "The seven Spirits before the throne in 1:3 and "the Spirit and the bride say come" in 22:17.

These are but a few, many other similarities can be seen by close observation, but this will suffice to see this pattern is clearly there, and is the intention of the Spirit. However, there is a purpose in all this, not merely a repetition of ideas rather a progression can be recognized in the design. This is most instructive, consider the said points again.

1) In the angel and the bondservants, the final passage adds the holy prophets. This manifests that the book of Revelation is the voice of God as from the beginning, now bringing to an end the process of inspiration and revelation. The warning of 22:19 could well be a reference to the whole Bible and not only this book. Note also that bondslave is in the singular, even John himself, he was the channel, the mouthpiece and writer to the other bondservants, someone has that privilege every time.

2) The fact of His coming in 1:8 is advanced, the word "Quickly" or soon is used three times in this conclusion, verses 7, 12 and 20. Again, 1:7 is to judge, tribes shall mourn because of Him.
   Here is the other side, the blessing and reward to his servants.

3) The mention of the name of John has greater import in the closing section from that of the first. "I John your brother", there based upon relationship, here the authority of what he had seen and heard, he is a man with a message. What a servant has to say is more important than who he is in Divine things.

4) The time is at hand in both sections, but has a greater significance in the second. In the first, the time is at hand is mentioned in accordance with the obedience of God's people. In 22:10 it is "seal not the sayings of prophecy of this book: for the time is at hand". Here the action is on the part of God, He is about to work, the other is the action of the believer.

5) The mention of the churches is again in advancement. 1:4 it is "John to the seven churches which are in Asia". Here it is "I Jesus have sent mine angel to testify unto you these things in the churches". In chapter one the churches are in Asia, but in 22 the Lord is in the churches in the person of the angel.

6) The first and last mention of the Spirit is also progressive. In 1:3 the Spirit is before the throne, representing the throne of God. In the final passage the Spirit has come out with a grand appeal, "The Spirit and the bride say come" (22:17) and the bride of the Lamb is associated with Him. How encouraging all this is, God is at work progressively. This last is especially very cheering, the Spirit has come forth in testimony with the bride the church, Peter says as much in his epistle, "they that have preached the gospel unto you with the Holy Spirit sent down from heaven" (1 Pet. 1:12).

This final section has a threefold purpose besides concluding the book. First, to establish the Authority behind the book, then to encourage John and all believers. Finally, to warn any that would meddle with its contents, either adding to, or taking away from the things written therein.

Consider the Authority first, even that of the Lord God Himself, and our blessed Lord Jesus. This Authority is presented in several ways to make the matter sure.

1) The same Lord God that inspired the prophets in their writings has inspired this book also in verse 6. This Revelation is therefore part of the sacred writings and a fitting end of the revelation of God in the Word.

2) This Authority is verily seen in the titles used in the section. The Lord Jesus is referred to in five double titles.

These each introduce a different view or attribute of the Lord.

The first is the Alpha and Omega of verse 13. These are the first and last letters of the Greek alphabet and therefore present the Lord as the Word. It is by Him that God communicates His Word to believers. According to John the title "The Word" includes the Lord in incarnation, coming into the midst of men to declare the Father. Communication then is the thought in this double title.

The second is the Beginning and the End in verse 13, and generally used in connection with creation. In the beginning God created the heaven and the earth (Gen. 1:1). This appears especially in Heb. chapter one. "Thou Lord in the beginning hast laid the foundation of the earth; and the heavens are the works of thine hands. They shall perish", the passage then goes on to teach that the Lord shall bring all to an end with the words, "as a vesture shalt thou fold them up". This double title presents the Lord as Creator.

Third, the First and the Last of verse 13 is usually to do with redemption. This is the use in 1:17, John in great fear fell at the feet of the Lord Jesus. The Lord stilled his fear by the use of this title. Again to the church at Smyrna in their passing through trial, the Lord encourages with this title. He is there from the beginning of their experience and will never leave or forsake those whom He has saved.

Fourth, the Root and Offspring of David in verse 16 is the title to do with the Dispensations. He is David's Lord and yet his Son, the root and offspring of David. In this title the Lord eventually shall reign over Israel and the nations.

Finally, The Bright and Morning Star of verse 13 is to do with His return and is especially a title to the church. Paul speaks of believers as sons of the day (1 Thess. 5:5), the coming of the dawn. The church awaits the morning star and the end of the night season.

These five double titles could be summed up as follows.

The Alpha and Omega —— His communicative title
The beginning and the end —— His creative title
The first and the last —— His redemptive title
The root and offspring —— His dispensational title
The bright and morning star —— His title of purpose and grace.

3) The lovely way the Lord speaks of Himself in verse 16 also lends weight to the authority. "I Jesus", this is beautiful coming in between the lofty titles of verses 13 and 16. Jesus is His Name, and is in keeping with His humanity and humility. But in the Name of this same Jesus every knee must bow. Here is the greatest authority.

4) The book closes with the full title of His Lordship. "The grace of our Lord Jesus Christ be with you all. Amen" (verse 21).

THE ENCOURAGEMENT IN THE CONCLUSION

The encouragement to John and to all servants is abundantly provided in this closing passage.

All shall soon be done in verse 6. Heaven may seem to be silent, but this is not the case. The programme is laid out by God and all shall be accomplished according to His purpose.

The blessing of obedience appears in verse 7. Obedience to Christ may bring forth the ridicule of this world, but the great blessing shall be entered into.

The time is at hand in verse 10 makes clear that soon these great prophecies will become history. He cannot fail.

The reward is sure, the Lord is coming and His reward is with Him. All patience and labour shall be righteously rewarded. The same statement "his reward is with Him" is found in Isa. 42:10 and 62:11.

The full blessing of salvation will then be entered into in verse 14. "Blessed are they who have washed their robes", this is the act of the human will in getting saved. The outcome of this is they have right to the tree of life, back to verse 2. The entering into the gates of the city goes back to 21:13, these shall be residents in that glorious city.

The believer is not alone in testimony and service. The Spirit is with him, and joins in that cry "Come" of verse 17. The word "come is three times in this verse 17, and the first is often applied to the Lord, after the promise of His coming in verse 16 the Spirit and bride long for and cry for His coming. This may be so, but the other mentions of "come" are to the thirsty soul etc.. Could not all three cries be an invitation to the sinner ? Such is the case in Isa. 55:1 where the word "come" again appears three times.

The coming of the Lord Jesus is sure, "surely I come quickly" a promise like this must be a great encouragement to all believers, principally to those who are suffering. His coming can never be doubted.

There is also great encouragement in the way the Lord presents Himself to John in verse 16 "I Jesus". This is similar to Acts 9 where Saul of Tarsus is afraid of the Lord, and the Lord replies, "I am Jesus". All fears were calmed, such is the case with every believer.

Truly a passage of encouragement, this really helps one to go on and to endure, these shall soon be realities, in the meantime we have His grace for every need in the closing verse (21).

GREAT FINAL WARNINGS

Scripture abounds with warnings and the most severe of these are to do with either attack or indifference to the Word itself. The Book of Revelation ends with this very theme.

The warning in verse 11 is to do with regard to the Word of God. The unrighteous and the filthy have refused the word of truth and gone in their own way. In similar manner the righteous were made so by the truth of the gospel, and the practising righteousness and sanctification again was by the leading of the Word. Here are two classes, those who refused the Word and those who believed and accepted the Word. The solemn warning then is the terrible "fixity" of the eternal dealings of God. The unrighteous and defiled go on in life this way, the way of their choice, but the eternal state of such will be the same. Gloriously so it is the same with the righteous and sanctified, they choose Christ, and their eternal portion shall be these delightful things throughout eternity. The two classes are very clear.

The two classes appear again in verses 14-15. Those who enter through the gates of the city and those who are outside, no entrance is permitted to them. This is not a reference to the saved nations of 21:24-26, rather those of 21:27. Again the thought of practising unrighteousness arises, and whose names are not written in the Lamb's book of life. Outside then, are the dogs, sorcerers, immoral persons, murderers, the idolater and the lover of lies. These persons had a complete commitment to these things, such have no place in the holy city and consequently are shut out of all blessing. This is negative to them, the positive side is seen in Rev. 20 the eternal lake of fire.

The meddling with the Word of God and its consequential warning comes finally in the book. The Lord Jesus is the speaker, "I testify" and the warning is to those who hear, alas, opportunity was given to embrace the truth as it is unto salvation, but refused. The warning concerns those who try to alter the truth of God, either to add to or take away from the prophecy. This no doubt could be enlarged to cover all the book of God, all is inspired and worthy to be received with thanksgiving.

It is instructive that Eve in the beginning fell into this fallacy and altered the Word of God. In one sentence she both took away from and added to the Word of God. "But of the fruit of the tree which is in the midst of the garden: God hath said, Ye shall not eat of it, NEITHER SHALL YE TOUCH IT, LEST YE DIE".

Eve added the word TOUCH IT, and took away the certainty of the death sentence by saying "LEST YE DIE".

The plagues positively promised and the negative taking away from the tree of life etc. do not refer to a believer. Salvation is not forfeited by any such action, nothing can separate from the love of God which is in Christ Jesus the Lord (Rom. 8:39). This is an unbeliever who hears the Word, refuses it, yea more, seeks to alter it to his own liking by omitting and appending according to his own whims. A true believer accepts all the truth of God, he may not understand all, but believes all.

These warnings stand out like beacons in this final chapter of the Revelation.

A FEW CONCLUDING REMARKS

In many chapters of the Revelation John himself shines in a searching way, sometimes in a poor light as in ch. 7 where he lacks interest in the great innumerable company, and sometimes in a good light, both examples are here.

John falls down to worship the angel in verse 8. Why this ? Note the words "which showed me these things" In other words, John fell into the error that so many sincere believers fall into. They admire even to adoration, the speaker who enlightens them in the Word, forgetting that he only is a channel. John the Baptist refused such eminence, making clear he was only a lamp but Christ was the LIGHT. Really, in many cases simple believers worship the very ground their favourite preachers walk on, and follow without thought. Christ must fill the picture. The very knowledgable angel refuses such a place and humbly speaks of his own service as a bondslave with John and the rest of the prophets who were humans, and as one with those who obey the Word. Such a lesson, the sad failure of John attracted to the channel and not the Golden Stream.

However, John shines in a very good light at the close of the chapter. Three times the Lord refers to His return, verse 7, 12 and 20. In the first, reference is made to the blessing of saints, but John does not respond. In verse 12, reference is made to the reward the Lord brings with Him, again no word from John. Finally in verse 20, when the Lord simply says "Surely I come quickly" with no mention of reward or blessing to believers, immediately John cries, "Even so come Lord Jesus". He is only interested in seeing the Lord, the prospect of His near return and the certainty of it makes his heart long for the event. Even so come Lord Jesus, he delights that the Lord shall come to enter into His glory as Lord of all. The aspirations of a sincere believer.

Throughout the ages troubled and suffering believers have faced perplexing questions. The understanding of this Prophetic Book of Revelation would have removed all such and brought much consolation to their troubled hearts. Therefore, read this Book and enjoy peace of mind.

Let us conclude this treatise with the words of our Lord to His own. "Let not your heart be troubled: ye believe in God, believe also in Me. In my Father's house are many mansions, if it were not so I would have told you. I go to prepare a place for you ... I will come again and receive you unto Myself; that where I AM, there ye may be also".

THE END